P9-BZJ-985

The Experts Praise
Branding Iron

The automobile industry is an ideal context to study brands because of the self-expressive benefits attached to many of the brands. *Branding Iron* tells with insight and humor how blunders in brand strategy destroyed brands and damaged firms. A great read.

Dave Aaker
Principal, Prophet Brand Strategy
Author, *Brand Equity* and *Brand Portfolio Strategy*

What a simple and practical concept. Branding sells products! That's a cornerstone of effective marketing. The authors show us clearly, through the use of a product category we're all familiar with—automobiles, that effective branding differentiates any product from its competitors and builds demand and sales. Well done!

Tony Alessandra, Ph.D.
Author of *The Platinum Rule* and *Non-Manipulative Selling*

Today, many marketers are suffering from the "lab coat" syndrome. The field is dominated by complexity, esoteric approaches, models rather than people, and fears of oblivion. *Branding Iron* recognizes that people still have practical needs, firms still face practical problems, and solutions still have to work in real life. The book conveys a pioneering spirit on how to be unabashedly great again. It goes beyond watching things happen or wondering what happened, and helps the reader to make things happen.

Michael R. Czinkota
Professor of Marketing, Georgetown University
Former Deputy Assistant Secretary,
U.S. Department of Commerce

One of the best books on branding I've seen in a long time. *Branding Iron* provides key branding and marketing insights for marketers in every industry. And, equally important, it shows a way out for those who find themselves in circumstances similar to this troubled industry.

Scott Davis
Senior Partner, Prophet Brand Strategy
Author, *Brand Asset Management*

Branding Iron should be required reading for every single person who aspires to be in business, let alone the automobile business, because it pounds into the reader the fundamental importance of, as Charlie Hughes and William Jeanes so eloquently put it: "standing for something, setting yourself apart, making a promise and delivering it in a well-designed experience." I would also like to give Hughes and Jeanes' excellent "Brand Triangle" to every college professor charged with teaching marketing. *Branding Iron* doesn't pull any punches, a style I can relate to, obviously—and when all is said and done it's a must read. And with today's tedious cacophony of blurred messages, two-bit pundits and frantic media overkill, that's saying something.

Peter M. DeLorenzo
Founder-Publisher, Autoextremist.com

Important lessons for any marketer who wants to avoid the automakers' troubles. And even more important, they don't just pick mistakes part, they provide a map to a more successful future.

Rick Kean
Managing Partner, Business Marketing Institute
Former Executive Director, Business Marketing Association

A first of its kind—the true story behind the auto industry. *Branding Iron* will supercharge your risk-taking batteries and fuel your brand-building strategies.

Thomas D. Kuczmarski
Preisdent, Kuczmarski & Associates
Author, *Innovation* and *Managing New Products*

This is one of the best, most coherent, readable and actionable books on brands and branding I have read in quite a while. The failures of the automobile industry provide cogent lessons for all senior managers tasked with growing their organization under highly competitive conditions. This is a veritable senior management manual on how to or, better said, how *not to* manage the most valuable asset the organization has: the brand. There are practical, useful lessons here that can be applied to any product category.

Don E. Schultz
Medill/IMC, Northwestern University
Author, *Integrated Marketing Communications* and *Brand Babble: Sense and Nonsense about Branding*

The power of brands is nowhere brought to life more vividly or more authoritatively than in the pages of *Branding Iron*. This book is a marketing thriller that every marketer should read, racing along from one automotive intrigue to the next, illustrating at every turn the fundamental importance of good branding, or, even more importantly, the terrible consequences of bad branding. Branding Iron is an advanced primer on the ways in which marketing makes the crucial difference.

J. Walker Smith
President, Yankelovich + Partners
Co-author, Coming to Concurrence: *Addressable Attitudes and the New Model for Marketing Productivity*

Automobiles are the archetypal product of all consumer interest, the perfect category to discuss 21st-century branding and business strategy. The "cowboy way" is an equally as perfect metaphor to engage you in the story . . . courage and good judgment. Hughes and Jeanes impressively point out that if everybody's thinkin' the same way . . . then somebody ain't thinkin' at all. A truly engaging book.

Watts Wacker
Co-author, *The 500-Year Delta: What Happens after What Comes Next* and *The Deviant's Advantage: How to Use Free Ideas to Create Mass Markets*

Branding Iron is an in-depth analysis of how to incorporate branding into what you build, and not just slap a pretend image on what you've already got. Filled with stories that that make the point—with specifics —this book captures the good and the bad. Where things went wrong and where things went right. Everyone from advertising to engineering should read this book!

Alan Weber
President, Marketing Analytics Group
Author, *Data-Driven Business Models*
Adjunct Professor, Kansas University

Using a compelling narrative, the authors teach us that there is no more important business endeavor than building brands. By showing that branding is not simply an activity for marketing communications after the product is developed, *Branding Iron* teaches marketers in all industries and cultures how to convince others in the organization why branding must be everyone's responsibility throughout the product lifecycle.

Roy Young
Co-Author, *Marketing Champions*
Vice President, MarketingProfs

BRANDING IRON

Branding Lessons from the Meltdown of the US Auto Industry

CHARLIE HUGHES
WILLIAM JEANES

Foreword by **DAVID E. DAVIS, JR.**
Editor in Chief, *Winding Road* magazine

Racom Books/Racom Communications
Chicago, Illinois

Cataloging information available from the Library of Congress.

For further information, contact:
Racom Books/Racom Communications
150 N. Michigan Ave.
Suite 2800
Chicago, IL 60601
www.racombooks.com
312-494-0100

Editor and publisher: Richard Hagle
Page Design: Sans Serif Inc.

This book is printed and bound in the United States.

With affection and gratitude,
the authors dedicate this book to our wives,
Barbara Hughes and Susan Jeanes.

CONTENTS

FOREWORD

"Brand," is perhaps the most overused and misunderstood word in modern marketing. Yahoos who know nothing about their customers and even less about their company's products, retire behind a fogbank of brand-talk whenever they're asked to explain why their product has lost twelve percent of market share in the last three business days. "Brand" is the adult equivalent of a baby's pacifier. Slip it into the assistant marketing manager's mouth and he is instantly reassured and optimistic.

With this book, *Branding Iron*, Charlie Hughes sets out to restore respectability to the concept of brands and branding. He has pulled together several decades of automotive experience at the higher levels of industry and commerce and poured it into this book. And it is an amazing book, in that it provides all kinds of practical guidance about how to turn the automobile—the most complex, expensive, and confusing consumer product in our lives—into a sought-after brand, and is at the same time a truly enjoyable read. This may be because Mr. Hughes made the altogether felicitous choice of his friend William Jeanes as a thinker/planner and co-conspirator to help him turn his collected wisdom into riveting prose.

Whatever the cause, this is a very enjoyable look at the imploding automobile industry from the inside. Charlie Hughes is not even-handed in his evaluations of executive performance in the case studies he presents. Idiots are idiots, fools are not suffered gladly, and the good men who get it right are celebrated. He presents a scenario in which this once great industry seems to have forgotten or willfully abandoned everything it ever knew about new product development, proper investment of resources, the optimal role of the CEO, customer focus, the importance of profits as opposed to mere growth, and the fundamental necessity of great product as the engine that pumps life into every other discipline.

Charlie Hughes spent thirteen years of his life as CEO of Land Rover. His task was to introduce an English sport utility vehicle in the United States, a country which had almost no confidence in the ability of British managers or British assembly line workers to build a vehicle that would work satisfactorily for American drivers in American conditions. Charlie's hand-picked team of "conspirators" not only pulled it off, but in so doing created a booming market for an entire new category of personal transportation—the luxury SUV—in the American marketplace. Then, in a series of miscues and good-intentions-gone-wrong, Land Rover was taken over first by BMW, and next by the Ford Motor Company, and that brand is now spiraling downward in the same flushing mechanism that seems to have captured Ford itself.

The disciplines and methodologies of brand development and brand strategy put forward by Charlie Hughes in these pages are so sensible and straightforward that one is inclined to smack his forehead in a "Eureka!" moment and snap, "Idiot! Why didn't you think of this? Why aren't you running your own business based on these rules?" In fact, I am rather hoping that I'll be the first reader of "Branding Iron" to examine my own new product launch in the bright light of Hughes' wisdom and experience.

There is ample evidence that the North American automobile industry, with its horror of real change and real innovation, might have been saved if a hundred key people could have read Charlie Hughes on brands and branding two decades ago, and if twenty-five of that one-hundred could have understood that they had not a moment to lose in the implementation of his disciplines. It didn't happen, and it may never happen. But there'll be vast opportunity for the dozen or so smaller companies that spring up from the ashes of Ford and General Motors to profit from the mistakes of the giants, and be guided by this book!

David E. Davis, Jr.
Editor-in-Chief, *Winding Road* Magazine

ACKNOWLEDGEMENTS

It is difficult for your authors to accept that we have a combined 60 years of experience in the car business. We worked with many admirable people, some lost souls and a few bad actors. We've learned from all of them—sometimes it was fun and sometimes it was painful—which is the nature of business. We want to thank a few of those who helped us, directly and indirectly, with *Branding Iron*.

Charlie Hughes

My knowledge of branding traces to my love of cars and the car business. In my teen years this obsession with cars flourished—despite my parents' determination to steer me away from an automotive career. My mother used to say, "You don't have to work in the car business to own a nice car, you just have to be a success." Later, of course, they saw the light.

Many kind and talented souls reshaped my misspent youth with cars. Among these were Dick Teague, Brock Yates, David E. Davis, Jr., Eric Davison, Bob Reese, Bob Levenson, and Bill Bernbach.

As my career progressed, I took on a series of marketing jobs that expanded my views on branding. At Fiat, I worked for Dick Reccia whose enthusiasm and leadership were unbounded. I met Norm Suslock, who ran his own direct marketing company, but served part time as my mentor.

At Porsche-Audi and Volkswagen, I worked for Jim Fuller, a forceful personality if ever one existed. We did not always see eye to eye, but Jim was a great teacher who understood branding and who also had a strong pragmatic streak. I never got to thank him while he was alive, and I owe him much. Thank you, Jim.

Also at VW I became friends with Bill Young, who somehow proved that a touch of larceny and a kind heart could go hand in hand.

Land Rover was a do and learn experience, an opportunity to act on our beliefs. Bob Sinclair and Mike Dale were steady CEO voices from the outside. I reported to Chris Woodwark, Tony Gilroy, and Tom Purves—three different bosses, each excellent in his way. Throughout my years there, the Land Rover executive team comprised overachievers who pushed the concept of branding. Especially Jim Lehmann, Joel Scharfer, Howard Mosher, Bill Baker, Dave Schworm, and Jim Newell. Chip Sleeper and Diane Rothschild at Grace and Rothschild, Tom Coyne at Coyne Communications, and Lee Carpenter at Design Forum were key co-conspirators. I am indebted to the entire team at Land Rover and thank them once more.

Three people had a major impact on my thoughts about leadership, branding, culture, and creativity: Roger Ball, Jim Bernthal, and Roy Grace. Roy and Jim are no longer with us, and I miss their friendship. Roger played a strong role in the development of *Branding Iron*.

This business would be no fun without dealers. And I've enjoyed the counsel of some great ones: Mark Hennessey, Bill Jacobs, Warren Zinn, Mike and Brian Lazarus, Barney Garver, Norm Gregerson, Eddie Bradley, John Symes, Robin Bacci, Joe Dockery, Bill Cook, Paul Sansone, and Karl Schmidt.

Steve Shipley was my gentle shepherd on this project, and Jim Sanfilippo kept the pot aboil on automotive branding controversies that arose daily.

Writing a book like *Branding Iron* benefits from observant opinionated authors and fortunately this book had two. Thank you William.

William Jeanes

For my part, as the so-called professional writer/editor on this project, I want to first thank Charlie for doing most of the work. Some call this delegating; others use the word laziness. In addition, I thank those of my friends and colleagues who generously provided invaluable information and opinions. Several of these have worked overtime through the years to help me understand the car business. These include David E. Davis, Jr., Joe Schulte, Leo Levine, Carroll Shelby, Don Hufford, and Jim Ramsey.

I cannot overstate the benefits of knowing, in the years I ran *Car and Driver*, men such as Ford's Don Petersen, GM's Bob Lutz, and Mike Dale at Jaguar.

Peter Schweitzer, who for years headed the Ford account for J. Walter Thompson, proved by example that sound management and humanity are not mutually exclusive. In the brief time that I served as management supervisor of the Ford Division account for JWT, Lou Lataif and Doug McClure also taught me that gentlemen have a place in client management.

The editors and reporters at Keith Crain's *Automotive News* could, I think, teach anyone about the world of automaking. And Peter DeLorenzo of autoextremist.com could, in his informed and acerbic way, give the thickest student an understanding of marketing, advertising, and branding as they relate to cars and trucks.

A number of persons cannot be recognized here for reasons of job security (theirs), but they know who they are, and I thank them once again. A mercifully small number of executives for whom I toiled provided landmark examples of what I call management by bellowing. They also know who they are, not that they would read this book. Let alone understand it.

Last, and first, I thank my Irish grandmother, Dora Lynch Hanley, who kept a journal. And inspired me to write.

Finally

Co-authoring a book provides you with more information about your co-author than most people can tolerate. This project grew out of mutual respect and friendship, which, astonishingly, remains intact.

We thank William Brown, our literary agent, who withstood several re-writes. He proved to be a calm patient man, never a bad thing.

Rich Hagle, our publisher, has been a good and gentle guide as we completed our first book. Fortunately Rich has a well developed sense of irony, enjoys getting things right, and remains passionate about publishing and marketing.

With two authors you have twice the number of people to acknowledge and double the opportunity of overlooking folks out who have made a big difference in our thinking. To all of the people who have supported us and worked to increase our knowledge of branding, we thank you.

ABOUT THE AUTHORS

Charlie Hughes, co-author of *Branding Iron*, is one of the few men alive who has created a car company that's still in business. The New York native has worked for six automakers on eleven different brands that include Cadillac, AMC, Jeep, Fiat, Lancia, Ferrari, Porsche, Audi, Volkswagen, Range Rover, Land Rover, and Mazda. He headed three different automotive marketing groups and was CEO of two auto companies.

As founder and CEO of Range Rover of North America, which became Land Rover North America, he built a car company from scratch, beginning in 1986 with an investment of $7.5 million. Eight years later, this had grown to a market value of $200,000,000.

"In the car business, being head of Land Rover was like being the owner of a four acre ranch in Texas," Charlie told an interviewer, "But we built one of the strongest brands in the industry and had fun doing it. We were mavericks all the way."

In 2000, Ford Motor Company hired Charlie as president and CEO of Mazda North American Operations. There, he revitalized the Mazda image and repositioned the brand in the crowded US market. When he arrived at Mazda, Charlie found a company with over $5 billion in sales but no profit. It was also lost in the marketplace. Mazda made a profit in his first year and a larger profit in his second—during the most cut-throat-discount market in modern memory.

Today, Charlie heads a marketing consulting consortium, Brand Rules. As its founding president, he describes the firm's mission simply: "In an over-branded marketplace, we help you learn what sets you and your company apart . . . and how to cut yourself out of the herd."

Mississippi native **William Jeanes**, co-author of *Branding Iron*, has spent the last three decades closely associated with the auto industry. A graduate of Millsaps College and a former Lieutenant in the US Navy, his first writing job was as feature editor at *Car and Driver*.

After three years at *C/D*, he left to become a copywriter at Campbell-Ewald (Chevrolet's ad agency). He became an associate creative director and after two years moved to SSC&B:Lintas in New York (now Lowe & Partners). He remained there for five years, becoming a senior vice president and gained experience in packaged goods advertising and marketing. In 1982, he moved to J. Walter Thompson/Detroit as a senior vice president and director of the Ford Division account. There, he learned first-hand the research, marketing, and advertising decision-making processes at a major auto company.

He quit JWT in 1985 and returned to writing. His writing has appeared in a score of the world's automotive publications and in *Sports Illustrated, American Heritage, Smithsonian Air & Space, Playboy, Parade,* and *The New York Times*.

In 1987, he became editor-in-chief of *Car and Driver*. He led *C/D* to a million-plus circulation and made it the envy of the industry. During his six years as editor, he appeared regularly on "CBS This Morning" as its automotive expert, and his radio commentary on Detroit's WJR reached 19 states each week. In 1993, he became a senior vice president and group publisher at Hachette Filipacchi Magazines.

Despite rising revenues, William forsook publishing to become the founding editor of *Classic Automobile Register*. Later, at American Media, he founded *Auto World Weekly*, the first US automotive magazine aimed directly at new-vehicle buyers.

INTRODUCTION:
Heroes and Villains

This book is about branding iron, as in Detroit Iron, as in cars. Applying both a scalpel and an axe to the world of selling cars, we examine the role that branding has played in shaping the way Americans think about the cars we buy. And, sadly, an auto industry where the art of branding has fallen on some very tough times.

Branding Iron is about grit, the kind our forefathers used to tame the American West. They were rugged individualists—mavericks who carried six shooters and used them. Hard-nosed men and brave women who lived tough, often short, lives. They never owned a cell phone or read a marketing textbook, but they had the bravado to run the herd, not become part of it.

What has happened to us? We've gone safe, soft, and somnolent. And in the process we've lost our nerve. We've become Generation B: bland and boring. We equate risk with trying vanilla flavoring in our latte. We've joined the herd. Most of us, anyway.

The car business is over a century old, yet it remains one of the most dangerous, daunting, and dynamic businesses on earth—an arena characterized by unthinkable financial risk, homicidal competition, and constant change. The car business provides a window on the world of branding and, more specifically, on how the value of a brand can disappear overnight—and how an industry can devalue the entire concept of branding and thus commoditize its own product. This trend is not limited to the auto industry, yet events and practices within this industry make it a showcase for costly muddled thinking.

For some time, much of the auto industry's management has displayed muddled thinking about marketing and branding. Over the last decade, trends—short-term sales focus to name one— unfavorable to brand building have accelerated. During this same period, too many auto executives have embraced faulty group-think concerning what it takes to be a success. Because competition is suffocating, price has become all important. With that has come an almost obsessive focus on cost reduction. The drive to reduce costs is not wrong, but the dominant approach being used sacrifices much of what we know it takes to build great brands.

Branding is a tried-and-true business strategy with this underlying premise: if we distinguish ourselves with a defined audience, we will actually shift the demand curve positively. We will either be able to sell more cars at the same price or the same number of cars at a higher price. As competition has become super-heated, the clarity of that goal has been lost on all but a few. We continue to talk about branding and invest in branding in ways that are not supported by our results. *In short, most companies view branding too narrowly, ignoring that branding must permeate every facet of an organization.*

What makes a Ford a Ford, a Pontiac a Pontiac, a Jaguar a Jaguar, a Mitsubishi a Mitsubishi? Too many potential customers reply, "Who cares?" People have spent years of their lives and billions of dollars designing and marketing cars so that people can ask who cares. Isn't that comforting?

Because the industry views itself as a serious business, its leaders demand fact-based answers. Yet much of what they do rests on their views of the future and how customer's tastes will evolve over time. When forecasting the future, one must go beyond available numbers and rely on experience and intuition.

Branding Iron will challenge you in several ways. We know that many readers would like us to provide lots of facts and figures to substantiate everything we say, thus proving we're correct, in the process providing a formulaic approach that can be used in arguments with all of the fact-finders out there. First, we provide a few basic benchmark facts that demonstrate the all-too-obvious. Second, for more specific facts and figures, just look to the media. The stories are becoming repetitious; only the names change. Third, and most important, readers who want all that are missing the whole point. We wrote this book to prod you into action, to stimulate your thinking, to ignite your imagination and creativity, to urge you to go beyond rote regurgitation of numbers and tap into an energy field that lies beyond the obvious.

If nothing else, brand building is a creative endeavor. With more than 45 automotive brands to choose from, standing out in a positive way is damned hard. It is a daunting task that takes all the creativity and courage you can muster.

The creativity of which we speak goes beyond the artistic, though artistry often can be a part of it. But it's more than creating logos and clever ads; it's thinking creatively about customers and markets, about one's own strengths and abilities, and about those qualities and attributes one must have. It also takes experience that is deeper than conventional wisdom—plus a keen eye, nose, and ear for what consumers are telling you and what you must fathom on your own. Too often, branding is relegated to the marketing group when in fact the most inspired branding permeates everything a company does. Everything.

All great stories have tension. *Branding Iron* is about an industry that is both fearless and cowardly. It is fearless in investing large sums of money. It is cowardly when it comes to standing for something in the marketplace.

It is a business that is most comfortable with the expense side of the profit equation (Profit = Revenue minus Expenses). Billion dollar bets are placed every day on new plants and on new models. It is an industry that focuses on continually reducing expenses and, when times get tough, will quickly pare expenses to the bone. It is an industry comfortable with buying, because buying forms the expense side of the equation.

Oddly, for one of the world's largest revenue industries, it has a growing discomfort with the revenue or selling side of the profit equation. It is an industry that loves control, which is a succinct encapsulation of the buying process. When we buy, we are in control.

By contrast, when we sell, the customer is in control, and that annoys and rattles many executives. They grudgingly acknowledge that enticing the customer is an art. An art with which most of the top leaders in the industry have very little real-life experience.

Industry executives become gun shy and timid when called upon to differentiate their brand in the marketplace. While they ceaselessly proclaim the importance of brands, they lack gut-level understanding of the art of branding.

When these top decision-makers find themselves on the shaky battleground of selling, what do they do? They research the industry and competition to death. They copy, they imitate, they play follow the leader. They try to play it safe, and in the process they squander billions of dollars of brand equity. They are the industry's villains.

Branding is a strategy designed to attract customers, set expectations, and draw them back again. Done with verve and intelligence, branding increases demand. Done poorly, it decreases demand. A few companies understand this, and they are our heroes.

The auto industry is busy with the business of growth and shareholder value. Too many of its executives have lost their single-minded focus on the customer. Not just any customer, *their* customer. They have lost sight of the need to do something so important for their customers that their company becomes a standout in the marketplace.

Instead, they concentrate on internal activities such as business plans, market equations, profit plans, and recovery plans. Too much time is allocated to planning outcomes and not enough on the actions they must take to win over customers. Doing right by the customer has been replaced by doing right by the shareholder. And in the process brand value has suffered. We seem to have a growing comfort level with being more and more alike. And the bottom-line result is that everyone—shareholders, customers, and the brand itself—is diminished.

For our part, we never fantasized about being just like everyone else. No one with any sense dreams about being plain looking, achieving median income, or working at an unsatisfying job. Do you dream about having average athletic ability, average intelligence, and an unremarkable personality? Good God, let's hope not. You dream about being rich, successful, popular, well-loved, the life of the party, a great athlete, the perfect Mom or Dad, or whatever puts the giddy in your giddy-up. You want to stand out. To be special. To achieve your dreams requires courage, and that goes double for branding.

What is missing in the car business? In the halcyon days of branding cars, people would have said the leaders had moxie, a street-smart combination of courage and judgment. It is a word that has fallen out of favor, but it is an apt description of what the industry needs.

We are optimists with a contrarian point of view: As the value of branding diminishes, an opportunity opens to build brands that add real value. The Me-Too attitude so pervasive in business today opens up startling opportunities for risk-takers. This means that Job One is to cut yourself out of the herd, a move that takes uncommon courage backed up by vision, judgment, and gut-wrenching commitment.

Branding Iron speaks from the perspective of a CEO or leader who is in a position to change the things that need to be changed. It will cause you to ponder your own behavior and how that behavior may have thwarted the development of your brand.

Branding Iron will drive you on a quest to build a brand that leaves a real mark on this world. A mark made the old-fashioned way—burned in with a red hot iron.

1

Dead Brand Tales and
The Evil of Conventional Wisdom

> "He's a good manager, I just don't get the
> sense he has the vision to dare fly in the face
> of conventional logic."
>
> *Todd Turner, President of CarConcepts, commenting on*
> *Tom LaSorda's promotion to CEO of Chrysler, August 2005*

Toyota will soon displace General Motors as the world's largest automaker. Once a company that Detroit was going to "push back into the Pacific Ocean," Toyota in mid-2006 had a market value more than ten times that of GM.

The root cause of this financial cataclysm mystifies many of the players, particularly at GM. But the numbers tell a clear story. Since 2000, GM's market cap fell from $66 billion to $12 billion (April 2006). In 1980, GM sold 45 of every 100 cars that rolled out of showrooms in the US. It now sells 24.

By any yardstick, this is a crisis. Numerous factors have contributed, but the main source of this crisis can be traced directly to branding problems. Like many a crisis, this one has been brewing for decades.

What happened? GM lost touch with the market and its customers, and lost sight of Alfred P. Sloan's strategy of "a car for every purse and purpose." In contemporary parlance, how to differentiate its many brands. GM in the 1950s and 1960s was a paragon of brand portfolio management. Today, GM's appalling lack of brand sense has industry analysts using words such as "bankruptcy" and phrases such as "Chapter 11."

The headlines offer a different interpretation. They say that legacy costs, poor cost control, ill-advised investments in other automakers and in undistinguished products—all of which are serious issues—caused the trouble. That's wrong. Or at best incomplete. What is killing GM is its inability to attract a growing number of customers to its numerous brands, many of which seem almost irrelevant.

Automotive branding is losing its cachet through misguided management of growing brand portfolios, a natural outcome of industry consolidation. Ford was the last company to buy a healthy brand, paying $6 billion for Volvo. Would anybody pay that kind of money today for any of GM's brands? Not if they thought about it.

Before you can successfully run a brand portfolio, you must know how to make one brand a success. In an overbranded car business that truth seems to be problematic for far too many executives. Everyone talks a good game, but few show evidence of really knowing what they are doing. Innovation and risk taking have been replaced with a herd mentality, a way of thinking driven by conventional wisdom.

Conventional Wisdom

We maintain that *conventional wisdom* is an oxymoron, and nowhere do we find more supporting evidence for our assertion than in the auto business. Other marketing universes, from shampoo to mutual funds, are infected with the same tried—and rarely true—bromides that plague our industry. You will recognize most of them.

In the car business, the appalling thing about hiding behind conventional wisdom is the money at stake. When British Aerospace owned Land Rover, its chairman had extensive experience in a conglomerate that specialized in commodity products like bricks. He once asked: "Who in their right mind would invest a billion dollars in a new product without knowing the outcome?" Good question. Without knowing who you are as a company— and who wants what you stand for—investments of that magnitude are terrifying. If the market is ignorant of what you stand for or, worse yet, *you* are ignorant of what you stand for, the investments are downright suicidal.

Which is why executives grow fearful and seek the safety of conventional wisdom. If the company fails, an executive who used methods and marketing that worked for other companies in the past can hardly be blamed. Right? Wrong. Anyone who believes blindly in the following conventional wisdom deserves worse than blame.

"Product Is King"

Really? Then why do so many uninspired and downright unattractive products contaminate the marketplace? It's bad enough that too many people in the car business act as if they don't really believe this. What's worse is the raft of poorly differentiated cars out there that give the lie to the product-as-king theory.

Product is crucial, of course. The product is what the customer drives every day. Each time a car owner turns the ignition key, one of two thoughts pops up: "Why did I buy this can of garbage?" or, on a more positive note, "I'm proud to be driving my [Brand Name Goes Here]." But product alone won't cut the Grey Poupon. What the brand *stands* for can be just as important, and so can the retail experience. More times than the industry will admit, customers have gotten excited by a product only to go to a dealer who treats them like a bucket of shark bait. Good-bye sale.

"Customers Are Smart"

Some are, many aren't. Some are too stupid to be believed—otherwise vinyl tops and opera windows would not have sold as well as they did. But all of this is beside the point. What you can count on is that most customers follow the herd. Not surprisingly, opinion-leading consumers (*e.g.*, the office car nut) helped along by *Consumer Reports* and some better than adequate automotive magazine writers, generally get it right. So herd members who do their homework make defensible choices. Herds are like steamboats, however, slow to change direction. This means that some buyers will continue to select brands that are well past their expiration dates.

"Let's Research It!"

Can you see a group of lost cowhands saying, "Let's ask the cattle which way to go"? You can ask customers how they feel, examine what they do, and ask them what they like in terms of their tastes today. That's fine, but customers are not futurists. That job falls to you.

One look at the cars on sale tells you that research is an imperfect tool. The Pontiac Aztek was an arrestingly ugly example. At its first showing, when the press questioned GM management's sanity, the response was that the team had thoroughly researched the vehicle and it would be a hit. Research notwithstanding, it was a total failure. Research does have a role, but that role is to *augment* your judgment. You must have sound judgment, and then you must have the courage to listen to it.

If you accept that customers by and large are followers, then it's your job to get them to follow *you*. How can you use consumer research to help you turn customers into followers? Well, you can start by ignoring most of it.

The car business spends more money on consumer research than any endeavor other than politics. Much of its research is syndicated and available to everyone. Buyer studies, shopper studies, consumer satisfaction indexes, buyer intention studies, transaction studies, dealer satisfaction studies, service studies, and on and on and on. What has all this research accomplished? In the auto industry, it has acted as a homogenizer. It can do that for your industry, too.

An entire industry poring over the same data—and believing it—produces few original thoughts. The data can possibly forestall a dreadful mistake, but so can sitting on your butt. Excessive reliance on research, as sure as a branded cow's flank hurts, leads to mediocrity. Incredibly, there are executives who find comfort and refuge in creating research-based mediocrity. At meetings, you can hear them muttering, "Isn't that what the customer wants?" or "That's what Toyota is doing, so shouldn't we?" Circling the wagons never got a single pioneer closer to California.

"Advertising Sells"

You can just hear the conversation in the leather-lined conference room. It begins with denial and moves on to delusions of salvation.

- "Our products are competitive." Wrong.
- "Our pricing is in the ballpark." Also wrong.
- "Our retailers are putting forth a good effort." Maybe.
- "We are just not on enough shopping lists." True, but we aren't about to face up to *why* this is so.

You can just hear what's coming next. "We need more punch in our marketing. Get the word out. We need to be more creative, like the guys across town. The Agency needs to get off its ass, or we should put the account up for review."

Finally, "We'll turn things around with a brilliant new ad campaign!" No one mentions that customers are at least half smart or points out that, with the diffusion of media, it now costs twice as much as it once did to reach half the audience. Ninety-five percent of that audience, by the way, is as eager to hear from you as it is to welcome an IRS tax auditor.

Bill Bernbach, one of the great minds in advertising history and the driving force behind the Doyle Dane Bernbach Agency, relished saying that nothing kills a bad product faster than great advertising. Great advertising will convince consumers to try a product. If that product disappoints, they will tell everyone within earshot that the product sucks like a Hoover.

Only rarely do advertising expenditures correlate with sales results. That's because advertising is not a stand-alone activity. Advertising can build awareness, it can help create an image, it can increase buying consideration. But seldom by itself.

The proliferation of media—from cable TV to the Internet to cell phones to little posters in the back seats of taxis—has brought with it confusion and resentment. Consumers feel assaulted by unwanted advertising and are fighting back. The notion of advertising that irritates your customers—while trying simultaneously to sell them—doesn't make sense. Do people yell at their romantic partners when expressing affection? Only if they're deaf. But that's what we're doing to our audiences—rendering them deaf to our messages.

More, we submit, is not always better. But this intelligence has not reached the advertising community, which is burning up the customers'synapses with too much boring, look-alike advertising. This overkill makes it harder and harder to reach our target market, even when it *wants* to listen. How many brands can you burn into a cow before it either bites back or plays dead? This relentless barrage of advertising makes it all but impossible for your message to stand out.

Traditional advertising can be a powerful tool or it can be a black hole. Either way, it is not the final answer, and it is becoming less effective through overuse. Interactive marketing on the other hand, represents real opportunity to those who understand the concept of one-on-one marketing.

Any doubts? In the spirit of encouraging the intelligent use of research, check out *Coming to Concurrence: Addressable Attitudes and the New Model for Marketing Productivity*, by J. Walker Smith *et al*. The book draws on extensive research by the Yankelovich Group, one of the premier market research organizations. Among other things, the research and the authors point out that one of the hottest-selling categories on the market today is products devoted to helping consumers *avoid* being sold to. Another tidbit: during the opening hours of the institution of the national telemarketing do-not-call registry, more than 20 million names were recorded by people who called in to say "no sale."

"You Can Charge More for a Brand-Name Product!"

Now that our nation's marketing wizards are branding every-thing in sight, the attendant dilution and confusion has con-sumers re-assessing the value of brands. This is apparent in the increase in sales of private-label merchandise sold at chains such as Wal-Mart and Costco. Why buy Kleenex tissues when Kirk-land, Costco's in-store brand, is 20 percent cheaper? Given the proliferation of brand messages, customers may now trust Costco more to begin with. And guess what? Many savvy cus-tomers know that some private brands are actually made by the brand name manufacturer.

More important, strong brands theoretically belong at the high end of the spectrum and generics at the low end. You re-member generics—products with ugly, plain labels that sold on price alone. Even this pecking order is upset. We now have gener-ics, near-generics, house brands, and multiple levels of "real" brands. At the bottom of the generic ladder, price can constitute 100 percent of the purchase decision. In between, the consumer's willingness to pay a premium varies.

To this marketing morass, we must add another problem: the American consumer's love of the deal. Compliment a friend on a new suit, and nine times out of ten the friend will say, "Thank you. And the best part is I got it on sale." Americans take pride in smart shopping, and even the most sought-after brands—and their advertising and marketing mavens—must face this bother-some character flaw. Ask yourself why name-brand outlet stores are such runaway successes. But also ask what they do to the brand's long-term value.

Overintellectualizing and overmanipulating has diluted the value of all but the most desirable brands. Even as you read this, executives in boardrooms across the country are wildly overestimating the value that consumers place on their brands. Yet in this benighted environment, a few enlightened companies are not only giving their brand's equity the proper care, they're increasing its value. How they perform this miracle we'll examine in later chapters, but we tell you now that fakery has nothing to do with it.

"The More You Pay, the Better the Product!"

Life would be grand if this were true, but it isn't. Buying a new or used vehicle is a complicated purchase, one with innumerable twists and turns. Furthermore, all manufacturers operate at differing efficiency levels—and when they are less efficient, they try to pass on those added costs to guess who? A lot of companies don't play the game honestly, which is where the dark side of brand development comes into play: marketers work round the clock to create a false impression of worth.

Some brands command a premium long after their product superiority has eroded. Up-and-coming brands, even those that offer world-class products, must charge less because they are less well known. Many car companies are not consistent, so some of their cars are truly great and some are embarrassing. Faced with overwhelming breadth of choice, the consumer will learn that price isn't the barometer of product goodness it once was. Some learn faster than others.

When Lexus and Infiniti entered the luxury performance category back in the 1980s, executives at BMW and Mercedes-Benz—especially those resident in their home country, Germany—reacted as if a one-legged man had announced his intention to play for a World Cup champion. Listen to the Germans' tune today. Does it sound different?

"More Expensive Brands Are Higher Quality!"

Did you ever wonder why, year in and year out, Toyota has dominated the J.D. Power quality sweepstakes? Not Mercedes-Benz or Cadillac or BMW—although Lexus, Toyota's luxury nameplate, often finds itself atop the list. Within the auto industry, it is accepted that Toyota consistently builds the highest-quality cars and trucks. The measures include fit and finish and reliability. Toyota brand vehicles are not the most expensive.

Using a broader definition, Mercedes-Benz unquestionably puts higher-quality materials and more sophisticated engineering into many parts of its cars. And the Germans will tell you that the absolute durability of a Mercedes-Benz is greater—if you can afford the expense of driving it that far. But dollar for dollar, does that make a Mercedes-Benz better than a Toyota? No.

The automobile industry has made enormous strides in improving the quality of its cars, and the overwhelming majority of new vehicles have superb dependability. The plain fact of the matter is that there are no cars on today's market that are of the shoddy quality common 20 years ago. This means that quality is nowhere near the differentiator it once was. Another area of potential brand superiority has been diluted.

"Adding Brands Creates More Synergies"

Let's see, we'll acquire another brand or two, downsize and integrate the acquired company, put some of our folks in to help them run it, combine back offices, share a higher percentage of components wherever possible, and, because we will be more efficient and effective, we will reduce our total costs *and* increase market share.

Put another way, we will strip the acquired company of its personality, its individuality, spend a fortune on redundancy and relocation costs, bring in new management that knows little about how the acquired company works and less about its brand personality and market, invest in redoing systems, create products that are more alike than distinctive, slow everything down by combining suppliers who then require a learning curve, and reduce the focus of management in the acquiring firm. And all this is supposed to deliver greater savings and increased market share? Good luck.

We've seen it when BMW acquired Rover Group. It has played out in the misnamed DaimlerChrysler "merger of equals."

Ford is enjoying a taste of it with Jaguar and, unless we miss our guess, will also have problems with Volvo and Land Rover.

What is at play here? Pure hubris. Never underestimate the value of focus. Or the high cost of sacrificing desirability in the cause of efficiency.

Proliferation, Fragmentation, and Ego

The car business, like most businesses, has gone through a protracted period of proliferation and fragmentation.

Here is conventional wisdom as it might be stated by a car dealer: if a little is good, a lot must be better. If my competitor has four models of one truck, then so must I. In the name of fighting to maintain or increase my market share, I *must* have an entrant in every segment—even if an intelligent sales forecast says I can't make any money doing this.

If we were talking about one or two big players in a market, the above might make sense. But the whole industry acts this way and has done so since at least the 1970s. The amount of choice has gone far beyond an interesting or manageable level.

In 1987, when the Range Rover was introduced in the United States, buyers could choose from among 19 sport utility vehicles. Today, 95 models vie for your business, and more are coming. The segment got hot in the 1990s, and everybody jumped in, including such luxury brands as Lexus, Infiniti, BMW and Porsche—none of which had any prior SUV experience or heritage. With its 450-horsepower Cayenne, Porsche has even brought a venerable contest to the SUV segment: the horsepower race.

There are truck-based SUVs (body on frame), and there are car-based SUVs (unibody). Some could go around the world; others are best used for going to the wine merchant.

For example, the first Lexus SUV was the LX 470, a gussied-up version of Toyota's capable and established Land Cruiser. Lexus next developed a "crossover" vehicle, which is what the industry calls a vehicle that looks like an SUV but drives more like a car. This was the RX 300, based on the Camry car platform, and it sold like water in the desert. Lexus rightly believed that there were many customers who wanted the looks, layout and prestige of an SUV but did not need any off-road capability. These buyers gladly traded off-road capability for lighter weight, better fuel economy, and more car-like handling.

Thus, the growth of the SUV segment led to an increase in the number of choices in the overall market. This success led to more offerings in that segment, which led in turn to fragmentation and even *more* choice. And far more confusion.

It seems as if every manufacturer rushes to each emerging segment determined to gain its fair share and then some. This stretches the resources of many companies to the breaking point. And to spread the cost of development and broaden market reach, executives encourage platform sharing. Ford offers the Ford Explorer thinly disguised as the Mercury Mountaineer and Lincoln Aviator. The Ford Expedition is also built as the Lincoln Navigator. GM offers its largest SUVs as Chevrolets, Hummers, GMCs, and Cadillacs. Its midsize SUV platform has been offered as a Chevrolet, Oldsmobile, Buick, GMC, Isuzu, and even a Saab.

Is this the kind of choice customers are looking for? Are any of these derivatives truly different? Of course not. Do they really represent the core values of the brand? Looking at these vehicles, you know what a patently silly question that is. *What* brand values?

More amazing, the industry is staffed with executives who believe this is smart. Most of them simply do not grasp the negative conditioning effect this is having on consumers and how it is destroying the very value of the brand they are meanwhile going on and on about. If you believe that your name is an important way to attract customers, why put it on undistinguished products?

The Briefest of Automotive Primers

Before we go further, let's pause and examine a few definitions of automotive terms that you will encounter throughout the book. They're easy, and there will be no quiz later. But you will understand some of the inside terms common to our industry.

Dealer Body

Cars are sold by dealers, not by automakers. In the branding wars, dealers are sometimes victims and sometimes villains. Some dealers are "dualed," meaning they sell more than one brand. A Pontiac-GMC dealer is an example. At Ford, Lincoln-Mercury is one division, effectively making all Lincoln dealers duals. Dealers provide the interface between the manufacturers and the customers. There are about 21,000 new-vehicle dealers in the US.

As the business has grown, automotive dealers have gone through their own form of consolidation. Thirty years ago, most stores were owned and operated by individual dealers who owned only one store. The better operators started buying additional stores, generally from the poorer operators, thus creating what the industry calls retail chains. One individual could own 2, 8, or 12 stores that were privately held and with their name on every store. Then in the late 1980s a few publicly owned automotive retail companies were formed—AutoNation, United Auto Group, and others. They have brought bigness to automotive retailing and yet another potential level of branding and brand confusion.

Nameplates and Models

We use the word *nameplate* to identify the overall brand of a car company and/or its divisions. Ford is a nameplate. Explorer and Mustang are models (though its long-term success has made many observers argue that Mustang is a brand). Toyota is a nameplate. Nissan is a nameplate. Camry, Corolla, Maxima, and Altima are models.

General Motors has eight division nameplates today: Buick, Cadillac, Chevrolet, GMC, Hummer, Pontiac, Saab, and Saturn. Within these divisions are about 70 models, and the calculator does not exist that can add up the permutations (different trim levels, options, transmissions, engines, body styles, and so on) within models.

Don Runkle, then head of GM advanced engineering, told

William Jeanes in 1987 that if one took an index card for every possible permutation of all GM cars—including variables such as interior colors, wheel covers, and paint selections—the stack would reach the moon, 225,000 miles away. And that was with the cards stacked flat, not laid end to end. To GM's credit, that can't be said today, but it would still be a hell of a stack.

Platforms

Platforms, sometimes called architecture, are the underpinnings of cars—the bits that are not visible to the naked eye. A platform is not a rigid set of immovable components but rather an assembly of parts that can, to a degree, be rearranged to make a vehicle marginally wider, longer, taller, or shorter. But the common parts are essentially the same, and the advantage is that they only have to be designed and engineered once and can then be ordered in large production runs. This creates what the bean counters call economies of scale.

A company might, for example, design and engineer a new midsize car. Underneath the skin would be an engine and a transmission (or transaxle in the case of a front-wheel-drive car) that transmits power to the wheels. At each of the four wheels would be suspension components—springs, shock absorbers, and the pieces that attach the wheels to the suspension and, in turn, the suspension to the car. The brakes are a part of each wheel-corner assembly.

In the old days, before unibody construction (a body welded together as a unit before the engine/transmission/suspension components are attached), a car's body was positioned on what was called a ladder frame—two longitudinal beams with cross-pieces that looked like, well, a ladder. The frame, in those days, was essentially the platform. You can see that a number of bodies could be placed on the same design ladder frame.

In today's world, a platform consists of the components we mentioned, but some or all of the components might vary and still be used within the original design specifications. A more powerful engine might be added, for example. This might call for heavier-duty brakes, and if the engine itself were substantially heavier than the base engine, the suspension and transmission might also need beefing up. Yet, the vehicle would retain essentially the same dimensions.

This procedure allows a basic group of parts, with greater or lesser differences, to be used to create a Chevrolet Malibu, a Pontiac G6, and a Saab 9-3. Underneath, they benefit from sharing parts instead of having to design each component for each car. The exterior skins can and should differ, but here again, they must remain within certain size parameters. Ditto the interiors, which can be more luxurious or less luxurious as the brand requires.

The temptation that comes as baggage with the shared-platform system is to do *too much* sharing. Once, for example, all GM divisions did their own engine development. With the exception of some Cadillac applications, that's no longer true. The same engine might appear with a supercharger in some brands and not in others.

Obviously, the same platform will not work for cars that differ materially in size. The Cadillac De Ville and the Buick Le Sabre might share a platform, but the De Ville and the LaCrosse are quite different. In simple terms, if your brand offers a subcompact, a compact, a midsize and a full-size car, you'd likely need four distinct platforms.

Crossover vehicles and SUVs, it should be noted, also share platforms. The Volkswagen Toureg and Porsche Cayenne constitute one example, and the new Saab SUV is in reality a Chevrolet TrailBlazer.

Badge Engineering

Earlier in this chapter, we mentioned that some respected manufacturers of brand-name packaged goods—soaps, cereals, face creams and the like—in some instances also manufacture the generic house brands sold by giant retailers. Same product, different name. In the automotive world, we call this "badge engineering." This is different from using a single platform to build multiple vehicles.

Here's an example: the Neon, Chrysler Corporation's small

car entry in the late 1990s, was sold as both a Dodge and a Plymouth. Only the name on the car—the badge—was different. Plymouth, of course, was on its way to Brand Cemetery at that point, so it hardly mattered. But it was badge engineering at its purest and worst.

Earlier, Chrysler had attempted to create a whole badge-engineered car line, though a narrow one, when it concocted the Eagle brand. Eagles were intended to appear at Jeep dealerships—which became Jeep-Eagle dealerships—so that a Jeep dealer could have a car to go along with his aging lineup of SUVs and Wranglers (the traditional Jeep). The original Eagle line was composed of vehicles that had been intended to wear American Motors nameplates. (In 1987, Chrysler had bought AMC principally to get the Jeep brand). After about five years, those disappeared and were replaced with vehicles built on Chrysler assembly lines and which differed from the Dodge Intrepid only in their badge, minor styling differences, and the availability of all-wheel drive—at that time a genuine—if unsuccessful—differentiator. Another Eagle, the Talon, was built at the Mitsubishi plant in Illinois and was a thinly disguised clone of the Mitsubishi Eclipse. The public was not fooled. Eagle sales never met expectations, and the name disappeared after the 1998 model year.

Ford vehicles are shared with the corporation's Mercury brand, and the Ford Taurus and Mercury Sable stood for years among the more blatant exemplars of the badge engineering tactic. Another example, one that even the general public understood, was Rolls-Royce and Bentley, which before they were sold to BMW and Volkswagen respectively, differed only in the radiator design. Most everything else was the same, and people thought it charming that one could claim understatement by purchasing a Bentley instead of the in-your-face Roller.

On a broader front, General Motors hurt itself badly by badge engineering. Under Chairman Roger Smith, GM destroyed the company's old structure wherein the various divisions—then Chevrolet, Pontiac, Oldsmobile, Buick, and Cadillac—operated almost autonomously. A great many bits and pieces were shared between and among the various brands, of course, but in the eyes of the public a Pontiac was a Pontiac and an Oldsmobile an Oldsmobile. Engines were developed independently by the divisions, and so were other components. Even though there were similarities between the body shells, enough exterior styling differences existed to maintain reasonable brand separation.

By the time Roger Smith's cost-cutters and efficiency experts were finished with the GM divisions, all the engines and transmissions—with minor exceptions—were exactly the same, and, what's worse, from a distance of 50 yards the cars all looked the same. By the end of the century, the once-proud Buick Roadmaster and the Chevrolet Caprice, were essentially the same automobile.

The Brand Portfolio

What is a brand portfolio? Simply the portfolio of brands a corporation markets, such as Toyota with Toyota, Lexus, and Scion; BMW with BMW, Rolls-Royce, and Mini; and Honda with Honda and Acura.

Years ago, the Motor City was a poster child for the power of branding, but times have changed. The industry has murdered some once-great brands and maimed most of the others. General Motors provides a sad example of how to flush billions of dollars worth of brand equity down the toilet by getting it wrong. And, with the resurrection of its Cadillac Division, a fine example of getting it right.

Growing one brand is difficult in today's market. Growing three, four, five, or more is even more difficult. And here is where the temptation to resort to badge engineering raises its ugly head.

The purpose of having multiple brands is to increase your appeal to different customer groups, to go beyond what you can accomplish with one brand. The issue plaguing the industry is the balance point between differentiation and cost cutting. Companies such as GM and Ford who have large brand portfolios consistently err on the side of reducing costs by sharing too much product and too many components among brands rather than creating clearly defined roles for each brand and applying the focus and funds necessary to make them distinctive.

The inability to get this right has led to the death of two well-known and once popular brands, Oldsmobile and Plymouth.

Oldsmobile: Centennial and Funeral

Everyone reading this book has some favorite product that's been interred in Brand Cemetery. Most often these are cereals, beers, clothing labels, or soft drinks, but even large brands—given enough bad caretaking and neglect—can disappear.

Some high-level, low-octane executives play games that are anything but harmless. Their belief that customers can be fooled with transparently worthless strategies is nothing short of moronic. By putting enough stupidity into the strategy mix, anyone can be responsible for killing a brand. Oldsmobile and Plymouth are two testimonials to this kind of anemic, muddled thinking.

Oldsmobile, named for automotive pioneer Ransom E. Olds, opened for business in 1897. Olds, not Henry Ford, instituted the first moving assembly line (Ford perfected the device). That kind of innovation, plus product excellence, made Oldsmobile one of the industry's early best sellers. A popular song of the early twentieth Century urged, "Come away with me, Lucille, in my merry Oldsmobile." The car was a household word.

Oldsmobile became a part of General Motors in 1908, joining Buick to become GM's second division. By the postwar years of the 1950s, most people felt they knew what an Olds was. Certainly they knew that it operated, along with Pontiac, between Chevrolet and Buick on the GM ladder of nameplate progression.

An Oldsmobile carried the first production Hydra-matic automatic transmission in the late 1930s. In the postwar period, its "Rocket 8" engine made Oldsmobile the darling of the fast-driving set. Its six-cylinder model, the 76 series, disappeared after 1950, leaving two models, the 88 and 98. Both were strong performers, and the 98 delivered near-Buick-level luxury as well.

In the 1960s, except for the Volkswagen Beetle, imports were not a threat to mainstream US car companies. Soon, however, imports had 10 percent of the US market. This led the nation's automakers and their dealers to conclude that there must be small cars at all dealerships—just as later market conditions would convince one and all that everyone must have SUVs in at least two sizes.

With the coming of the 1980s, Toyota, Honda, BMW, Mercedes-Benz, and others had become a serious force to combat. The Big Three were no longer competing only among themselves. One of the fallouts of this pronounced change in the marketing landscape was that every dealer body began to demand that they have cars to compete in every segment.

The postwar marketplace, where an automaker might have a convertible, coupe, sedan and station wagon in two trim levels—standard and deluxe—were gone forever, replaced by so much choice that choice became overwhelming at some dealerships. There is such a thing as too much choice, particularly when the choices are between too-similar vehicles.

By the mid-1970s, the Oldsmobile Cutlass had become one of the hottest, most sought-after cars in America. In 1970, buyers took home 200,621 Cutlasses, making Olds the fifth best-selling division in the US. By 1975, Olds stood third, and 319,531 Cutlasses left the showroom out of 628,720 Oldsmobiles sold. It was a car that had a following, that said you were a hip, smart buyer. But over the next ten years they went from hot to irrelevant. That is no simple trick, and it indicates that GM management's thinking was straying farther and farther from the reality of the market and from the way their customers were trending.

Life had changed so much for Oldsmobile that, in 1988, it informed the world that Oldsmobile was no longer a relevant brand. They accomplished this singular feat by adopting a new advertising tagline: "It's not your father's Oldsmobile." GM poured millions of dollars into this self-written epitaph. You could conceivably defend this by saying that Oldsmobile marketers were at least facing up to the truth about what the market thought of them, but the defense would be half-hearted at best. In one line, Olds managed to devalue its entire heritage, insult Oldsmobile loyalists, and turn off anyone else who might have been even vaguely interested in an Olds.

Twenty years earlier, the Olds Toronado was advertised as "The all-car car for the all-man man." That, citizens, is some comedown, even allowing for political correctness. Speaking of which, Olds could possibly have made things worse by saying, "It's not your parental unit's Oldsmobile," but we doubt it.

Oldsmobile made itself irrelevant by not keeping in tune with Oldsmobile buyers, an oversight that led to an array of undistinguished and undesirable cars. By the end of the 1980s, Oldsmobile offered a four-cylinder Cutlass Calais plus two other Cutlass series, the Ciera and Supreme. The Calais had four separate versions, the other pair each had three, and there were permutations of each version. An Olds Cutlass was therefore available in almost endless variety. The Cutlass name dated to the early 1960s when it was a version of the F-85, Oldsmobile's first compact car. The model later became a major success on its own, as just plain Cutlass. What better way to recognize success than by slapping the Cutlass badge on 19 Oldsmobiles? *Nineteen.*

Some honor. But that's what Olds had done by 1989. In addition to the glut of Cutlass models, Olds dealers could also sell you an Eighty-Eight Royale, an 88 Royale Brougham, a Custom Cruiser wagon powered by the only V-8 in the Olds lineup, a Ninety-Eight Regency, a Ninety-Eight Regency Brougham, and a Toronado. All told, there were 29 possible Oldsmobiles. Which one was the real Oldsmobile? Your guess is as good as ours, though we'd say none of them. The Oldsmobile marketing and product plan could have been titled, "How to water the whiskey and weaken your brand."

Oldsmobile sold 653,000 cars that year. In both 1977 and 1979 it had sold more than *one million* cars. Cars that were still perceived as Oldsmobiles, not generic GM vehicles with Oldsmobile nameplates on them. The public was learning fast.

Remember the flap over Oldsmobile installing Chevrolet engines in some models? That was one of the public's first exposures to the reality of badge engineering, and it was one more indication that GM was good at saving money but insensitive to the potential for damaging brands.

In another depressing footnote from the 1970s, note that this was the decade in which General Motors and, to a lesser extent, Chrysler and Ford began putting stand-up hood ornaments on selected models. This was an *homage* to Mercedes-Benz, which had used its famous three-pointed star hood decoration for decades. The stand-up ornaments were meant to signify luxury. Even had they not been so dreadfully cheesy, the ploy would never have worked. More bad branding in action.

But back to Olds. The division's last hurrah came with the introduction of the Aurora, a reasonably competent sedan that compared favorably with import competition, and the smaller Alero and Intrigue. But they were too little and too late. A major division revamp called the Centennial Plan was scrapped.

A badge-engineered minivan and SUV, the Silhouette and Bravada, did little to help. Had Olds stayed in touch with the marketplace, it would have seen the growing migration from cars to SUVs. But it didn't. Because Oldsmobile cars were already insipid, hurrying some badge engineered, average at best, "trucks" to market only accelerated Oldsmobile's loss of credibility. Not for the first time, GM believed that the customers would not know the difference and that the Olds name would carry the day. What Olds name?

Olds dealers had pleaded "something for everybody" instead of clamoring for an Oldsmobile line that stood apart and meant something. Dealers having the power they do, GM went along. This was no smarter than the cookie-cutter cars GM spread across its divisions in the 1970s. Saving money by tracking the platform permutations instead of customer wants and needs "saved" GM from continuing a once-hallowed brand.

Once the third-best-selling car in the US, Oldsmobile celebrated its centennial in 1997, its marketing in disarray, its product line spotty and confused, and its brand equity hardly worth the ink it took to write "Oldsmobile."

Seven years later, General Motors killed the division. A wise move, but a sad one. A CNN poll taken during Oldsmobile's last week of existence showed that 38 percent of the respondents checked "Who cares? It's just a car."

The Plymouth Saga

More than three-quarters of a century ago, a new nameplate sailed into the automotive world with an ambitious target: challenge Ford and Chevrolet's dominance of the high-volume low-end segment. The nameplate was Plymouth, and for many years it did just that. In 1973, dealers sold 882,000 Plymouths. Today there are no Plymouths.

This aggressive newcomer to the low end of the car market cleverly and effectively positioned itself as one of the "low-priced three," the other two being Ford and Chevrolet, brands that even in the 1920s were American icons.

Plymouth was a player from the outset, yet on the brand front, it suffered somewhat from the beginning. The Chrysler Corporation never intended to have stand-alone Plymouth dealers. The Plymouth brand was dualed with Chrysler, DeSoto, or Dodge, the three nameplates aimed respectively at Buick, Oldsmobile, and Pontiac. On the positive side, this meant that Plymouth took the field with a ready-made dealer body. By 1930, it was the corporation's best-selling nameplate, a distinction it retained through the 1978 model year.

The Plymouth name derived from Plymouth Rock, and the car was rock solid from day one. It promised dependable, low-cost transportation, and it delivered just that. Plymouth began the 1950s with just two model series, the Deluxe Six and the Special Deluxe, both inexpensive and reliable. Of course, this meant that no lad or lass wanted mom and pop to buy a Plymouth. By the 1970s, that had changed.

Beginning with its 1956 Fury model, a V-8-powered coupe with good performance for its day, Plymouth began adding more and more performance coupes to its lineup. With the stunning success of the 1964½ Ford Mustang, which created the "pony car" category, Plymouth stepped up its internal pace. By the early 1970s, it was a popular nameplate in the youth market. Cars such as the Barracuda, the Road Runner, and the Duster were fast— and often more affordable—alternatives to Fords and Chevrolets. Many in what would become known as the Baby Boomer Generation thought Plymouths were hot and desirable. A few still do and have bid over a million dollars for classic restorations of Hemi-powered Plymouth Barracudas and Super Birds.

The Plymouths never approached the Mustangs in volume, but they were competitive in the hearts and minds of younger buyers. In 1970, Ford sold just under 200,000 Mustangs while Plymouth sold fewer than 100,000 Barracudas, Dusters, and Road Runners. The car that started the performance years at Plymouth, the 1953 Fury, was by now a full-size car that, although it offered V-8 power, was something of a slug in the eyes of pony car buyers.

By 1989, there weren't many more models than the two Plymouth had offered at the start of the 1950s. The 1989 Plymouths included Horizon, Sundance, Reliant and Acclaim and, of course, the Dodge Caravan minivan clone called the Plymouth Voyager. These were all shared with the corporation's Dodge and Chrysler divisions. Only the badge and grilles changed. An aging throwback sedan, the Gran Fury V-8, was in its final year. Even the most optimistic Plymouth executive had to see that the nameplate was in deep trouble and headed for worse.

Chrysler did not announce the death of Plymouth for another 10 years, in 1999, but the lack of new product exposed its intentions long before the announcement. Plymouth started the 1995 model year with only the Acclaim and the new Neon subcompact—also sold as the Neon at Dodge dealerships—plus the Voyager minivan.

Only the introduction of the 1997 Plymouth Prowler gave the faintest indication that Plymouth might have a future, and that turned out to be a false hope. The Prowler, a beautiful modern interpretation of the classic American hot rod, was to be a "halo" car for the Plymouth brand. It would, so the marketing story went, add the magic so absent from the rest of the line. But there was just too big a disconnect from the Prowler and all other "Plymouths." They shared nothing in common. The now-invisible ordinary Plymouths sold on one attribute: price.

The startling act of making the Prowler a Plymouth—Dodge by this time was the designated "performance division" of the corporation—could have conceivably revitalized the Plymouth name had Chrysler chosen to make its PT Cruiser a Plymouth instead of a Chrysler. But even with the sales success of the PT Cruiser, Plymouth would have still been saddled with the cloned Neon, Breeze, and Voyager.

The Prowler was a desperation Hail Mary pass in a game that was already over. A management that dried up the product line finally had to face the results of its thinking. It could surely be argued that Chrysler didn't need three divisions, but the leadership would have saved time and money if it had displayed the courage to do away with Plymouth much earlier than it did. It might also be argued that Plymouth dealers had enough clout to delay things, but because virtually every Plymouth dealer was also a Chrysler or Dodge dealer, this is doubtful.

Plymouth, like Oldsmobile, missed the movement away from cars to light trucks. It had only the minivan. No sign of a pickup truck or an SUV—which would in any case have been shared with the Dodge Division. With so many "old" brands competing in what had become a dwindling car segment, some lackluster brands inevitably had to go.

By 1999, the year Chrysler Corporation handed down Plymouth's death sentence, there indeed was little point in trying to save the brand. It had been thoroughly devalued by then, and only the Prowler was exclusive to Plymouth. From the beginning, of course, there had been no stand-alone Plymouth dealers, so Chrysler-Plymouth dealers became simply Chrysler dealers, and Dodge-Plymouth dealers became Dodge stores. The products at both kinds of outlets remained the same except for trim and content levels; only the nameplates changed.

The Evil of Conventional Wisdom

Almost to the bitter end, executives at Oldsmobile and Plymouth claimed to believe that the divisions could be saved. An exception to this charade was John Rock, an outspoken bear of a man whom GM sent in to run Oldsmobile in its declining years. GM executives probably wished they had sent someone else, because Rock really did believe that Olds could survive, and he did not shy away from saying so. Rock had a product plan, called the Centennial Plan, to work with, and it might actually have produced enough cars with enough character to achieve the impossible. His dealers would probably have followed Rock into hell, which in the minds of many was where they already were, but his leaders at GM were another story.

The plain fact of the matter—leaving aside some sane arguments that no company needs more than a couple of divisions—is that, year after year, executives in charge did not have the courage to stand up to top management. They should have said, "Our product lineup is not competitive, not exciting, and it is going to sink us if we don't do something about it." Instead, they swigged down the corporate Kool-Aid and continued to march until the poison stopped the suffering.

Top management, meanwhile, continued to cling to the belief that sharing platforms would save money. Obviously, that's true from the bean-counter standpoint. But it won't save a damn thing if every car looks like every other car, with its badge as the major differentiation. And if it's boring to begin with, that just makes matters worse. The consumer is not stupid. Not *that* stupid, anyway. And the end result is a model, replete with efficiency and money-saving devices, that no one wants to be seen in. Bottom line: you can lose money by saving money if you lack the courage to preserve your brand's value and integrity.

A brand that has no value—having lost it through an endless series of cowardly compromises—and which bores the consumer comatose cannot be saved by brilliant marketing. In the cases of Oldsmobile and Plymouth, the marketing was closer to moronic than magnificent, once again because no one would stand up for what any sensible auto executive knew to be the right way.

The auto industry is in many ways like a cattle herd—lots of followers and a handful of executives courageous enough to be the bell cows. At its worst, the industry makes lemmings look like rugged individualists. Ask yourself this: if it costs around a billion dollars to bring a new car to market, why do so many of these "new" vehicles look like things someone else has already done? Because, like cows following the herd, it just feels safer that way.

You can always look at the market and see what your neighbors are doing. Examine their products, marketing, advertising, Internet activity, whatever. See who is having success with what. Then follow them. Just try not to moo.

What's wrong with imitating success or adopting conventional wisdom? After all, isn't imitation the sincerest form of flattery? What's wrong is that imitation rarely sells as well as something fresh. Worse yet, it continues to muddy the water in terms of who you are and what you represent to the buying public. How many look-alike, Me-Too products do you think the public wants to keep track of?

As we said at the outset, we think conventional wisdom is an oxymoron. Those hoary mantras may be conventional but they rarely represent wisdom. A blind devotion to following them, coupled with a lack of the courage to question them, will ensure that you never set yourself or your brand apart.

Do you see the irony in taking the safe, conventional, cowardly way out? We do. The safe way, once the results are in and the disaster can be quantified, invariably turns out to be the most dangerous path you could have taken.

2

The Market

"Many brands want to be American. However, there is no uniquely and consistently American brand in the auto industry."

Ford Executive Vice President Mark Fields
at the 2006 Los Angeles Auto Show

The Test of Perspective

It is easier to subscribe to the beliefs of the Flat Earth Society than to convince yourself that you can disconnect yourself from the consumer and still grow a business. Amazingly, a great many executives believe exactly that. In this chapter, we introduce you to the test of perspective and to the career-saving Brand Triangle, which will keep you from being among the misguided.

What does the test of perspective mean? It is a test of your ability to put the market in perspective—the capability or talent to place things in their true position or relative importance based on your experience and insights. You are able to see the market as it is and, more important, as it might be. Having perspective is the necessary precursor to vision. And it demands a great familiarity with the market and how it works. The success of Saturn was based on an independent team's incisive view of the marketplace and the company having the *chutzpah* to introduce a new way of selling cars.

The Story of Saturn

"A different kind of company, a different kind of car," was Saturn's original advertising slogan. A lot has been written about Saturn, which was one of the rising stars of the car business until GM starved it of new product. Going back to the beginning, what exactly did Hal Riney & Partners mean when they wrote this line?

In the mid-1980s, as GM began to lose serious market share to the Japanese, it embarked on an odyssey to build a brand that could fight the Japanese successfully in the small-car market. GM did not believe it was possible to do that with any of its existing brands. The company invested billions of dollars, built a new plant in faraway Spring Hill, Tennessee, and got the UAW to agree to an innovative new labor contract. Then it took years to get to market and, in the end, produced some remarkably ordinary cars.

Yet for years Saturn was a resounding success. Why? Because as the company attempted to rewrite the rules on building a small domestic car, it took a hard look at the entire ball game—how to engineer a car, how to build a car, and how to sell a car. Saturn's brain trust made the decision early on that they wanted to be different from both their fellow GM divisions and the Japanese. And they succeeded in doing just that. Saturn showed the marketplace a fresh and different face.

Saturn and its newly minted dealer body gave themselves permission to dissect the methods by which cars were being sold at the time. It was not a pretty autopsy. Customers, in the main, hated the buying experience and hated the service experience. This insight was hardly groundbreaking, but their drive to change things was. They understood the market, and they knew the customers they were targeting. They knew that most customers did not like to haggle on price and still wind up feeling as if they had been hosed down like a muddy pickup truck. Customers, in Saturn's view, wanted to learn more about the product and were willing to pay a fair price. And they wanted to feel good about their purchase because it represented an important decision for them.

With all that in mind, Saturn and its charter dealers designed a selling process that began with everyone paying the same price: Manufacturer's Suggested Retail Price(MSRP) or "list." This bold strategic decision ignored standard practice, defied prejudice, and to a degree skirted the law. Getting rid of the undesirable price bickering attracted an entirely different type of salesperson to Saturn stores: men and women who wanted to sell a product with pride and to make buyers happy. Saturn focused the sales process on listening to the customer's needs and building a relationship based on trust.

Saturn steeped its sales force in product knowledge and paid them a flat fee for the sale of each car—not a commission based on how much they could squeeze out of each hapless customer. In a burst of marketing genius, Saturn did not send its early prototypes to the scrapyard crusher. Instead, it made cutaway display cars like those seen at auto shows and placed them in dealerships. This enabled the salespeople to discuss with customers what lay beneath the Saturn skin. Customers were encouraged to take test drives and took comfort from knowing they would all pay the same price.

Then Saturn took the delivery process to a new level. With precious few exceptions, most dealers were no better at delivering a car to a customer than the counter person who hands you a Big Mac and mumbles something about having a nice day. Virtually everyone did little more than hand customers a set of keys and wish them good luck. Maybe the car contained enough fuel to get to the Exxon station, maybe it didn't.

Saturn made its retail buying experience less like slaughtering cattle and more like a celebration. Before delivery, every car was thoroughly inspected, cleaned, and topped off with gas. Then, when customers picked up their new Saturn, all salespersons were invited to join the buyer in the dealership's separate delivery room. There they cheered and shouted congratulations as the buyer had a picture taken standing next to the new car. Customers loved the experience and couldn't wait to tell their friends about it. Prospective buyers who happened to be in the showroom when a new car was being delivered were impressed by it as well. You could almost feel the generation of favorable word-of-mouth.

Saturn also tackled the service process through technology and hospitality. Each dealership had to have its own IBM AS400 computer that was online with the Saturn mainframe computers. When a customer brought a car in for service, its VIN number would be entered into the system, causing all previous maintenance and recall work performed—no matter at which dealership—to show up on the screen. That provided the service writer with more information and maintenance history than was available at any other brand's dealership. If this was the second time for a repair, the service writer could discuss that with the customer and work hard to ensure that they fixed the problem this time, thereby pleasing the customer and avoiding expensive lemon-law problems. The service department could also use the AS400 to download revised software to the computers on board the car—commonplace today, but considered Space Age high-tech at the time.

The dealerships didn't stop there. They offered doughnuts and coffee to all their customers. Saturn was not the first company to think of this, but they executed it smartly and in every store. Saturn insisted; it did not rely on local dealers doing it only if they thought it was smart or felt like it. The company even ran a clever Hal Riney commercial featuring a customer driving across the country conjuring up problems that would justify a stop at different Saturn stores for the jelly doughnuts. The Saturn folks saw through him, but never let him know they knew.

Saturn's secret to success was a fresh perspective on the market, how it worked, its shortcomings, and what their customers truly wanted. The company looked at the same old bad habits that everyone else saw, but it used a different eye, one focused on the changes needed to find a better way for its customers. Saturn had the courage—and it took real courage—to attack bad sales and service practices that had been defended for decades by the nation's car dealers. More than 15 years on, Nissan, Toyota, Honda, and many others have yet to effectively address these issues.

Perhaps one of the most telling measures of Saturn's brand strength came when it invited all Saturn owners to Spring Hill, Tennessee, for a "family reunion" celebrating its tenth anniversary. Despite Spring Hill's remote location, an astonishing 44,000 owners showed up. And remember that Saturns were painfully ordinary cars. Dependable but undistinguished. No flashy design. No high performance. But they stood for something with a specific group of customers: dependable performance and respect for the customer. That, students, is brand power.

The Saturn brand was created by a leadership group convinced that, to compete against the Japanese, they had to build a stand-alone company independent of mainstream GM management and processes. Isn't it ironic that at the same time, General Motors was stripping its traditional brands of their autonomy and distinctiveness? History is whispering, none too softly, that GM identified the right problem but applied the wrong fix.

How the Marketplace Works

That a man or woman can rise to the top of a major company and not have a basic understanding of how the marketplace works is one of the miracles of modern American business. This aberration is all but beyond comprehension in a society where aerobic shopping has been elevated to near-Olympic status and where almost every person has at least some shopping experience.

A marketplace is a place where buyers and sellers meet to buy and sell goods and services. Is that clear and straightforward, or what?

Too many executives ignore the most important truth about the marketplace: it's about choice, stupid. Many choices made by many parties. For the hearing-impaired, **"It's about choice, stupid!"** And we're not talking about providing more choice; we're talking about providing *clear* choice.

Car buyers have more choices than a glutton at the buffet table, yet branding, the device intended to set products apart, just doesn't seem to be, well, setting them apart any more. Auto companies seem to be lacking the insight and the will to stand out in a terribly crowded market. They fail repeatedly to make themselves attractive to buyers. For many of these companies, the failure traces to a lack of understanding how the market has changed and how—and why—they must change with it.

Just remember, customers can choose someone else. If you don't give them a good enough reason to choose you, they *will* look elsewhere.

Conventional Wisdom

"We need to sell to our customers one at a time." It may be conventional, but is it wrong? No, but most companies mouthing that adage didn't mean it. At the time this wisdom was being trotted out at every major auto show press conference, the industry was buying media by the pound. Network television's cost per thousand (CPM) ruled the advertising mindset. "This audience skews too far female." Or, "That's okay because it only costs us peanuts per thousand for the 35-to-55-year-old males that we want."

Does this sound like selling one at a time? Of course not. We bought ad space and time by the ton and not by the individual. We talked individual marketing, but we behaved mass marketing—in a world where only one-half of one percent of the US public buys a new vehicle each month. Market fragmentation has now driven the industry to the point where it really needs to sell one vehicle at a time, and expanded media choices allow it more chances to buy "individually." Successful marketers must embrace and adopt selling to one individual at a time, because customers are now in a position to demand it. And the car industry is beginning to do just that.

Advertising Age, in its "2005 Interactive Media and Marketing Awards" issue, selected Chrysler as the interactive marketer of the year. Imagine, an automaker was picked over companies from every other industry. In her article covering the award, Jean Halliday of *Advertising Age* said:

> The maker of Dodge, Jeep and Chrysler vehicles has built interactive into its marketing strategy and backed it with heftier budgets over each of the past few years. At the hub of it all is the desire to pull consumers into a voluntary, ongoing dialogue.
>
> Jeff Bell, VP-Jeep and Chrysler brands, says the marketer dialed up its interactivity early for three reasons: the splintering of media, relative affordability and more measurable return on investment.

The world has gone from "The audience for my FM radio station is classic rock enthusiasts" to "My audience is people who buy an iPod and download their music from iTunes. They then listen to exactly what they want to hear." Add to the mix the phenomenon of podcasts, downloadable programming that appeals to very narrow audiences—perhaps to some of your buyers. And the fragmentation continues.

In November of 2005, the three major networks announced that they would sell prime-time programming through video on demand so that customers who were willing to pay could watch the show at their convenience and not the network's. Selling to customers one at a time—and selling them what *they* want to buy, not what *you* want to sell—has arrived. And it is profoundly changing our consumers' mindset.

Trends Founded on Contradictions

Reading tea leaves or chicken entrails is difficult business because it leaves so much open to interpretation. Reading the automotive marketplace is slightly less esoteric but fully as controversial. Right now, five trends, each based on a contradiction, are having a profound effect on the car business. They are:

1. Brand Distinctiveness/Brand Portfolio
2. More Choice/Less Choice
3. High Growth/Low Reality
4. Brand Value/Insane Discounting
5. Low Risk/High Reward

Chances are, you can identify with all five to a greater or lesser degree. In any event, your task is to understand these obstacles to success and find a way past them.

Brand Distinctiveness/Brand Portfolio

For some time now, the auto industry has been going through a consolidation. Because it is a mature industry, this is not altogether surprising. Volkswagen, which added Audi many years ago, has now purchased SEAT, Skoda, Bentley, Lamborghini, and Bugatti. Ford has purchased Jaguar, Aston Martin, Volvo, Land Rover, and a controlling interest in Mazda. Daimler-Benz purchased Chrysler and was in the process of acquiring Mitsubishi when the Novocain wore off, and it reversed direction. General Motors purchased Saab and then pursued a different tack by buying minority holdings in Suzuki, Isuzu, Subaru, and Daewoo. GM also entered into an ill-advised agreement to buy Italy's Fiat and ended up with about a $3 billion dollar hangover when it unbundled Subaru and walked away from the Fiat purchase in 2005. Renault bought a controlling interest in Nissan, and Hyundai now owns a controlling interest in Kia. And the list goes on.

In each one of these acquisitions, the acquiring company talked about the value of the brand they were buying, its unique character and loyal customers, and how they would grow that brand while finding savings through synergies in ways that would not dilute the distinctiveness of their new brand. Looking at how well they are doing, it seems as if many of them sold themselves a fairy tale.

There are success stories. Renault's approach with Nissan has allowed Nissan to grow at a rapid rate. Renault concentrated on making Nissan a healthy company and then a strong brand without launching an immediate search for synergies between two quite dissimilar companies and cultures. In 2005, Carlos Ghosn became Chairman and CEO of both Renault and Nissan, and it will be interesting to see if he allows the drive for greater sharing and efficiency to have the undesirable effect of diluting both brands.

Mutual dilution has happened in too many instances. The Jaguar X-type is built off the Ford Mondeo platform, and the Saab 2-X and 9-X are built, respectively, off Subaru and Chevrolet Trailblazer platforms. The automotive press, with some accuracy, called the Saab 2-X the Saabaru. The efficiency gene seems to be the dominant gene. This "synergistic" brand consolidation has been a primary contributor to the next trend.

More Choice/Less Choice

How is it possible that more choice can lead to less choice? We've discussed how proliferation and fragmentation have expanded the amount of choice the market offers today's car buyers. In 1995, buyers could choose from 256 models. In 2005 there are 316 models with more coming every month. Even as car companies consolidate, the number of individual offerings keeps growing. The US car market is the most profitable automotive market in the world. Naturally, everyone wants to be here, but it is jammed to the rafters now, and the Chinese have yet to make their entrance. (But you can hear them moving around outside the barn.)

The market has grown, yet as industry sales have increased, the average number of unit sales per model has gone down. One might conclude that, with a mature market, the industry had to offer more choices tailored to smaller segments, thereby stimulating interest. But the contradiction is this: there's lots of choice, but very little of it is properly differentiated. Customers are *not* being offered clear, meaningful choice; they are being offered overlapping and "virtually the same" choice. Proliferation does not necessarily bring with it a raft of individual and attractive personalities.

For example, GM offers four minivans: the Chevrolet Upland, Pontiac Montana, Saturn Relay, and Buick Terraza. All these, with the exception of some minor styling differences, are the same vehicle. Is this choice? It's like giving names to each biscuit in a Pillsbury container. The same by any other name is still the same. They are almost indistinguishable and equally mediocre. Do meaningless choices add more selection or just more confusion?

Undistinguishable, meritless choice leads to a climate of diminished real choice for the consumer. It makes the job of sorting out all this "choice" hard work for buyers. It takes a manufacturer with uncommon backbone to provide clear choices.

High Growth/Low Reality

Each year the auto industry gets to demonstrate its version of voodoo mathematics. It occurs when the car companies trot out their sales forecasts for the coming year. An annual Laurel and Hardy fire drill, these forecasts generally produce a sum much higher than the total industry will sell. It's laudable to have ambition, but runaway ambition can get a company into trouble. Conventional wisdom says that you are either growing or declining. It fails to emphasize that growth must actually occur, not just be talked about. Carried too far, belief in an excessively rosy future can cripple a brand.

The car market is both mature and cyclical. Certainly not growth-oriented enough to encourage marketers to believe that next year's sales increase will be a result of market expansion. But that's hardly an alarming detail for most of the companies projecting sales increases. They state openly their intent to increase market share by conquesting sales from the competition. A small stumbling point even with voodoo on your side is that all companies can't grow in a flat market. What drives this folly?

The explanation is simple: expectations. Whether executives have the faintest idea of how to deliver sales growth, few are so dense as to not know what the higher-ups expect. Forgotten is the quaint notion of sales growth as an outcome of *earning* your way in the market, the act of making yourself more desirable to more customers. Fantasies don't count.

Yet these very same fantasies can ruin your day if not your career. Bad things happen when you mismatch sales goals and market reality. Companies base billion-dollar investment decisions in plants and products on their forecasts. Understanding this begins to explain to you how an industry can create 24 million excess units of production capacity.

Bogus forecasts and false assumptions neuter the planning process. Precious time is wasted on plans doomed to fail. People know when plans are unrealistic—*e.g.,* "We will raise our prices, reduce our marketing budget, and sell more cars" or some variation thereof. It demoralizes and disempowers the people you are counting on to deliver. Companies then start the tango of mid-course corrections and "road maps to recovery" as they desperately chase numbers that were foolish from the get-go. Watching a major part of the industry churn this way is embarrassing.

When you get it wrong, the sales and marketing team comes under tremendous pressure to deliver the numbers, realistic or not. This bends their heads toward short-term solutions, short-term *expensive* solutions. Most of your hard-earned brand value goes out the window when you look to pricing as your salvation. Even whispering the possibility of potential long-term damage to your brand is viewed as unacceptable obstructionist behavior.

Meanwhile, the sales department flails about like a wounded sea tortoise and tells themselves "any day now." Getting the promised numbers becomes paramount to shareholder value, and it makes us lose focus on what's important to our customer. As we chase more sales, the incremental cost to sell each additional car skyrockets. It all has a very psychotropic drug-like feel to it. And there is no joy in Mudville.

Brand Value/Insane Discounting

A good example of this trend occurred a few years ago when all GM executives showed up sporting lapel pins with the number 29 on them, signifying the goal of 29 percent market share. Was this goal based on a great product plan? No. Was it based on creative marketing that would sell the customers on the wisdom of buying products from one of their brands? No. It was based on a belief that they could flex their marketing muscle and buy market share.

Immediately after 9/11, GM introduced a zero-percent financing plan that kept the American economy rolling and pushed GM to the forefront of the market. The sales came not because the products or brands were more desirable, but because customers were flocking to "the deal." In an efficiency move, GM pooled its considerable advertising dollars and promoted zero-percent financing under the corporate banner. Someone forgot to remind GM leadership that General Motors, like Proctor & Gamble, is supposed to be a holding company, not a brand.

GM fell into a trap. First, it spent huge sums telling the market that the only reason to buy a GM product was the deal. Furthermore, by advertising it under the GM flag, the corporation underscored the lack of real differences between most of its brands. That all the cars and trucks were in the same distressed-merchandise bin sent the message that they were all equally in trouble.

The second part of the trap is that all great "deals" require large marketing expenditures, vast sums of money that could have been spent building brand equity. For example, telling the consumer what makes Buick great. But that act would have presupposed that GM believed in Buick's greatness.

Over the last four years GM has shown how hard it is to kick the discount addiction. In the summer of 2005, it launched the "Employee Discount Plan" in which all customers got the GM employee discount. It sold cars, but again at what price to brand equity and future sales? Is it just a coincidence that EDP are initials associated with Ross Perot, the man GM bought off its board in 1988 for telling the truth?

True, we live in a discount world, and all car companies offer discounts. But compare Toyota, with per-car incentive costs for 2005 of around $1,000, to GM's $3,600 per car. When you lean continually on discounts to save your bacon, you embark on a downward spiral that is difficult if not impossible to arrest. You dissipate brand value and take away resources necessary to compete on an equal footing. In short, you commoditize your brand—gut it of any distinctive perceived value—when you sell on the basis of price. You lose.

The scariest part of all of this discussion is that it's old news, or at least should be to all the MBAs in the auto industry charged with the task of keeping up with such matters. Nearly 30 years ago, Robert Prentice, a Lever Brothers promotional-marketing executive, developed what he called the "consumer franchise building" approach to promotion.

Prentice had tracked a wide range of promotions for a wide range of products for more than 20 years. The result was the identification of two kinds of promotions—franchise building and franchise destroying—and the differences were painfully simple. Franchise-building promotions were those that emphasized or gave the consumer the chance to experience some distinctive quality of the product, thereby making the consumer more inclined to buy it based on a new appreciation of its value and benefits. Franchise-destroying promotions didn't. Instead they emphasized something unrelated to the intrinsic value of the brand.

The best examples of franchise-building promotions are sampling and product demonstrations. They make the product and the brand experience the star of the show. Franchise-destroying promotions include coupons, contests, sweepstakes, rebates, and discounts—all things that emphasize something other than the product.

A lot of time has passed since Prentice developed his original idea, so this isn't—or shouldn't be—new, and it has been restated and rephrased numerous times over the years. But it's still accurate and maybe more relevant than ever. When you sell based on price, you tell your prospect that the stated value isn't the real value. You also emphasize the least important element of the brand and its potential benefits to the buyer.

Low Risk/High Reward

The entrepreneurial spirit is alive and well in America, yet at many car companies it seems to be on life support. Of late, the industry's entrepreneurial muscle has not been exercised much beyond embracing risk avoidance. Can you imagine some of the recent entrepreneurs in the consumer electronics business saying, "Let's create a new toaster that is a bit larger, a bit faster heating, and is garnished with a bit more chrome"? No. Camera phones, iPods, satellite radio, and the near death of Kodak at the hands of digital camera makers were engineered by people who loved risk and were in a hurry. They were in a hurry to make markets, be the first, and to be on the cutting edge of technology and style. They were not the people who created the Ford Five Hundred.

Entrepreneurs know that success requires risk. And that the longer the odds, the greater the potential payout when they bring it off. Notice we say "when." Entrepreneurs seek risk knowing that chance-taking is what separates them from the corporate drones. And that big risk leads to big payoffs. They thrive on the challenge, the adrenaline rush.

That's not an endorsement of recklessness. It's simply the nature of risk and return. Innovation thought leaders such as Thomas Kuczmarski will tell you that if your new products are "succeeding" at a rate much above 35 percent, they probably aren't true innovations. They are line extensions. And they might make sense to your product line and/or to your customers, but they aren't genuine innovations. Genuine innovation means risk and a relatively high degree of failure. And the potential for high payoff. That's what makes innovations special and unique—and not mere knock-offs

The car business, on the other hand, is run largely by corporate milquetoasts. An examination of how successful automotive executives moved through their careers would show how few were exposed to entrepreneurial experiences. Having profit-and-loss responsibility, though important, is not entrepreneurship. Running established businesses or divisions barely qualifies, given the number of decisions that need upstream approval. Start-ups and turnarounds provide the closest approximations, but few automotive executives get to practice these skills in their early careers. Instead they learn patience. And fear.

Yet the car industry is big business. And it arrogates to itself a solemn pledge to safeguard shareholder money. Putting shareholders first means that conservatism reigns. No one in the industry wants to make a big mistake, or even a small one, so most executives walk around with their heads at about belt level. They become one of the herd. That is a mistake. Their world is saturated, and becoming part of the marketplace wallpaper is a big and costly mistake. To succeed, you must stand out, which takes uncommon courage.

Despite the undoubted wisdom of the above paragraphs, many executives still believe that they can take a low-risk path and end up with substantial rewards. You need only look at the plethora of Me-Too cars and Me-Too marketing to see how many believers there are. It is the car business's answer to fool's gold.

How can you rise above these trends or turn them to your advantage? How do you balance the drive for cost efficiency with your desire to build a world class brand? Start by seeing, clearly and honestly, how customers perceive your brand. And use that information as a first step toward making your brand world class. We have a way of looking at brands that should help.

The Brand Triangle^{sm}

Before you can set yourself apart, it is important to understand how customers view brands. To help you visualize what they see and experience, we introduce you to a marketing tool that just might save your career. It's called the Brand Triangle[sm].

The premise of the Brand Triangle is that consumers experience a brand through four key areas. Each of the four areas affects not only the public's view of the brand but also shapes their perception and expectation for each area. The areas include the brand's *image,* the *product,* the *retail experience* and the glue that holds it all together, the company's *culture*—how a consumer experiences the brand, directly and indirectly, through the actions of the company's people.

The Brand Triangle provides a way to assess the current strengths and weaknesses of a brand. What is the *main* attraction of your brand? Is it the brand's image, the product, the retail experience, or the culture? If your main attraction is product, what are its strengths over the competition? How do the other aspects of the Triangle have to work in order to support your key driver? And in every case, does your culture play a strong role in bringing your brand to life?

We will discuss the Brand Triangle as if your brand already exists, but it is equally helpful when you're starting from scratch and must create everything. Let's see how it works.

At the top of the triangle is *Brand,* in essence what you stand for. This encompasses the brand's image, its desirability, its momentum, and its overall importance to its target customers. What is the level of awareness of the brand and what are its image strengths and weaknesses? Where does it fit in the marketplace? Is it a mass, specialty, or niche brand? Does it stand out from its competition in any meaningful way? What characteristics do customers really appreciate in the brand? Is it exciting or boring? Is it rising or falling? Does it have any energy and momentum? Do we know and like who we are?

At the lower left-hand corner of the triangle is *Product.* How do owners and third parties such as the trade press rate it? Is it regarded as competent, competitive, or best in class? Does it have a clarity of benefits that trumps the competition? Is there a consistent theme throughout the product lineup? Over time, has it

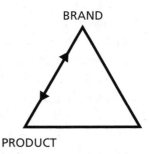

carved out a unique or compelling spot in the market? Is it considered to be high quality? Does it garner high praise and loyalty from its owners? Does it generate high customer satisfaction scores? Does it consistently lead in technology? Do we love our product, and is it a source of strength for the brand?

The lower right-hand corner of the triangle is *Retail*. While the importance of the retail experience varies with different industries, it is often a critical factor in how people view the brand. Is the experience branded, and if so, by whom? The retailer or you? If by the retailer, how does that affect a customer's view of the brand? Does the retail experience enhance the purchase experience, or is it a handicap to be overcome? Can your customers find your product? Are you well represented in the store? What does the store look like, and what does it say about your brand? Being sold in Saks Fifth Avenue says one thing; being sold in Wal-Mart makes an entirely different statement. Both are perfect for certain brands and won't work at all for others. Are the people who represent you in the stores well trained and highly motivated? Do they do a good job of representing your brand? Do they do a good job with after-sale service? Do you sell on the Internet? Does your Internet activity support your physical retail activity and vice-versa? The questions can go on and on and on—and should.

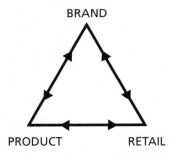

To be in business you must sell something. Yet not all businesses include a retail component. In a business-to-business operation you can substitute the word sales for retail. The same questions are relevant: how do your customers experience the purchase of your products, and how does that affect their view of your brand and products?

In the center of the triangle is a company's *Culture*, and it is essential to your success. We define culture as "who we are and how we do things." In terms of the Brand Triangle our interest lies with how culture affects a person's view of the brand. We believe that culture is the glue that holds brands together. Haven't you had experiences where you've been totally won over by the people representing a brand? Sure you have. And you've also experienced the opposite.

Wrestling with each of the four areas is productive, yet the power of the Brand Triangle lies in seeing and understanding how they interact. Clearly, the brand's image affects people's initial opinion and expectation of the product. Great products, over time, have established a brand's image. Conversely, a series of misfires on the product front have undone more brands than you can shake a worthless stock certificate at.

A brand's image sets up an expectation for the retail experience, and that experience can make or break a purchase decision. A potential customer's opinion of the product creates expectations for what he or she wants from the retail experience. This has been a hard lesson for the car industry to learn, and just as difficult for its dealers.

Culture, in the center of the triangle, drives the other three. Sometimes it works behind the scenes as companies develop their products and programs. Or it can be working with customers, whether at the retail level or within the company itself. Help lines, customer assistance, field staffs with both retail and customer exposure, and all employees who influence the marketing, public relations, and product development contribute to the image of the Brand. The employees must first "get it," otherwise there's not a hope in hell that your customers will understand and believe in your brand, let alone form a relationship with it. No matter how brilliant a product or marketing campaign you create, the first employee a customer encounters can cement or destroy that relationship.

When working with a new group, we like to take them through the concept of the Brand Triangle and then ask them to rate their own situation on a simple five-point scale. This lets them ascribe a point value to their own view of their brand, product, retail experience, and culture.

In industries where there is sufficient research—and here the auto industry is certainly an overachiever—you can decide what research best describes how the customer views each of the four areas relative to your competition. Not all industries have access to such comprehensive consumer research and must rely on a combination of available quantitative data and the Delphi method.

Not surprisingly, when you work with people who have devoted years to a particular industry, you'll find that their rating of each area generally mirrors the research. When you are making important and expensive decisions, it is of course preferable to have valid consumer research.

When Charlie Hughes joined Mazda in 2000, he tried this method with his executive committee, the company's top 60 managers, and with 15 dealers from the dealer advisory group. Across all three groups, the ratings were remarkably consistent. Brand was rated as C-minus. The minus shows how all groups resist being pinned down to whatever rating scale you put forth. The product was given a solid B. The retail organization was given a D by company personnel and an F by the dealers. They were not asked to rate culture because, at that point, they had no common understanding of the concept.

Subsequent research from J. D. Power, Allison-Fisher, and others showed that the Delphi ratings were generally accurate. As was true at Mazda, what surprises people when first exposed to the Brand Triangle is how it reveals the intricacies of the relationships between all four components. It helps you visualize what is working, what is holding you back, and on which areas you need to concentrate.

Go ahead; give the Brand Triangle a test drive. Rate your brand for each component. What does that tell you? Do you have brand clarity? Is your strategy working? Does each area support your brand position? Together, do they provide your customers with what they are looking for?

The Brand Triangle does not argue that you be best in all four areas; it does prod you to be *you* in all four areas. You decide in a world of finite resources where you need to have the greatest impact on your customers. Most likely that will fall into a single area. You then must orchestrate the remaining components so that they reinforce your strategy.

Testing Your Courage

Building brands is a test of courage, your courage. To be fair, courage is not a black-and-white issue. In building a world-class brand, you will face trials in many aspects of your business, tests that will challenge your character. Tests of perspective—vision, engagement, skill, inclusion, will, emotion, and conviction—will work to knock you off course. If you are not up to these tests, the best you can hope for is being as unremarkable as the rest of the herd.

Sizing up the market, as we have discussed in this chapter, will test your *perspective*. Limited market perspective makes these other tests a moot point. However, if you have keen insight into your market you will face these seven additional tests.

1. Finding a way to set yourself apart, to *differentiate* yourself, will test your *vision*.
2. Building a culture that brings your vision alive will test your ability to *engage* folks.
3. Developing products that stand out will test your *skill* as well as your competitive spirit.
4. Enrolling all those you need to travel with you on this journey, building a conspiracy both inside and outside the company, will test your sense of *inclusion*.
5. To be a strong flavor you must not dilute yourself. This requires a consistency throughout all that you do and is a real test of *will*.
6. Beating tough competition requires passion, and that is a test of your *emotion*.

7. Business is the world's longest marathon. It must be approached with patience, and it will test your *conviction*.

It sounds like a never-ending series of trials, and it is. And that is the fun part, for this game gets played each day. And day in and day out you have the opportunity to move your brand forward, sideways, or backwards. Bring all the grit you have. Know going in that, most often, it's easier to do the wrong thing. After all, conventional wisdom would be on your side. But then you would be like most other people: common.

To help you avoid being common, we discuss in the following chapters what you need to think about in order to pass these seven tests.

Differentiate

> When you reach for the stars, you may not quite get one, but you won't come up with a handful of mud either.
>
> *Advertising legend Leo Burnett*

The Test of Vision

We are immersed in a world crammed with choice, yet much of it is depressingly ordinary. To build a brand that stands out requires a vision in which you combine market perspective, creative thinking, and an appetite for risk—creativity aimed at doing something better, having the backbone to stand up and declare it, and then delivering on your promise. Differentiating a brand is tough, we know, but being ordinary just makes life tougher.

A "Mini" Case Study

When you look at success through a rearview mirror, why does it look so obvious? The second generation of Mini by BMW is a smash hit in terms of impact if not in terms of absolute volume. Knowing BMW, it's a profitable hit. The Mini is successful because BMW knew its audience, was not afraid to differentiate, and because its values led it to bring an authentic product to market.

BMW introduced the current Mini in 2002, but Mini is a product with a much longer history. Mini came to life in 1959, a product of the fertile imagination of Sir Alec Issigonis. It was a revolutionary car: front wheel drive, only three meters long, and equipped with a decent interior package and a hydro-gas suspension. A generation of kids throughout the British Empire grew up with a Mini. The vehicle was class-blind and appealed to buyers ranging from landed gentry to students to dock workers.

In 1994, BMW purchased Rover Group, ostensibly to acquire the Land Rover and Mini brands. They also took on the Herculean task of trying to make Rover cars a success, but not even BMW's magicians could sweep the muck out of that stable. The Chairman of BMW, Berndt Pischetrieder, a nephew of Sir Alec Issigonis, had an understandable love for the Mini. At the time of the purchase, Mini was 34 years old, long of tooth, and selling in significant numbers only in Japan.

After the purchase, BMW set up competing teams from BMW and Rover to design the next Mini. The teams took quite different approaches, each playing to their cultural tendencies. The Brits were in love with innovation and wanted the new Mini to be as *avant garde* as the original, a tall order. The Germans leaned far more toward incremental change and brilliant execution. In terms of technical layout, one of the competing concepts was adventuresome, and the other was pedestrian. Not surprisingly, the more conservative German concept won.

If any automaker knows its market, that company is BMW. Its market comprises people who can afford well-crafted, expensive, fun-to-drive cars. BMW believed that a market existed for a small car with those qualities at the lower end of the market. Not cheap, you understand, just less expensive than a BMW. The Rover Group sales and marketing team struggled with this concept. They saw a car that was styled like a Mini but on a commonplace front-wheel-drive platform. To the Brits, the new design, a meter longer than the original, looked like a Mini on steroids.

When it came to deciding price point and production volume, the discussion got really interesting. BMW envisioned a car priced at a 20- to 30- percent premium to other front-wheel-drive cars of the same size. To keep the price even that low, dealer margins would necessarily be thin. To augment profitability, BMW and its dealers would have to persuade buyers to purchase an expensive array of dealer-added accessories. Furthermore, unless the sales group agreed to higher prices, there would be precious few funds for marketing and advertising.

Two conflicting perceptions, both of which later proved to be inaccurate, clashed. They were: "No one wants an expensive small car," and "BMW is not capable of building an inexpensive anything." History has proved the first one wrong. As for the second, BMW chose not to build an inexpensive car and stayed above the small-car discounting fray by building a car that created its own category. How smart.

The car had its handicaps: ordinary front-wheel drive layout, a cramped but good looking interior package, low-tech engine, relatively high price, small dealer margin that demanded heavy accessorization, no ad budget, and a doubting sales group. In Detroit, the car would never have made it off the drawing board.

Yet the Mini had some heavyweight advantages: the Mini heritage; BMW standards of design, engineering, and materials; brilliant handling; and enough power in its supercharged form to provide vigorous drivers a first-class rush.

BMW hit a sweet spot in the market—drivers who wanted a car that made them look hip and who could afford a $20–25,000 small car that looked great, had an enviable heritage, and was a ball to drive. The year it was introduced, it won the North American Car of the Year award and a raft of other accolades—each and every one inevitably described as coveted and prestigious.

With typical BMW panache, the company had turned apparent disadvantages into advantages. Low volume—place it in a limited number of BMW dealers as a store within a store. Small dealer margin—persuade dealers to use one-price selling at list price but in a customer-friendly manner. Heavy accessory load—create desirable accessories that allow the customer to personalize their vehicle and the dealers to raise their profits. Minuscule advertising budget—devise an antitraditional media marketing approach that relied heavily on public relations and innovative marketing tricks such as placing a Mini on the roof of a large SUV and driving it around the largest cities in the US. Mini also created a captivating Web site and arresting direct mail and print materials that reinforced the hipness of Mini. Their buzz factor sailed off the graph paper.

Buying a Mini is smart, just like a BMW. For its market, it is an affordable, desirable, no-excuses car for a mere $8,000 more than a similarly sized Honda Civic. Note that no one ever mentions these two cars in the same conversation.

Mini's success can be attributed to BMW's way of doing business, its attitude about where it wants to play in the market, startlingly innovative marketing and brilliant execution. And, as in most things, a pinch of good luck. BMW knew its audience and discriminated against all buyers who were buying small cars because of price and affordability. It set itself apart by building an expensive small car and selling it as an inexpensive prestige car. They marketed their new concept in a new way. Finally, they were authentic. BMW stayed true to itself by building a small car to its existing high standards and capitalizing on Mini's heritage.

Conventional Wisdom

We hear all the time that the market is saturated with brands, products, and marketing campaigns. Everything has been done to death. We are into our "re" period, as in refreshening, repeating, replication, recreate, retread . . . really.

We can hear Peggy Lee singing "Is that all there is?"

Most of us need to take a brave pill, let our imaginations roam, and release the reins on our creativity. True, we see occasional flashes of brilliant creativity—witness the Mini—but the amount of uninteresting product and marketing that surrounds us would put a cocaine user to sleep. Do not be overwhelmed by this dreary sameness—the insightful and imaginative executive sees this as fertile ground.

Given how fragmented the market is, a company's instinct often leads it to conclude that it must broaden its appeal. Break out of the shackles that have constrained its sales figures and stop being so, so much like itself. The company's leaders think that if they execute properly this breakout from convention, new customers will come running.

Execute what properly? Stop being ourselves? Become or imitate someone else? Spread our investment even thinner? What the company is considering amounts to a great strategy for shedding huge chunks of its brand equity and becoming as distinctive as a paving stone. You may be saying to yourself, "Isn't it counterintuitive to conclude that a crowded market is the right place to walk away from your identity?" Of course it is. Just ask VW how successful it was in bringing a luxury car, the $65,000 Phaeton to market. Not very; VW gave up after three years of demonstrated futility.

Ask yourself how any company's management not using hard drugs could conclude that being simultaneously special and common is a good thing?

Dangerous Trends

Perhaps it is the pace of change that has so muddled corporate thinking. We are to a degree in uncharted waters. As you think about ways to distinguish yourself, we have identified several overarching trends that you will do well to understand—because you will surely have to deal with them.

More Choice/Less Choice

As we discussed in Chapter 2, wide choice between items not much different from each other creates tedium. Boring choices don't get people's attention. Much of that tedium of choice comes from companies with brand portfolios that have no clear vision. Companies that view differentiation as something for the little guys and that don't understand the basics of marketing. How can you have a brilliant marketing campaign when you have nothing meaningful to say?

Given how much sameness of thinking and of product permeates the market, one must conclude that setting yourself apart has a low priority number. Perhaps companies have grown to the point where the number of products they must design and build has worn out their enthusiasm. And because so many others have fallen into the same trap, the companies might be unaware of just how uncompelling they have become.

Dialogue Marketing

We are firmly in the age of dialogue marketing, an age in which the customer expects to be able to talk back to you—and have you listen and respond. That was never possible in the heyday of network television advertising. Corporate spending on media designed to reach their customers continues to grow. But everywhere there are more media choices available to the advertiser, and advertisers are allocating their dollars in new and diverse ways.

For decades, television was everyone's favorite advertising venue but even that medium has fragmented into network, local, cable, and satellite. In 2000, television accounted for 51 percent of total media spending. In the first half of 2005, according to TNS Media Intelligence, only 38 percent went to television, a drop of 13 percentage points in less than five years. That 13 percent has been reallocated to other media, much of which allows dialogue with the consumer: The company talks and they listen; then they talk and the company listens. If we listen well to our customers and apply our vision to what we hear, we will surely set ourselves apart.

Visions of Outcomes

The whole notion of vision has fallen on hard times. There are many reasons for this, among them impatience, short CEO tenure, focusing on expenses, high reward/low risk syndrome, and perhaps imagination-challenged leadership.

Visions have a history. In the 1980s and 1990s, corporate America went gaga over vision statements, mission statements, and corporate values. These items were a trend of that time, and, as with all trends, some grasped the purpose of doing them and most did not. We have been involved with companies where every working department felt it needed its own vision and mission statements. Most of these endless documents were pure unadulterated nonsense. A complete waste of time. Almost all of them could be summed up as, "It is better to do good than to do bad."

Eventually, even the dullest executives caught on to the notion that these "statements" were as worthless as last year's desk calendar and did not alter much of anything. A fatigue with the whole concept set in. This fatigue left a vacuum, and we have now gone from "We want the happiest most satisfied customers in the galaxy" to "We want to be a billion dollar company"—all without much thought to the power of the original concept of vision.

With our laser-like focus on expense control, we have become a business culture obsessed with numerical outcomes. Yet we do need goals. The best definition of goal we have heard is "a dream with a deadline." And we need a plan to hit that goal. Having a vision of who we want to be in the market and how we propose to get there is absolutely essential. Being a billion dollar company is an outcome, not a marketable identity.

Companies with the best brands spend more time worrying about the actions required to win in the marketplace and less time on moving numbers around a Ouija board. Success is not laboring over a plan and optimizing the numbers; success is beating the competition in the marketplace with better products, better marketing, better retail, better people, and, consequently, better profits. Vision helps guide you through the actions that are appropriate for you. Concentrate on the actions, execute properly, and the outcomes will follow.

The Newest New Thing

The world's most active—and spoiled—shoppers crave entertainment. The old bores them; the new captivates them. A sizable minority of shoppers in almost every category and segment are early adopters. They want—and must have—the newest new thing.

This provides yet another obvious reason why you must set yourself apart. Anything boring, bland, or unimaginative instantly puts a dinosaur button on your lapel. This trend, like so many others, tells you that being Me-Too is a risky strategy.

How to Set Yourself Apart

The test of vision gets played out on the world stage daily. Consumers admire and gravitate to companies that display a compelling vision—a vision executed in a way that differentiates them in the marketplace. With equal speed, companies without vision fade into the clutter of the marketplace. It is easy to illustrate the difference, just listen to two leaders, Helmut Panke, Chairman of BMW and Nick Scheele, the now-retired COO of Ford Motor Company.

At the 2004 Automotive News World Congress, Helmut Panke said:

> You cannot successfully be a bit of everything. If you try to stand for everything, you end up really standing for nothing . . . a brand is not just a label or a marketing campaign. A brand is a promise, a promise that the products of a brand [will] provide substance, authenticity, emotional appeal and heritage.

Panke's thoughts show rare thinking for the car business and explain why BMW has been such a success over the years. BMW, the ultimate driving machine, knows what it stands for, and so do we. At most companies, executives see their brand in shades of gray.

Contrast Panke's clarity with the words of Ford's Nick Scheele at an annual automotive industry conference held in 2003. A reporter asked Scheele, then COO of Ford Motor Company, what Ford stood for. Scheele replied, "D2ADE." And Mercury? "A little bit more of that." And Lincoln? "A lot more of that."

Has branding been reduced to the meaningless? Nick Scheele is a man we not only know and respect but also like. He knew that D2ADE was current Fordspeak for "desirable, dependable, affordable driving enjoyment." There's a catch phrase that rolls off the tongue like flypaper. In any case, he knew it and the world didn't. Nick didn't invent D2ADE. It came from a lot of research and is what Ford believed constituted its brand DNA. But what does it really mean? WWHHT? What Would Henry Have Thought about D2ADE? NBM—Not Bloody Much.

Sadly, the D2ADE cleverness, if you can call it that, is not an isolated example of corporate branding jargon. Is that kind of thing benign? No. Neither the organization nor its customers have a clue to what you are saying. In a funny but overt way it avoids the whole reason for branding, which is to set yourself apart and not look or sound like the other players.

What are we afraid of? Losing a customer? By establishing who you are and defining what you stand for and whom you serve, you implicitly—or explicitly—say who you aren't, what you don't stand for, and whom you won't serve. The trouble is, too many auto executives either fear and loathe doing that—never mind that it's the essence of branding—or else lack the insight, discipline, patience, and tools to do it right.

So ask yourself, what sets you apart? Why is such a simple question so hard to answer? Could it be that nothing sets you apart? And that the decision not to be set apart is intentional?

What sets Ford apart from Chevrolet? What sets BMW apart from Mercedes-Benz? What sets Nissan apart from Toyota? What separates Built Ford Tough from Dodge Ram Tough from Chevrolet's Like a Rock? More than just words? What sets Cadillac apart from Lincoln? A lot, actually.

So what can set you apart? Some qualities and examples follow:

- **Imagination**—Chrysler bringing out the original minivan.
- **Creativity**—Land Rover creating Land Rover Centres.
- **Perception**—Saturn betting the ranch on the retail experience.
- **Vision**—Subaru deciding to go exclusively all-wheel drive.
- **Drive**—Hyundai making quality a strength.
- **Passion**—Chevrolet bringing to market the C5 Corvette.
- **Execution**—Toyota making Lexus a synonym for quality.
- **Risk**—Cadillac's current edgy in-your-face styling.

What does not set you apart? Having so few of the qualities listed above that you settle for copying others. Corporate Me-Tooism. Monkey see, monkey do. Copycatting will get you exactly what you've earned: a cloak of invisibility.

What drives this rush to mediocrity? Is it that everyone—or what appears to be everyone—in the industry wants desperately to be loved by everyone? To be *popular*? Exactly. Executives discuss branding in terms of being well known or having high levels of awareness. They want to be well liked, in the sense of having a good image. They want to be inclusive and appeal to virtually everyone. Like a supermarket, something for all. No buyer goes unserved.

That is nothing less than a total misunderstanding of branding.

At its core, branding is about discrimination—persuading buyers to select one brand over another based on what each brand stands for. Something meaningful that the company is committed to. What you stand for should not be veneer or cake frosting slathered on by the marketing department. What you stand for runs right to the heart of the company and is what makes the best brands authentic.

Is it any wonder that the automobile business is struggling with branding? The lack of three qualities—discrimination, differentiation, and authenticity—has done them in. Flimflam is not a substitute for any one of the three.

Face it. To absolutely, positively set yourself apart, you will first need courage. You must carefully select your target buyers and abandon the rest. You must do something that unquestionably distinguishes you in the market. And you must act like what you want to be. This attitude must extend right to the core of your business. It takes vision as well, but courage comes first.

Your Imagination

As children, we often played games all day long that required the one piece of equipment we all had: imagination. Somewhere along the road to adulthood, evil spirits reined in this imagination. Imagination can be wild and scary, incredibly successful, and, of course, demonstrably foolish. That's why most parents, teachers, and employers distrust and discourage it.

Display imagination and your business associates will ask you for facts and figures. They'll point out that your idea is not in step with the market and that no one is doing anything like that. What are they afraid of? Their clear message is that you must be wrong or crazy. Probably both. As a result, too many of us have conditioned ourselves to corral our imaginations or to put them up in the loft with the hay. Left unused, the gift of imagination will atrophy.

The pressure cooker we put our business leaders in—the pot containing both high expectations and a pathological fear of failure—hardly encourages those leaders to be imaginative or take any risk greater than those already established as acceptable. It is a sad paradox that so many "leaders" view differentiation as riskier than aping their competitors. Fear seems to invite copying. The most desirable brands are expressions of clear compelling visions. Visions spring from your imagination. Take a pull from the courage bucket, let your imagination soar, and be creative.

Choose Your Customers . . . Wisely

Some years back, when Chrysler introduced its new Ram pickup, which had a front end that looked like nothing so much as a Peterbilt, Chrysler president Bob Lutz said, "We don't care if half the pickup buyers hate it. If ten percent of them can't live without it, we've hit the ball out of the park." Chrysler at that time had maybe three percent of the lucrative pickup truck market. Do the arithmetic.

More recently in the fall of 2005 as Ford missed its financial targets and the debt-rating agencies downgraded its debt, Ford put together a team to design a plan to turn Ford around. Named "Way Forward," this group had the task of "fixing" Ford's sales declines and cutting costs in accordance with the current market reality. Such programs are extremely painful, but often some very good things come out of them. In this case one of the group's key tenets was, "Quit trying to sell Fords to people who won't buy them; focus instead on likely prospective customers." A true breath of fresh air at Ford.

Your first step should be defining the market arena you want to play in. That should be easier than dozing at a conference table, right? Wrong. If it is so easy, why has Mercedes-Benz developed a small, inexpensive front-wheel-drive car—its A-class—to compete with the Volkswagen Golf? And what in God's name was the management of DaimlerChrysler smoking when it developed and marketed its upscale $325,000 Maybach—instantly rendering the Mercedes-Benz S-Class a second-best luxury choice, something the competion had never managed to accomplish? We say the culprit is massive ego, which in the car business more often than not trumps market reality.

. Defining one's market arena is difficult because it is the first step in paring down your potential market. You must decide your place in the market, select your target customer, and be willing to forego all the others. Give yourself permission to exclude whole segments of the market and concentrate on where you want to be strong.

There are basic market-arena questions you must answer. Do you want to be up market or down market? A niche player or a mass marketer? Are you a boutique or a supermarket? Are you cheap, entry level, mainstream, accessible, premium, or super expensive? And which product segments do you want to compete in?

No one ever did this better than General Motors during the 1950s and 1960s when it achieved an unthinkable 50-percent-plus share of the market. GM did this using Alfred P. Sloan's "A car for every purse and pocket" philosophy, which dated to the 1920s. GM did not just define the market territory of one brand; it successfully defined the market territory of *five* brands: Chevrolet, Pontiac, Oldsmobile, Buick, and Cadillac. While there was some overlap among these brands, they each stood for something different. This was the first important step—defining the divisions' target markets—and for decades GM exercised the discipline to keep its divisions both physically and conceptually separated.

As the market has evolved—and suffered from fragmentation, proliferation, and growth mania—it's tempting to conclude that times are so different you really don't want to fence yourself in. Porsche brought to market the Cayenne, an SUV. Such a move would have been unthinkable ten years ago. Porsche says it appeals to its existing customers, who bought SUVs in addition to their Porsches.

The Cayenne rapidly grew to more than half of Porsche's sales in the US, and most pundits hail it as a success. Time will tell, and there is no doubt that Porsche has expanded its market arena. Just as surely, they've diluted their hard-core, purist image. Porsche's most recent move was to announce a forthcoming four-door sedan, sending the purists back to the fainting couch. We'll be watching.

Another question is, "Who is the enemy?" On their best days, Chevy and Ford fought like wildcats to beat each other in the market. They were different flavors fighting for the same customers, and competition improved both. Mercedes-Benz has benefited similarly from the Quant family's purchase and resurrection of BMW. Great growth and profit grew out of this intra-German competition and made each company far better than it would have been had the other not existed.

All of this is prelude to the tough part, the part most car companies just can't seem to face up to: asking the question, "Who is our target customer?" Specifically? "Males 35 to 45" or "Males making more than $100,000" does not answer the question.

Business is personal; you want a *person*—many persons—to buy your product. These persons don't view themselves as interchangeable, and you shouldn't either. You need to love them, entice them, and please them. But first, you must know them. You must know who they are, and who they are not. You must turn some people on, turn some people off, and allow hordes of people to tune you out instantly when they learn that you're of no interest to them. You must do this intentionally and with purpose.

Here's an example. In 1998, Mazda's sales goal was about 300,000 vehicles. Looking for 300,000 buyers raises obvious questions: What do Mazda buyers have in common, and how do I identify them so I can target my products and marketing to them? Do they share anything in common other than purchasing a Mazda? Demographics? Previous purchase patterns? Psychographics—lifestyle, values, and beliefs? Are there regional differences? What makes them different from buyers who did not put Mazda on their shopping list or who shopped Mazda but bought another brand? Who can be taken off the list because they have no interest in Mazda and never will?

By going through this difficult questioning process in 1998–99, Mazda gained a decent handle on its target customer by 2000. First, it embraced eliminating a large portion of the market in order to identify the group that it could cultivate by just being Mazda. Mazda's diluted image further complicated this task. The target market they would go on to woo had little interest in what Mazda had become, but a lot of interest in what Mazda had been before losing its way.

For Mazda, the defining area was psychographics, the grouping of potential buyers based on lifestyle and value considerations. This narrowed the market down to 25 percent of light vehicle buyers. Ignoring 75 percent of the market is a real gut check, but even so, the remaining 25 percent held more than four million buyers from which to find Mazda's desired 300,000.

Mazda knew what these buyers shared in common and what Mazda had to be in order to win big in its defined target market.

Some industries have far more buyer data than others, and as you might guess, the car business has truckloads. There's data from buyer studies done by Maritz, purchase intention studies from Allison-Fisher, customer satisfaction studies from J. D. Power, media usage studies, and in-house research done by all car companies.

Adopt a discriminating attitude as you analyze as much data as you can get your hands on. Who is buying your product, who is not, and who is your most natural target? Not every industry is blessed with so much buyer data, but you get the point: identify your target customers and learn all you can about them. Target buyers need to become your folks, people you want to develop a relationship with and to know better than your competition does. Without thoroughly knowing your customers, how can you possibly design a product, or a marketing campaign?

What—who—could be more important?

Define Your Brand Unequivocally

If the task of developing brands with real value was an IQ test, most automotive companies would score in the two-digit range. What must change to improve this? Perhaps the very perception of what makes a brand great must change before you take another step.

We need a new definition that holds a gun to our head and hollers, "Do something!" A strong statement that sets you apart. Give yourself permission to be different. Demand it! Anger some people and get others to love you. And don't give a damn about buyers who don't give a damn about you.

We see great brands as *a promise wrapped in an experience*.

Grow up. Promise to *be* something—something that can be delivered through an experience that *only you* provide. Make a *commitment,* a word that scares the bejesus out of marketers. Get *active*—because commitment means you must deliver on it. And know that it is *personal*—a promise from *you* to each and every customer.

The best brand promises are clear and compelling and they communicate your commitment. No equivocation, no wiggle; just straightforward intention. What could be simpler?

Clarity is the acid test of your commitment to make a promise. What kind of promise have you made if you cannot express it clearly in a simple declarative sentence? Most likely you haven't made one. If it takes you a paragraph and lots of qualifiers and modifiers, you and your customers will be lost. It is excruciatingly hard to focus a vision in a simply stated promise. But in simplicity lies power. A clear promise will help target all your communications and will make attracting and holding on to customers much easier. Why? Because both you and the customers will know who you are and what you've committed to deliver. And so will your team.

Making your promise compelling depends on knowing who your target customers are and what you can do to turn them on. To make a compelling promise, you must embrace risk. Compelling is again a discriminator. Compelling to some is repelling to others. What compels buyers to select you also becomes the core of what they will expect from you.

And last but by no means least; your promise must inherently communicate your commitment.

Oh, one more thing: *you must keep your promise.* No one can be perfect, but in the car business there are notable success stories based on kept promises. Toyota has kept its promise to build high quality, reliable transportation. BMW has given us genuine "Ultimate Driving Machines." But can you name a promise—one promise—that has been made and kept by Chevrolet, Ford, or Mercury—to name just three automakers?

Chevrolet: An American Revolution

Ford: Bold Moves (formerly Built for the Road Ahead)

Mercury: Reach Higher (formerly New Doors Opened)

Let's get personal. Has the company you work for made a real promise? If so, can you say it in a few words? Has the company made it clear and important to its customers? Does it excite your fellow employees? Have you delivered it unequivocally? Have you lived this promise for years? A yes to all those questions says powerful and positive things about your company, things that applied to only a couple of the many companies we've worked for.

And so we don't sneak one past you: a compelling promise most often means that you are promising to be *better* at what you do than anyone else—to add value to your customers' lives in ways that others can't match. This thought, perhaps more than any other, discourages and defeats most companies. It is a brutally competitive world. To stand out and to succeed, you must set your sights on being a better "you" than the competition.

And being a better you means defining your essence. That is another little secret: differentiating yourself requires a hot streak of creativity. Accept that every last bit of information implicit in a brand promise cannot be packed into one word or even one sentence, but it can be distilled to its essence. Land Rover's original promise to put you behind the wheel of the "Best 4 × 4 × Far," as good as those words are, doesn't begin to capture the rich tapestry of images that has grown over decades of Land Rover remaining true to its promise.

When people think of Land Rover, they conjure up much more than an SUV. Land Rovers are: British, tough, strong, utilitarian, brute tech, fit for purpose, expeditions, military, the Serengeti, conquering the world, used by the Royal Family. And on and on. Trust us, the whole brand is in there, and it damn sure didn't get there because someone wrote and circulated a 3,000-word mission statement. What separates Land Rover from lesser brands is a simple, clear promise: We sell the "Best 4 × 4 × Far." And it consistently delivers on it.

The promise is your brand's foundation. Yet it is the experience you orchestrate that provides real value to your customers and pays off the promise. A simple empirical equation we first heard from a friend of ours in the business, Mark Rikess, says it all:

Commodity +Experience = Price/Value.

Just ask Starbucks. Likewise, your customers will decide through their experience whether you delivered on your promise.

Our world has attempted to commoditize most products. How do you increase the price/value ratio of these goods? You wrap them in an appealing experience. That experience is in the product, the service, the environment, and a thousand other areas. Here is where art enters the picture. What you most certainly do *not* do is sell on the basis of price. Quality and value? Of course. Price? Discounts? Of course not.

Bringing your promise to life through a value-added experience requires knowing your customers and their expectations— and then *designing* an experience that brings acceptance and smiles. Sound easy? It isn't. That experience is woven into everything the customer senses, whether you planned it or not. And the Brand Triangle can help you do just that.

The Brand Triangle provides a direct way to assess the current strengths and weaknesses of a brand as well as help you decide how you want your customers to experience your promise. What is the *main* focus of your experience? Is it the brand, the product, the retail, or the culture? If your main focus is product, which product characteristics need to be superior in order to deliver on your promise of superiority over the competition? How do the other aspects of the Triangle have to work in order to support your main focus? And in each case, how does your culture become a driving force to bring this experience alive?

The Allure of Authenticity

As we work through setting ourselves apart, we need to ask ourselves one more question about something that is becoming increasingly important:

Are you real, authentic, and genuine?

Our guess is that you know instantly, because this isn't something that one has to ponder. Authenticity is a concept most people either get or don't. The car business is living proof. Toyota,
Porsche, Land Rover, Ferrari, BMW all get it. Most others don't
get it and don't believe that authenticity is important to customers. Yet the industry constantly worships (and personally
wants to drive) authentic brands.

We think anyone who downplays authenticity is missing a
crucial point:

> Authenticity distinguishes you in both a natural
> and compelling way. Like all differentiation, it is
> both enticing and limiting.

We toss around words like authentic, genuine, and *bona fide*
easily. Yet marketers, in their haste to be clever, often take liberties,
so let's be clear. To be authentic is to be real, actual, exactly as
claimed—as opposed to being false or an imitation. Being authentic means being true to one's own personality, spirit, or character. Authentic, genuine, and *bona fide* all imply trustworthiness
and good faith.

So much marketing these days is contrived or copied. This
has made authenticity even more compelling. To some, words like
authentic and genuine seem quaint. Being "actual and exactly as
claimed" does not appeal to the charlatan streak in so many business folks. To be true to yourself sounds so sophomoric. It also
sounds like hard work, and please, for God's sake, don't tell me
this is what customers want. Can't we just fake it? After all, how
can the latest thing be authentic if it's so new?

With enough choice to choke on, authenticity is a concept
heaven sent for this time and this market. Why then is there such
resistance among marketers? Perhaps because their attempted du-
plicity is not being sufficiently ridiculed. If authentic brands are,
well, authentic, what are inauthentic brands?

The best characterization we've come across was created by
Jonathan Hill and Ian Hilton at WCRC/London. They came up

with the notion that there are *conviction* brands and *confection* brands. We applaud this distinction and find it a useful concept. Without even hearing their definitions, the labels ring true.

Here is how they define them.

Conviction brands result from companies that have strong points of view on both products and the market. The source of inspiration for their products comes from within the company. The goal is simple and unambiguous: to lead consumers, to take them were they want go, by unlocking unrealized consumer wants and needs. We would call these brands authentic.

Confection brands lack that strong point of view and leadership drive. They look at the market with a blank sheet of paper approach. They examine consumers and let them dictate the company's point of view and product. As a result, their product development process churns out undifferentiated Me-Too products. And what are they left with? Marketing as their prime differentiator. Bottom line, there is no substance to these brands and little value.

Pause for a moment and think about brands in your market. Can you readily identify which are *conviction* brands and which are *confection?* We bet you can. And whose employees do you think get up in the morning just proud as hell to be working for their brand?

This brings us to a dilemma: To be authentic requires that you know who "you" are to begin with. And that you like what you see. It implies self-awareness, world awareness, and decisiveness— decisiveness you must demonstrate every day.

One of the more subtle points of being authentic is that perfecting your act becomes second nature, as natural as breathing. You love being you, and you constantly learn and work at getting better at it every day. Being the best at what you do is great motivation. Ask anyone who works at BMW.

Consumers seek authenticity for a number of reasons. You stand for something. This distinguishes you from all the wannabes. Words like character and concepts like being true to yourself, imply trustworthiness. Surrounded by so much you *can't* trust, you can rest assured that this strikes a chord with buyers as well as with you. Buying an authentic product says good things about the buyer—things such as smart, discerning, and savvy.

A Different Ending

Difference is your job. You must write a different ending to your company's story by making it a different company. Different from the herd. Differentiation, the test of vision, is not a test you can fake, cheat on, or mail in. You need to be perceptive in viewing the market to get this far. Finding your special spot in the market, finding your customers, and winning them over is a pass/fail test you must ace if you are going to have a worthwhile future.

The other tests you will face, while challenging, only matter if and when you have successfully determined how you will set yourself apart.

Culture

> "Culture eats strategy for breakfast."
>
> *Sign in Ford Motor Company's "Way Forward"*
> *restructuring war room, December 2005*

The Test of Engagement

Culture, put simply, is "who we are and how we do things." Getting your culture right is worth every lick of the fight it will require. Does most of the water cooler talk center around Little League games, Fantasy Football, or the Christmas party? If your answer's yes, trust us, it's time to pour Lysol into their whiskey.

Culture is nothing more than a test of engagement. Can you get your troops fully engaged in building a world-class brand based on a shared vision? Is it a group anxious to do whatever it takes to win in the marketplace "our way"—and market-savvy enough to know what that way is? Does the team understand that "who we are and how we do things" is both the catalyst and the foundation for the experience we want our customers to have?

How to Build a Culture in One Week

Imagine you were given the opportunity to start a car company from scratch in the US. What would you do first? What would be most important to you? These and many other questions faced Charlie Hughes when he began the task of creating Land Rover of North America in January of 1986.

In startups, only fools fail to keep things simple. Charlie's priorities were a vision, a team, and a plan. He envisioned nailing down the strategy first, then executing it. While still distilling the vision, he recruited his executive team, seeking out experts in their respective fields who felt passionate about building a new and different company.

It took Charlie five months to select the right team. At their first meeting, the group established a seemingly unreasonable goal: quickly create a business plan that would build an entire business in just nine months. If that worked, maybe they could add world peace to next year's goals. Here, in Charlie's words, is the story.

The first person to come aboard was our general counsel, Jim Lehmann. These days, getting your attorney in harness first seemed smart. The rest of the team included Roger Ball, our resident Brit, as head of marketing; John Horner, head of sales; Dave Schworm, head of service; Bill Baker, head of public relations; Dudley Cohen, head of advertising, and Joe Gumienny as head of both IT and parts.

Except for Jim Lehmann, Charlie had worked at one time or another with each of the executives, but the majority of team members did not know each other. We were still without our chief financial officer, Joel Scharfer, who took another three months of persuading before joining up.

Our first meeting, on Sunday night, June 1, 1986, kicked off an intensive week developing our business plan for launching Range Rover in the US. In addition to the new hires, Chip

Sleeper, the account executive from our new advertising agency, Grace & Rothschild, also joined us for the week.

We had inherited a general, high-level business plan from the home office in England, but it lacked flesh and bones and local knowledge. Otherwise it was fine. The new team had been given a pre-meeting homework assignment: read *The Unbeatable 4 × 4*, a book by Ken and Judy Slavin. It would ground them on the history of Land Rover and provide historical context for the company we were about to build.

Jim Bernthal, a brilliant industrial psychologist, was my co-architect for our first week of meetings. Together we crafted a week that was intended to be, and indeed became, the genesis of Land Rover North America.

As we wrote our business plan, we also began to formulate our culture. We would have to learn to work together even as we built a company from scratch—an opportunity that excited all of us.

Sunday night, we set the tone for working together. We began by having each person draw three pictures that described who they were and what they would contribute to the team. We followed that with a quiz on the homework and a discussion of *The Unbeatable 4 × 4,* setting the precedent of holding each other responsible for doing assignments, even homework. We wanted to ensure that our first conversations were limited to Land Rover, not wasted on sending team members to detention hall.

I laid out my vision for the company, a vision that took full advantage of the parent company's years of experience promoting Land Rover worldwide. After all, it would be silly—and wasteful—to create a "new" vision for the US when Land Rover's worldwide image couldn't have been stronger. The Land Rover vision had been distilled over time to the simple yet powerful line: "The Best 4 × 4 × Far." Put into the context of a promise wrapped in an experience, that line held most of the raw material we would need to start building the company.

Declaring this vision at the beginning simplified life in several ways. In the recruitment interviews, we could point to our stated desire to be the best at what we did. *The Unbeatable 4 × 4* message had removed any internal doubt about the line's validity. Finally, because Americans love superlatives, it seemed like a perfect vision.

Our vision, however, was broader than the "best 4 × 4" line. We agreed that we wanted to be a British car company, but British with a small b. We wanted to be a company that had conquered the world, a company full of adventure and adventurers, and a company altogether at home off the paved roads of the world.

We agreed that our company's cornerstone would be love of product. We knew that our vehicles would be expensive, and we believed that we had to love the products before we could expect a group of strangers—customers—to love them. Bringing to market the "Best 4 × 4 × Far" became the foundation of our identity.

We visualized the company we were about to build as a boutique company, but one with a voracious appetite. A giant killer, if you will. Land Rover products were unconventional, and we wanted to be the same way. We actually used the expression "the mouse that roared" among ourselves, but the cliché cops thankfully kept us from going public with it.

We covered one other piece of business that evening. Never having worked together, it was important to lay out working values that went beyond our decision to be product centric. I put three values on the table and had some fun discussing them. The team never debated them; instead we embraced them, nurtured them, and lived them for the next 14 years.

The first value was "maintain high standards." On a primary level, all members of the group had been selected for their accomplishments at other companies. On a secondary level, we knew we would face pressure in building a company in only a matter of months, and we wanted to take no short cuts. We wanted our work, at a minimum, to live up to our prior personal standards.

The second value was "allow ourselves to grow." Again on a primary level I came clean and admitted that I had never been president of a car company. Jim Lehmann owned up to never having been a general counsel, and so on through the team. The message was this: if anyone started strutting around with an inflated ego, the rest of the group was encouraged to get out the hatpins. On a deeper level, we were about to build a company from scratch, and we did not want to make it in the image of Volkswagen or Volvo or Buick or any of the other places we had worked. We wanted to give ourselves some rope, even knowing that rope is sometimes used for hanging.

We wanted to take chances, to do things differently, to work smarter and better—to develop ways that would become our way, not someone else's way. Taking risks, we knew, meant making mistakes, so we agreed to use our mistakes as learning experiences. We would discuss what went wrong, not who went wrong. We lived that principle, but it took a lot of coaching.

Finally, the third value was "support one other." When you have ten people in a room aiming to build a car company in nine months, you will need mutual support. Our goal was to build a company that disdained politics, a company driven only by the desire to become a great car company. This would require supporting each other.

Although we spent only about 30 minutes discussing these values, the team instantly recognized and embraced them as appropriate for what we were about to do. The notion that we so clearly wanted to build a better car company created an energized environment.

On Monday morning, you might think we would look at

the existing business plan from the home office and then spend the next five days fleshing out that plan, identifying and assigning all the tasks required to get the company up and running. But you would be wrong. Remember, we intended to do more than formulate a business plan that week; we would build a branded culture.

We began our simultaneous tasks by identifying with our customers. Monday we conducted our first "love of product" day. We spent the entire day evaluating the Range Rover and other sport utilities on the market at that time. First, using a static display, we filled out a questionnaire just as we ask customers to do in research clinics.

Next, we drove and rated all the vehicles on paved roads, evaluating their ride, handling, acceleration, braking, steering, quietness, controls, and sound systems. We spent the afternoon at a Virginia farm testing the vehicles off road. Off pavement is perhaps a better description because most of the driving was done on dirt farm roads, but at the time it seemed adventurous. We saw for ourselves how superior the Range Rover really was.

At the end of that day we enjoyed a barbeque at the farm, talked about the products we had driven, and discussed what we felt our customers would see as the strengths and advantages of Range Rover.

With the driving done, Tuesday's the day for the business plan, right? Wrong again. On Tuesday we took the group to a local Volkswagen dealership where we spent the day taking two of our Range Rovers apart and putting them back together again. We became intimately familiar with all the features and components of the vehicle and learned how to do some of the easier mechanical work. At the end of the day we had a competition to find six faults we had purposely implanted in each vehicle.

The message? As a team, we would not only know and love our product intimately, we would also get our hands dirty when circumstances demanded.

On Wednesday, having learned a few things about the product—and each other—we finally sat down to create the business plan. We reviewed in broad strokes what we were trying to achieve and then broke into two-person teams, each composed of a function expert and a coach. The teams worked for two hours to generate a complete list of things that each function expert needed to do before we could sell the first Range Rover in March of 1987—just nine months away.

We generated lists for four function areas and then switched team members and roles so that each member of the team could work with a new partner in a new area. Those who had been coaches became the experts and vice-versa. After each round, the whole team listened to the experts present the work that they felt needed to be done. This allowed us to see the breadth of our task. It also allowed members to comment or raise any concerns. The process permitted the experts to generate the work plan for which they would be responsible—and to work with at least two other members of the team. We learned from the start to help each other, coach each other, and support each other.

After the two-member team exercise, we asked everyone to refine what they needed to do and to generate a comprehensive list of tasks complete with time lines. This took all day Thursday, but by the end of the day we had a set of charts showing all of the tasks and projects we needed to complete.

"Daunted" falls short of describing the lengthy to-do list's effect on us. Stunned was more like it. We would be a small company, yet we would have to do the same things that General Motors does in order to sell and service cars, from accounting to warranty. That we did not run for the door indicates the depth of our enthusiasm, which was now *informed* enthusiasm.

The plan was finished by Friday, but one important step, called R Charting, remained. We knew all the tasks, and it was clear that considerable cross-function work would be required. R Charting sets forth clearly who is responsible for what. It's a simple form that lists all the tasks along the rows and lists all the players along the columns. Each player can be assigned an *AV*, which means Approval or Veto power; an R, indicating that a person has the responsibility; an S, meaning that a person needs to support whomever had the R in order to get the task done; or an I, which meant that you just needed to be informed but weren't going to be active in the task. For R Charting to work, there can be only one R per task, period. If any task appeared to merit two Rs, we either made the hard decision or subdivided the task.

Function by function we went through every task, making sure that everyone in the room knew who was responsible, who had the AV, who had to support, and who needed information. At the beginning, everybody wanted an I for everything, but within the first hour we came up with a new symbol called the dash. It meant "I'm busy, leave me alone." R Charting brought empowerment and a team-to-task clarity without which we would not have launched on time.

We completed all this work by close of business Friday and prepared for the arrival of our spouses the next day. Friday night we threw a memorable party celebrating the completion of an arduous but successful week. You've heard it before, but great teams work hard and play hard. That week a great team was born.

The next day we shared with our spouses all that we had done, and even the hangovers did not diminish our excitement at bringing our partners on board. Our partners also evaluated and drove the Range Rover and the competitive products. They were amazed at how much we had accomplished, which was reinforcing in itself.

We had called the week "Leading the Way," and indeed it led the way in building our company and its culture. We were smitten with the product and had a growing appreciation for our brand, the Best 4 × 4 × Far. We knew intuitively how these

RESPONSIBILITY CHART
SALES

CODE: R- Responsibility (initiates)
A-V Approval (right to veto)
S- Support (put resources against)
I- Inform (to be informed)

ACTORS → DECISIONS ↓	BAKER	BALL	COAN	GUMENNY	HORNER	HUGHES	LEHMANN	SCHWORM	SLEEPER	FIN	CSW							
DLR AGMNT/STDS																		
· CONTENT	I	S	-	S	R	A	S	S	-	S	-							
· DRAFTING	-	-	-	-	S	-	R	-	-	-	-							
· ENFORCEMENT	S	S	S	S	R	S	S	S	S	S	-							
INITIAL PACKAGE																		
· CONTENT	I	S	-	S	R	A	S	S	-	S	I							
· SHIPMENT	I	S	-	S	R	I	-	S	-	S	-							

SALES DEPT.

DATE 6/6/86

TASKS	JUNE	JULY	AUG	SEPT	OCT	NOV	DEC	JAN	FEB	MARCH	APRIL	MAY	JUNE
DISTRIBUTION													
· LR·L ORDER PAR.	SYS	OPS.	INITIAL ORDERS										
· SYSTEMS													
DEFINITION													
ORDERING				TEST	OPERATIONAL								
FORECASTING													
ALLOCATION													
REPORTING													
· PORT AGREEMENTS		?											
· INLAND TRANSPORTATION AGREEMENTS													

products would fit into a desirable lifestyle—a lifestyle we not only admired but wanted to share. Had we become zealots? You bet.

Did the week pay off? We'll tell you at the end of the chapter. But first, we'll expose you to some conventional thinking about corporate culture.

Conventional Wisdom

Ask yourself if the following paragraphs describe your company's culture.

- We spend a lot of time thinking about the organization and its culture. We are a flat organization, process-oriented with a participatory management style, and we are performance driven. We have a casual dress code and try to make our workplace friendly.
- Our personnel policy aims to treat our employees with respect. Our company has an up-to-date policy manual that tells our employees what we expect of them. Our manual spells out our review systems, employee ratings, succession plans, job classifications, job posting, promotions, annual raises, bonuses, travel, company cars, office size, training, and more. We have conducted sexual harassment training and regularly hold sensitivity workshops. These policies ensure that we obey the law and, moreover, they protect the company should an employee take us to court.
- On top of that, we pride ourselves on how well we communicate with our employees. We have a monthly newsletter and employee email news; anything else employees need to know they will find on our human resources Web site. To engender camaraderie, we have a summer picnic, we dress up on Halloween, and our annual Christmas Party caps the year.

Conventional wisdom says that doing all those things right will create a healthy work environment. Many believe those things form the foundation of a culture. Funny, but all of those things have to do with me—or you—and none of them have to do with the customer. Therein lies the problem. A big problem.

Too often we concentrate on employee pacifiers, many of which cost far more time and money than they're worth. In the process we avoid the important question: how do we get our employees engaged—engaged with the market, with the customer, and with our promise and experience? How do we make them love that engagement?

Trends

When you think of marketplaces, you may not immediately think of one market that directly affects our lives—the market for businesses. Success allows companies to grow and to acquire other companies and brands. Competition drives them to seek efficiencies, and failure leads them to reorganize. As this plays out in the car business, certain trends are having a universal impact on corporate culture.

Downsizing and Outsourcing

As companies such as General Motors and Ford continue to lose market share, they find themselves forced to downsize their operations. In the fall of 2005 General Motors discussed the need to reduce salary work force by 25,000. Ford soon followed with a plan to reduce its payroll by 25,000–30,000 and to close a slew of assembly plants. For years, Ford and GM have searched for suppliers and locations to do more work on an outsourced basis. Ford enlisted Caterpillar and UPS to help it with its parts and logistics operations. Both firms have parceled out software development to companies offshore.

Downsizing and outsourcing trends have been front page

news for some time now, and both trends raise the level of tension in the workplace. Even the most rosy-eyed optimist finds it hard to concentrate on the customer and the brand when valid concerns about continued employment haunt the workplace.

Industry Consolidation

BMW first bought Rover, then Rolls-Royce. Daimler-Benz bought Chrysler, and Ford bought Jaguar, Aston Martin, Volvo, and Land Rover. Volkswagen bought Seat, Skoda, Bentley, and Lamborghini and has resurrected the Bugatti brand. All these newly minted conglomerates inevitably go through a consolidation of operations. The consolidators seek efficiencies and make changes with a conqueror's attitude. Simply stated, "If *you* were so smart, you would have bought *us.*"

The new owner often imposes much of its culture on the acquired company. The first inoculation rarely takes because the purchased company's culture acts as an antibody—fighting uninvited changes to how it does things. Sound productive so far?

The intelligence nugget too often lost in all of this is understanding that the acquired company owes what success it's enjoyed to its people and its culture. This does not mean that one culture is better than another, just as one personality isn't necessarily better than another. But quash a culture too harshly, and you will remove the essence of the brand.

Brand Portfolios

Because of consolidation—and new homegrown brands such as Toyota's Scion and Honda's Acura—almost all of today's auto companies operate a portfolio of brands. The industry continues to wrestle with what it takes to make each brand special and desirable. Because the role culture plays in building great brands is largely unappreciated and frequently misunderstood, more familiar areas such as product and marketing garner the most attention. Some companies, *e.g.,* BMW and its handling of Mini and

Rolls-Royce, show a keener appreciation for its importance than, say, Ford's handling of Jaguar and Land Rover.

What happens is this: In the headlong stampede to effect efficiencies across a number of brands, the "synergizers," blinded by visions of reduced costs, lose sight of what made the brands great to begin with. A brand portfolio does not necessarily work using a one-corporate-culture-fits-all approach. There are so-called management development processes that absolutely snuff out the cultures of acquired brands. Consider the "generalist manager" approach where companies rotate "fast-track" talent from job to job in the belief that minimum exposure prepares them for maximum responsibility. Such approaches have had a destructive effect on the culture of companies that have a brand portfolio.

Companies that do not understand the importance of culture to a brand's success will sooner or later pay a high price for their lack of understanding. It makes one wonder about the money a company pays for blue sky—good will—when it acquires other brands. What intangibles do the acquiring company's executives think this money is buying? If it's good will and brand value, what do they think created that value and that good will? The difficulty in understanding this is pervasive. As described previously, GM management apparently didn't really understand what it had built and had got for its money when it created Saturn.

There's No "I" in Team

There is nothing older than ambition, and we live in a world that likes making an individual the star. Many of our measurements of performance reward individual efforts, reinforcing the power of one instead of the power of the team. As we have discussed, too many companies have a shareholder-first, customer-second mentality. Loosely translated, this means that we look after number one first, and that would be us. It's then a short leap from "us" being number one to "me" being number one.

What happens in companies that place too great an emphasis

on individual performance? Your pay, your perks, your promotions and your social standing depend almost entirely on how your personal performance and contribution are rated. People must of course be held accountable for their performance, but this approach communicates a value of individual first, team second, and the company evolves into a careerist organization. My win is a team win, because I am the team.

A careerist environment poisons a company's ability to design a culture focused on the outside world.

How to Brand a Culture

The question, "Who sets you apart?" seems too obvious. Your people, of course. But what sets your people apart? We know great companies have people, average companies have people, and companies teetering on the brink of abject failure have people. So what gives?

Know that consistently successful companies have strong branded cultures—cultures that reflect the company's differentiating point of view. A branded culture is a company's in-plain-sight secret weapon—secret because most company leaders think culture is what makes yogurt. Too many companies confuse culture with personnel pacifiers. They lose sight of the big motivator—culture itself—altogether.

We've defined culture as "who we are and how we do things." Every company has a culture, but does that culture work for it or against it? Who we are and how we do things is not necessarily a positive. The sad fact is in most companies, culture turns out to be a negative. And its "who we are" offers little support for "who we want to be" in the marketplace. Brand promise? What brand promise?

In our careers, we have identified two types of cultures: legacy and branded. They are easy to tell apart. The former talks about fantasy football and what the company is doing for me. The latter concentrates on winning in the marketplace, living the promise, and delivering a remarkable experience to customers.

Legacy Cultures

In our go-go business world, where we turn over CEOs and management teams faster than you can say "missed earnings target," few top teams remain in place long enough to design and then execute an effective culture. The defining word here is design, for most cultures are legacy cultures. Legacy cultures have been allowed to grow in an unplanned and unstructured way. Management is either unaware of the importance of getting it right or confuses culture with competent professional personnel policy. Many don't know enough about who they are to create a reinforcing culture.

Without getting too simplistic, legacy cultures are fueled by an environment that concentrates on outcomes such as sales, cash flow, or profit. They give less attention to customer-centric actions—product innovation or an excellent buying experience, to name two—that help you win in the market. There is an "in-house" and an "in-market" aspect to all companies, yet far too many live "in-house." How "we" are doing is more important than how "our customer" is faring.

In that regard, companies are like families in that most children model the behavior of their parents. If a company is more concerned with its outcomes than with its customers, then most employees will adopt the same attitude and be more concerned with their outcome than the company's.

This is why legacy cultures tend to be entitlement cultures, which concentrate on what my company is doing for me, what's in it for me, and how am I being protected from my big bad company. The social atmosphere is more important than what we accomplish together. Functional and territorial boundaries harden, resulting in there being no real common cause.

Over time such cultures erode and debilitate the ability of companies to compete. Such environments tend to retain mediocre performers and repel the best and brightest. A legacy culture company is generally loath to take risks because it lacks real market feel.

Legacy cultures are so prevalent in our business world that most of us have endured at least one experience in such an environment. Charlie Hughes walked into one when he joined Mazda in 2000. A survey conducted shortly after Charlie arrived allowed him to sum up the company attitude thus: "We've had five presidents in ten years. We've heard it all before. We didn't believe it then, and we don't believe it now." How utterly dysfunctional.

While Mazda had an interesting history, it had been on a ten-year slide. A losing track record encouraged almost every team in the company to have its own view—its own mini-vision—of what Mazda should be and how it should go about becoming that. Most of these visions weren't very original. Many were germane only to a specific area of the business. Worse, no one seemed fettered or even concerned by so many conflicting views.

The culture could be aptly called cynical chic.

One of the executives reporting to Charlie told him that he needed to fire half of the employees. "It's not that they are bad people, just that their attitudes are wrong. They will make good employees somewhere else where they cannot get away with simply blaming the company."

Yet, Mazda was a happy place to work. People liked each another, and a warm social atmosphere prevailed. A lot of good if misguided folks worked there. Mazda's successful past, and a few interesting cars, kept people believing that things would get better—something we could spend more time on once we stopped missing our sales targets.

Mazda suffered from no vision, little accountability, and less reward. When Mazda could not persuade managers to accurately evaluate employee performance using a three-point scale, it moved to a five-point rating scale. The change resulted in a company average of over four points. This is a company whose performance was mediocre at best. In spite of its past performance, Mazda's culture had evolved into one of entitlement.

Most tragically, Mazda's culture included no dreams.

Hughes worked to solidify the positioning of the Mazda brand. His team agreed that Mazda's promise should be "Always the soul of the sports car" and strove to make this a living vision within the company. When Charlie left Mazda, the dream had begun to take root. Mazda had gotten the press on its side. The product program was designed to reinforce Mazda's basic brand differentiation. Programs were conducted to give the majority of Mazda employees hands-on experience driving the products that had put smiles on so many customers' faces. Most telling, Mazda had spent so much time and resources talking to its potential customers that management felt it was beginning to know and understand their hot buttons.

Even companies that understand culture rarely have the stomach to change an existing, badly performing one. When you decide to design and implement a more effective culture, you incur sizable risk. People embrace progress but resist change— and some will resist it to the end. It is easier to change the *English Book of Common Prayer* than to change the culture in most companies. It takes enormous perseverance and no small amount of time to change a culture, but when you succeed, you put real purpose into the team. A strong branded culture will align the troops, provide motivation and inspiration, support constructive empowerment, provide censure where needed, and recognize individual performance. A strong culture breathes life into a brand.

Our competitive world drives us to be ever more efficient in all that we do, and no company is immune to profit pressures. But developing a branded culture has dramatic, albeit hard to quantify, positive value. Which is why some misguided executives believe that saving a penny here or cutting a program there is better than having an excited, effective, tightly focused team.

Burning Your Brand into a Culture

If a company's promise is quality, as Toyota's is, it seeks incremental quality gains in everything it does. It creates an environmental context such as the Toyota Way. If a company's promise is the "Ultimate Driving Machine," then it creates a culture that is totally product driven—which BMW has done. BMW claims that even a blindfolded BMW employee can tell a BMW from a competitor's car. We don't doubt that for a minute.

In these companies, leaders have been deliberate in immersing employees in the very essence of the company. They know the main ingredients required to burn a brand into their culture are vision, values, and market focus—flavored with some market success. Gaining the employee's interest starts with a vision worthy of that interest.

Vision

People respond positively to visions such as Ferry Porsche's dream to build the world's best sports cars. That vision, simple though it was, had real meaning. To say you want a generic outcome—a successful car company that has a four percent market share and six percent return on sales—is hardly inspiring.

A differentiating vision provides purpose and, rightfully, should emanate from the leaders. They must provide the conviction needed to make a real promise in the marketplace. Leaders must have not only a compelling vision, they must also have the confidence to test their vision—hold it up for public scrutiny, allow critiques and encourage co-authoring, all the while fueling people's imagination. Compelling visions express a strategic intent to *be somebody*. At the beginning, great visions are a reach—which makes them irresistible to some folks.

The question has been asked, "Which comes first, vision or talent?" Jim Collins, in his book *Good to Great,* makes a strong case for talent being more important than vision. Collins and his associates believe that, to achieve greatness, the 11 companies they singled out as great " . . . first got the right people on the bus, the wrong people off the bus, and the right people in the right seats—and then they figured out where to drive it. The adage, 'People are your most important asset,' turned out to be wrong. People are *not* your most important asset. The *right* people are."

Getting the right people on the leadership team is critically important, but in our opinion not sufficient. To be effective, a team needs a compelling vision fully as much as it needs the right people. We might add that our experience shows that the right vision invariably attracts the right people. In start-ups particularly, the leader's vision attracts talent to the team. Great teams are teams of leaders, and a shared vision is the glue that holds them together.

Look at it from an employee's point of view. Would you rather work for a company that constantly changes course or a company that in its heart—and in all its employees' hearts—knows right down to its spurs who it is?

Values

If cultures are who we are and how we do things, it follows that shared values strengthen your culture. Not general values such as "we tell the truth" or "we treat each other with respect," but values that support the real you and make you different from your rivals. Values in a culture abhor a vacuum. If a company does not develop and subscribe to a set of meaningful values, an *ad hoc* set of values will emerge.

Values grow out of observed behavior. As somebody once told Charlie Hughes at Mazda, "There are 1,100 employees here who are paid to watch everything you do." No matter what you *say* as a corporation, employees will take their lead from what you *do*. By observation they will determine what they perceive as the real values of the company. Discrepancies between stated values and observed values can create an aura of mistrust, internal self-doubt, and backbiting criticism—and that can kill a culture.

Values not only provide a mental safe haven for employees, over time they become a powerful mechanism for attracting and retaining the right people.

Focus

A branded culture brings focus to the team, and that focus is on *pleasing the customer.* Most organizations try to do too many programs, projects, new concepts, and initiatives at the same time, and they suffer accordingly. Making a promise sets your priorities. Studying your customers as you create the experience to wrap your promise in will teach you what they want and what is important to them. Once you know that about your customer, measuring your progress becomes easier.

As one of our friends puts it, "We want our employees to be talking about customers, what they want, and how we are going to provide it. We want them saying, 'How does what I do contribute to our success?'"

A Happy Ending

What happened after the Land Rover team's first week together? Everyone left the gathering radiating enthusiasm. There were some false starts, and some work required additional clarifying, but mostly people just got on with the work.

By December, however, it became apparent that the new Land Rover team was falling behind schedule in several—too many—areas. Charlie called a meeting to take a hard look at the overall project status and to learn what might not be done on time. On time meant March 17, 1987, our stated on-sale date. Opening the meeting with a request for candor, Charlie asked each person present to share the status of their projects and problem areas.

The first person called on to come clean on his projects' timing was Roger Ball, the marketing VP. Roger's area was not in the worst shape, but some projects had fallen behind schedule, and they would require a struggle to get them done on time. Charlie asked Roger, "Where do you stand?" Roger said in a clear voice, "Charlie, I committed to this group last June that I'd be on line, on time, and I will live up to that commitment."

"Roger, that's very commendable, but we're going to have to get honest about project status and see if there is some way we can help each other solve some of the issues that have thrown us off schedule." With that Roger said, "Charlie, I'm deadly serious, I committed to you and this team that I would have all this work done, and I will. I will find a way to do this; that is my commitment and I will live up to it."

Jim Lehman, our general counsel, then spoke up, "Charlie, I feel the same way. I've got some issues that are taking more time than I thought, but I made a commitment and I will be on line, on time, as well."

One by one, all the leaders reiterated their commitments and said they would get the work done. And they did. When we launched Range Rover on March 17, only one of all the many pages of tasks and projects was late. By three days.

Those early days formed the foundation for the company and created, as you might guess, a rich body of tribal lore. Because we were able to launch the vehicle on time—and with an entire new company operational—we tried, with a mixture of awe and insight, to ascertain reasons why the company went on to be a success. Vision and culture topped the list.

Understand this: culture runs the show and will determine your success. All cultures have strengths and weaknesses. But one of the strengths must be unwavering support for your brand's differentiation. Does the vision of the brand permeate all of the thinking done by the people who work in the organization? Do they get it? Do they dream it? Do they taste it? Do they hold each other accountable for making the brand live up to the vision? More important, do they evangelistically *sell* it?

The desire to run a successful business does not make a

culture. Having clear business objectives and the world's best business strategy does not make a culture. But knowing who you are and how you are going to win customers in the market-place is a damn good start on culture building.

Product

"We now have one, single global design and engineering budget. We've put an end to badge engineering."

Robert Lutz, Vice Chairman of General Motors.
Washinton Post, *March 5, 2006*

The Test of Skill

If there's one area where the courage of your convictions can't be overdone, it's product. Abraham Lincoln was right. Sooner or later, nobody is fooled.

Every month *Car and Driver, Road & Track, Automobile* and *Motor Trend* magazines feature new and exciting cars that capture the imaginations of millions of Americans. They have been joined by new electronic magazines such as *Winding Road*. They're all about excitement. Words like competent and practical get little play here. The most sought-after brands and the most exciting new products get the most coverage.

You would think that everyone in the automaking business

has the skill to build wonderful products that take the market by storm. Most of them do. The technical skills, anyway. The branding and marketing skills are another story. Here are two stories from the Pontiac history book that illustrate how skill, and the courage to apply it, affect a product's success. In the first example, skill works; in the second, it's far less successful.

Song of the GTO

In the summer of 1964, an obscure band called Ronny and the Daytonas sang of the "Little GTO," Pontiac's new lightweight two-door. The GTO, with its four-speed gearbox and whopper 389 cubic inch V-8 engine, was the culmination of a brand transformation.

In the mid-1950s, Pontiac's image was every bit as exciting as that of Herbert Hoover or Estes Kefauver. But from 1958 through 1963 Pontiac transformed itself, morphing steadily into a performance brand by offering ever more powerful V-8 engines in virtually all its models and body styles. Even its lackluster styling improved, developing an unmistakable cool quotient.

Pontiac cemented its image with the introduction of the 1964 GTO, a car that Pontiac division manager John Z. DeLorean snuck past GM's budgeting brass. The GTO used the simple automotive principle of a favorable weight-to-horsepower ratio. Stuff a big engine into a light body and, wham! Instant omigod acceleration and eye-watering top speed.

The Pontiac marketing lads did a great job of promoting the GTO. *Car and Driver* immortalized the "Goat" in a comparison test between a Pontiac GTO and a Ferrari GTO. Just mentioning those two cars in the same breath appalled every Ferrari enthusiast with a reading lamp, and *Car and Driver* infuriated them even more by saying that the Pontiac, at a fraction of the Ferrari's cost, was competitive. Throughout the rest of the 1960s Pontiac was a dominant player in the category it had just created: muscle cars.

By the mid-1970s, emission regulations, a fuel crisis, and a hostile insurance industry conspired to kill the GTO and its peers.

But by that time, the GTO had become such a revered part of Pontiac's history that its adherents, like Cargo Cultists, spent the next three decades waiting for Pontiac to wake up and bring back the GTO in some form.

No less a light than Bob Lutz, Vice Chairman of General Motors and the man GM brought in to straighten out its product offerings—and who has made signal progress in his assigned task—decided to do just that. This made him a momentary hero to the Pontiac faithful. Why momentary? In an industry where cost efficiency, not cleanliness, is next to godliness, Bob Lutz showed that even he could get it wrong, however pure his motives.

On a trip to Australia in 2002, Lutz fell in love with the Monaro coupe built by Holden, GM's Down Under brand. It was fast, handled reasonably well, and looked sporty in a generic non-threatening way. He announced to the press traveling with him that the Monaro would make a great GTO. Re-do the front end, put in a version of the Corvette engine, certify it, and away we go. In 2004, Pontiac introduced its new GTO. How smart, how straightforward, how cost effective. Did it work? No.

Industry pundits said GM introduced the new GTO in the wrong season, winter. They said it had bland styling and cost too much. No one said out loud that the real reason was that the car was a transparent phony. You can't make Francis the Talking Mule a racehorse by dressing it in Calumet Farm silks. In fairness, however, the car's handling and performance were more than acceptable.

Let's review. We have an Australian body designed for, of all things, Australians. We have a Chevrolet Corvette high-performance engine and a Pontiac front fascia. No one was fooled. Not that GM hid anything. In fact, GM bragged about its wisdom in combining existing bits and pieces to create a GTO. If nothing else, this exercise demonstrated that Pontiac as an authentic brand is just a memory—utterly lacking in authenticity. Its lead image car is a fake in a world where authenticity is a concept that connotes integrity. GTO sales declined in 2005 from 2004 when Pontiac sold about 13,500.

This brings up another question, if Pontiac is to be GM's "performance" or "excitement" division, what do customers have a right to expect? What makes a Pontiac a Pontiac? In an age of shared platforms and components, no clear answer emerges. For years, lots of years, Pontiac tried to create an aura of performance by placing cladding on the sides of their cars. We'll spare you a discussion of how futile that exercise was. Except for a few Firebird models, there were no performance Pontiacs. Its lineup of Sunbird, Grand Am, Grand Prix, and Bonneville models differed only superficially from products at other GM divisions with which Pontiac shared platforms. They shared engines, transmissions, suspensions, and brake components. Can cosmetic differences make a brand? If you believe, as we do, that General Motors lost 30 market share points for a reason, the answer is a ringing no.

To shore up disappointing first-year GTO sales, GM increased horsepower from 350 to 400, making this car legitimately fast. GM also tweaked the styling, adding two hood scopes that should have been there in the first place and a new rear bumper incorporating dual exhausts. Both the GTO and the Cadillac CTS-V now use the same performance engine originally designed for the Corvette. It's cost efficient, but it hardly builds brand authenticity.

The original GTO was conceived by people who worked at the Pontiac Motor Division, then a separate quasi-independent business as were all the other GM Divisions. Pontiac employees were consumed by the goal to make Pontiac different and better than its competition, never mind that some competitors were GM-owned. They believed in what they did, and they were good at it. They loved their "Poncho" engine and constantly improved it. Pontiac excited a whole generation of buyers, and it sold cars. Authentic Pontiacs. Buyers knew the difference then, and they know the difference now.

In 2006, Pontiac announced it would discontinue the GTO. The GTO could have been the first step in recasting Pontiac as a genuine performance brand. Instead, it has been a showcase for GM's flawed conception of how little it takes to build a desirable brand.

Conventional Wisdom

Conventional wisdom says that 80 percent of a car company's success is tied to its product. Yet, many auto executives act as if they believe their product is less important than Casual Friday. They repeatedly try to fool the public with thinly disguised common architecture and insignificant product differences. Could any rational human give you a reason to buy a Mercury Mountaineer instead of a Ford Explorer? Meanwhile, the leading Asian brands keep raising the competitive bar on quality and functionality and are beginning to make inroads into styling, an area where they'd traditionally trailed.

Regulations for safety, emissions, and fuel economy, plus global competition, industry consolidation, brand proliferation, and platform sharing have led to a dreary homogenization of products. Executives at Ford and GM say they believe that product is king, but they seem to have little time or stomach for creating compelling originality.

The industry believes that, as Ford used to say, "Quality is Job 1." Build the highest quality car, and the world will flock to your door. Companies are reluctant to say "Hey, well above-average quality is good enough. Let's put our money into other product characteristics."

Quality is of course important to customers, and they get angry when a manufacturer disappoints them. Just ask Mercedes-Benz, once the benchmark nameplate for quality. Yet cars have now improved to the point that quality is no longer a real differentiator; it's the ante chip. The quality race has got so tight that J.D. Power had to change its questionnaire and scoring method on its satisfaction surveys. Otherwise the survey simply could not properly differentiate.

You can still buy a poor-quality car. But you have to work at it.

Trends

The pace of new technology and the continuing effects of the information age are changing our world in ways that are hard to comprehend. The speed of change is dizzying, and it is having a profound affect on automotive product development.

The overarching trends of more choice/less choice, fantasy growth, and low risk/high reward are impacting product development in ways both obvious and subtle. Product is an identity test and then a skill test. Here are some of the trends that the industry must grapple with. While most are right out in plain sight, one of them is a stealth trend sneaking up on the industry.

Brand Portfolios . . . Platform Sharing

The trend of industry consolidation and subsequent collecting of brands heightened the issue of platform sharing. The tension between the need to reduce costs and the desire to sell products from multiple but differentiated brands is vexing the industry, and many of the players are getting it horribly wrong.

The question being asked is, "How much can I share on a platform or component basis before I start to dilute the desirability and equity of the brands in my portfolio?" Put a more cynical way, what is the minimum amount of differentiation needed to fool the public? GM and Ford in particular have consistently failed to find the right balance point. Critics within both companies have said that they have become neither as efficient as they need to be nor as brand sensitive.

Two examples from Ford tell how difficult it is to navigate this trend intelligently.

Ford owns Volvo and, in an efficiency move, decided to base its 2005 Ford Five Hundred, Ford Freestyle, and Mercury Montego vehicles on an excellent Volvo platform. The Ford and Volvo models do not look alike, and they have separate powertrains. So far so good, but industry observers claim that the platform was too expensive a starting point for a Ford vehicle. Furthermore, tooling only one plant to build around 220,000 units a year—in total—for all three models makes it hard for Ford to recover the costs of all the changes they had to make.

In 2002 Mazda, in which Ford holds a controlling interest, introduced the Mazda6 on an all-new platform that Mazda designed. Ford had designated Mazda as the center for midsize platforms that would become a series of US-market cars sold under other nameplates. The first of the cars went on sale in 2005 and included the Ford Fusion, the Mercury Milan, and the Lincoln Zephyr. Ford increased the dimensions of the platform to conform to American drivers' tastes and sizes. Consequently, they look nothing like a Mazda6.

Unfortunately, the three Ford brand offerings vary from each other mostly in styling, trim and equipment differences. When they were introduced, they even shared powertrains. Is that sufficient to convince the customer that the Lincoln version's $7,000 price premium is justified? Not the customers we talk to.

Globalization . . . Localization

We've heard all the lines: we live in a global village; the world is flat; we are becoming ever more alike. You would think that means that Honda could sell the same Honda Civic around the world, right? Well, yes and no.

Many products are sold throughout the world with only trim, equipment, and powertrain differences. Yet the industry must cope with two realities. The three major markets—Europe, the US, and Japan—all have different government regulatory statutes that must be met before cars can be sold in their markets. Some of those regulations vary widely. The other issue is local preference. Europe is in love with diesels; the US is not. The Japanese want small cars, smaller even than the Europeans want, and *much* smaller than Americans. Europeans like hatchbacks and small minivans. Americans don't. And so on and so forth.

These globalization realities make differentiation more complex and difficult. The most successful brands have found ways to align their brand essence with different market regulations and satisfy local market preferences. Many have not. Peugeot and Renault, two French brands strong in Europe, have given up trying in the US. Ditto Fiat. US-built cars do poorly in export markets.

The Fraying of Newness . . . Number of Introductions . . .

More brands and more models mean more new product introductions: This is a natural outgrowth of the proliferation and
fragmentation trends, and we have already discussed how more
apparent choice has resulted in less real choice.

Another aspect of this trend dilutes every marketer's favorite
word: new. We have gone from 25 to 30 new model introductions
a year just a few years ago to a forecast of 45 to 60 new model introductions each year for 2006 and beyond. This puts even more
pressure on the product development teams because being new is
just not the attention-getter it was only a few years ago. You must
be new in a way that commands interest.

Pace of Change . . . Fast Tech/Slow Tech

The car business is caught up in the same crazy pace of change as
every other business. Yet for all of its billions of dollars invested in
product development, the car business looks like a wandering
turtle when compared with the consumer electronics industry.
The consumer electronics industry now shapes customer expectations regarding speed of product development and change. Consumer electronic products get replaced every six to twelve
months, while vehicles usually get minor facelifts—freshenings—
every three years and are replaced every five to six years.

Apple was on the twelfth iteration of its iPod before the car
industry could engineer a way to hook an iPod into a car's
sound system. Customers are probably not yet aware that they
want the industry to pick up the speed of technological change.
But early restlessness can be seen in the accelerating demand for
hybrid vehicles. Hybrids don't pay off for the customer financially, but they are the newest new thing, and leading-edge customers crave them. The car industry finds itself behind the
demand curve.

The auto industry has, over the past decade, brought some
excellent engineering and design to market. The list includes

cleaner, more powerful engines that also get better fuel economy. Safety features such as air bags, antilock braking systems, and electronic stability control are electronic marvels. As are navigation systems. Yet much of this progress has felt more like continuous improvement, not breakthrough change.

Even though it is a mature industry, and even though years of rebates and discounts have diminished its luster, the car business—and other businesses—will do well to note the customer's growing familiarity with rapid change. Consumers are hungry for more.

The Skill Test Called Product

All new vehicles look good to their creators—right up until the day they confront the harsh reality of the marketplace. Product is the "you" that the world sees. When your new product appears, the whole world will know in short order whether you know who you are, whether you are who they think you are, and whether you have your act together.

Product, as important as it is, is only one element of an overall strategy to sell in a marketplace. Some successful companies choose a product-secondary approach. They adopt a strategy with another focus that they hope will appeal to their customers. A 100,000 mile warranty, for example. Or a "youthful image." These can work, but not if a company builds cars so unremarkable that the world concludes the company doesn't care about product. Then there's little to fall back on but price, and no automaker ever built a great brand on a price-only strategy.

The Brand Triangle helps you consider and decide where you want to place your emphasis—where you want to place *your* bet. Should you decide to place your primary emphasis on a different area—customer service and the retail experience for example—the product must at least reinforce the brand strategy.

Must your product be exciting, best in class, and a world beater? It helps, but those things are not always necessary. What the product must do, however, is deliver successfully on your promise and provide that aspect of the ownership experience that your customers expect from you. Cheap and cheerful? Great. Most reliable and lowest price? Terrific. Most fun to drive? Go for it. Muddy image and confused differentiation among your products? Sharpen your pencils; you'll need them for the discounting you'll be doing.

There is no substitute for a full understanding of what role your product plays in your brand's promise and what you want your customer's experience to be. Does the product deliver it? Does the product shout your promise or whisper it? Have you got the mix of product characteristics right? All complex products force trade-offs. Are your trade-offs supporting or undermining your promise?

Excellence and Character

Our friend Peter DeLorenzo is the founder of an insider automotive Web site appropriately named *Autoextremist.com*. A rebel with a cause, Peter, in his weekly "Rant," delivers perceptive and wickedly barbed insights. Speaking of what a new vehicle must do to gain serious consideration in the market, Peter wrote:

> . . . designing and building great products is just the beginning. It used to be that the "price of entry" for every manufacturer in the world had two basic components, quality and reliability. Without those two basics, a manufacturer couldn't expect to compete. But now that the quality gap is shrinking . . . the game has been changed and [the cost] raised to an even higher level.
>
> Creating cars and trucks that are excellent in every aspect of consideration is now the new "price of entry" package for every automobile manufacturer in the world. And with that intimidating set of parameters facing every automaker, differentiating themselves from each other becomes more and more complicated—and crucial.

And, might we add, exponentially more difficult.

The market drives a level of excellence that competitors must honor. The challenge is to know where you need to be strong, perhaps even the best, and where you only need to be competitive. Your promise and your intended experience should guide you to make appropriate trade-offs.

The Platform Trade-off

In an earlier chapter, we introduced you to platform sharing and the practice of what we call badge engineering—selling essentially the same car with different nameplates. Platform sharing can be done with success. Consider that the BMW 5 Series and 7 Series are built using the same platforms. And remember that a platform is usefully described as a collection of components that can be moved this way and that; it is not a rigid frame. The 5 and 7 Series BMWs have different personalities, one from the other, but both are unmistakably BMWs.

Platform sharing is not always bad, but it can be fatal if wrongly applied. We have repeatedly cited the mistakes made by General Motors under Roger Smith. You don't need to be a rocket scientist to know that cars with the same drive trains, the same dimensions, the same seats, and the same driving personalities simply cannot be differentiated by marketing and advertising—and nameplates—alone.

A more recent, and somewhat more successful, example is Ford's use of a single platform to build the Ford of Europe Focus, Volvo S40, and the Mazda3. The brands are quite different, and each brand's version of this shared platform does a good job of representing that brand's essence.

Another successful bit of sheetmetal sleight-of-hand is the Volkswagen New Beetle. Underneath, it's a VW Golf, but who would know? Or care?

When platform sharing results in look-alike cars, however, it's a sign of trouble. The trouble may not come today, but it will come. We've seen what happened to Oldsmobile, and we can see GM ridding itself of more divisions before we get much older.

And if you can tell us why someone with a single analytical bone in his body would pay more for a Lincoln Town Car, the automotive equivalent of the high-button shoe, instead of buying a Ford Crown Victoria (a less expensive high-button shoe) or its absolute twin, the Mercury Grand Marquis, we'll send you a rebate coupon good at any Ford or Lincoln Mercury dealer.

Who does platform sharing the right way? The usual suspects. Toyota shares components between Lexus and the Toyota brand without damaging either. Ditto Honda and Acura.

How We Build Cars

The platform-sharing discussion is part of a larger set of considerations. Remember our words defining corporate culture: who we are and how we do things? That has an obvious application to product, because product is what winds up in the hands of the customer and, together with the other elements of their experience, determines the fate of your brand.

If you went to the management suites at GM, Ford, Daimler-Chrysler, Toyota, and Honda, and asked the question, "How do you build cars?" you would hear different answers from each.

Doubtless, all would say they build product-first cars with the customer in mind, doing so with integrity, innovation, value, and fun-to-drive excitement. Well, maybe not the excitement.

What you would not hear is, "We build cars that our research can defend, that can only be sold with huge rebates and without regard to the damage we might do to our brand by creating Me-Too cars that make a snail race seem exciting." In short, cars conceived and executed with no executive left unprotected.

Yet, look at the public's perception of Toyota value as opposed to Ford or GM or DaimlerChrysler. Toyotas often sell for over $2,000 more than equivalent domestic vehicles. It makes you believe Toyota's statement that the company bases its management philosophy on long-term goals, even if that means sacrificing short-term profits.

A Disciplined Approach

Imagine that you're sitting in a Land Rover meeting in the UK in 1997. Present are the Discovery Series II product development team, the US dealer advisory group, and US sales and marketing executives. Product launch is less than 18 months away. The concept is past the approval stage, has reached the execution stage, and is not up to American customer expectations.

The dealers, as you might well imagine, were not pleased.

The product contained some bright thinking, but it did not address a number of concerns raised by existing Discovery Series I owners. It remained underpowered and unrefined, with a substandard interior package, difficult ergonomics and styling that would embarrass a bread box. While superior in many ways to the current product, it seemed out of touch and behind the curve. Land Rover, even as it attempted deliver on its Best 4 × 4 × Far promise, had left major holes in the experience. In too many areas, "rugged" had become "crude."

We use Land Rover to illustrate that even when you've made your promise and know the role you want product to play in the customer's experience, you can still get it wrong. Evolving tastes, escalating competition, technological advancements, not enough investment capital, holding on to the wrong parts of your product heritage, poor judgment, and weak execution are just some of the product-development pitfalls you can find yourself tumbling into.

Mazda, in 1999–2000, had wrestled with returning to its roots, using the positioning line, "Always the soul of a sports car." This expressed the company's promise to a taste of Miata or RX-7 in every Mazda. But the Mazda team hit a wall in 2001 when it came to launching its revised minivan, the MPV.

The difficulty stemmed from the image of minivans—vehicles designed for "soccer moms," not for drivers you could characterize as interested in driving pleasure. Conventional wisdom said you win in the minivan segment with superior features and functionality.

Did Mazda's target market—the 25 percent of buyers who

actually liked cars—buy many minivans? They did. Would they buy a minivan with sporting pretensions? The new MPV was a great-handling, fun-to-drive vehicle that just happened to be a minivan. That did not prevent an internal battle between people who felt Mazda had to promote customary minivan traits and those who wanted to position it as a true Mazda.

Despite considerable opposition, the leaders at Mazda positioned the revised MPV as a minivan with the soul of a sports car. This was consistent with the belief that you must be who you are everywhere. Period. To bolster this argument, Mazda launched the new MPV at Mazda Raceway at Laguna Seca. Where better to argue that your minivan had sporting blood?

At first, journalists were surprised by Mazda's audacity, and then even more surprised by how well the MPV performed. They drove the MPV around the town of Carmel, California, on a Gymkhana course at Mazda Raceway, and were driven around the race track in an MPV prepared by Mazdaspeed, the company's racing arm. The journalists left as believers.

Each product must deliver on your brand promise. If one of your products says one thing, another says another thing, and a third something else entirely, your promise becomes an average of the three. Which is to say average. How often do you see "to be average" among a successful company's list of aims?

How do you deliver your promise?

Cars are complex products, and those who build them must balance countless performance parameters because optimizing one characteristic of a product generally requires suboptimizing one or more other characteristics. Compromises must be made. The stickiest trade-offs occur as you try to build your dream vehicle for a price the market will pay. Through these trade-offs, the definition of your product emerges.

As the world evolves, the process repeats itself with every new or revised product. So as to not lose the thread or become old before their time, the brightest codify their promise in their product design process.

Mazda carefully defined its buyers' wants and then decided in which areas it needed to be the absolute best, where it needed to be very good, and where it needed only be competitive—or less. The process was called PALS (Product Attribute Leadership Strategy), and it provided the discipline part of the equation. It detailed 25 or so product attributes and rated each in terms of importance to Mazda's brand promise.

The rating system had four values. Attributes where Mazda wanted to be (1) the leader—number one or best in class, (2) among the leaders or in the top three, (3) competitive or top half, and (4) uncompetitive or bottom half. The attributes were all quantifiable automotive characteristics. Initially, the process drove a forced ranking and occasioned much soul searching.

With product priorities in hand, each product program required that Mazda analyze competitive performance and determine hard targets by attribute. What would it take to be the leader or among the leaders? Tough work, yet it had a liberating and invigorating effect on the engineering team. They knew in which areas they had to be the experts and in which areas they just needed to be competitive— a relief from the old days when marketing would best-ball them on all attributes.

Braking is an interesting example. Like many characteristics of a car, braking has both quantitative and qualitative aspects. For instance, one quantitative measure for brakes would be the 60–0 mph stopping distance. A qualitative measure would be brake pedal feel. When developing the Mazda6, the engineers had a clear quantitative target on stopping distance. It was a tough but appropriate target.

They then needed a target for the qualitative feel of the brake system. They choose the Porsche 911. They never intended to out-brake a Porsche, but they felt Porsche had the best brake feel in the industry. If Mazda could approach Porsche in brake feel, they would be light years ahead of Toyota or Honda. Such a sterling attribute would be noticed by journalist and buyers alike.

By decision, there were a host of areas where Mazda did not need or want to be the best. In areas such as ride or fuel economy they might only have to be competitive. And for an area like acceleration they might only have to be among the leaders. They could then quantify what performance level that translated into—such as 0–60 mph times.

There is one small problem. The competition is also busy improving its future products and does not willingly tell you their targets. So you must also do some qualitative future factoring. Undershoot what the competition will achieve and you won't clearly differentiate yourself. Overshoot by a ton and you may build in additional cost and complexity. Pushing the envelope not only takes investment, it can also take time—time the marketplace may be unwilling to grant you.

PALS and other similar processes write your promise in high definition. Priorities become clear yet much work remains subjective. For instance, if sports-car handling is important, some aspects can be measured and some have to do with "feel." How everything works together is also subjective. You can measure NVH (noise, vibration, and harshness), yet it is only a part of what creates an impression of overall refinement.

Tools like PALS bring discipline and visibility to the product development process, but the best companies then rely on their own expertise to fill in the areas that are still art. And who ends up with the real expertise? Those companies that continue to develop the skills that set them apart.

Your Look

The word *styling* sounded too much like flower arranging, so the industry now calls it design. It better connotes the challenges of blending form and function. Call it what you will, it is an art. And too much of this art is being judged by solemn businessmen in dull but expensive suits who have no demonstrated taste. We could say that these men should be hanging from light poles, but that would perhaps be extreme.

People who underestimate the importance of style should work for your competition. Style is a critical purchase factor that is judged, not measured. Most of the car industry appears to be too timid, which is why handsome looking cars stand out. For the record, you want to design attractive cars—cars that look good on the inside and outside—and exteriors and interiors that look as if they belong together. It is also necessary to create a "look"—*your* look. A look communicates your promise and becomes the face of your brand. That this notion is debated in the car business tells you a lot. Penguins, they say, are able to find their children no matter how crowded the ice floe; few customers want to work that hard. You want to stand out in an attractive way and in a way that lets your customers know it's you. And, if you require more challenges, your design needs to evolve continuously.

Designing and creating good-looking products is difficult enough for most automakers. Creating a genuine look is well nigh impossible. Some companies with established themes grow bored and move on to new themes. Each change redefines them more than they realize. It's part of the dance that keeps them a secondary player and tells the world they don't know what they want to be when they grow up. But the people who get it right are an inspiration to us all.

There are handsome vehicles on sale in 2006. The Bentley Continental GT, some of the Aston Martins, the Ferrari 430 Mondial, and, though it is conservative, the latest generation 911. There are some distinctive vehicles such as the Audi TT, Cadillac CTS, the Chrysler 300, the Dodge Ram Pickup, the Nissan Z, Mazda RX-8, the Infiniti FX45, the Nissan Murano, and the Volvo XC90. There are cars that are mildly more interesting than other cars in their segment such as the Nissan Altima, the Honda Odyssey, the Land Rover LR3, and the Infiniti G35. And then there are the undistinguished masses. Scores of cars and trucks that are indistinguishable. Rental car fleets are crowded with these beauties. So are dealer storage lots.

It costs the same to design a stunning vehicle as to design a boring one. The difference lies in the artist and the artist's environment. Some environments are just far more demanding of great work.

Okay we lied; it does not necessarily cost the same to build a boring car as to build a stunning creation. Some shapes cost more to tool than others. The cost of the detailing that goes into cars, sometimes called the jewelry—headlights, taillights, door handles and grilles—varies greatly by design and materials. If it looks more expensive, it probably cost more. Given this country's boom in plastic surgery, the lesson should be clear: Invest a bit more in how you look. Saving pennies to look homely even sounds ludicrous.

It is hard work to come up with a distinctive and attractive family brand look. Mercedes-Benz has done an excellent job of this over the years. BMW used to be the best example, but recent designs have strayed from their signature athletic, tailored look. Over the past five years, Cadillac has made great strides in developing a bold brand look.

Defining your look is difficult, and many automakers have found it even harder to keep it fresh. Mercedes-Benz has demonstrated it knows how to do it. Each new car is unmistakably a Mercedes, yet each one looks fresher and more attractive than the one before. Toyota is beginning to get the hang of it, and Nissan changed its look entirely—and for the better.

But you must first create and establish a look before keeping it fresh matters. That's a high hurdle, and it's frequently exacerbated by a collection of new designers brought in to save the brand. Getting there may be tough, but it puts you in rare company.

Quality. Striving to Get It Right.

Quality across the automotive landscape has gotten so good that it is easy to think of it as a given. It isn't—as Mercedes-Benz, which has had uncharacteristic quality problems over the past few years, knows. Mercedes has disappointed too many customers, and it will take years for the company to fully recover. Customers now expect an extremely high level of quality. It has become more of a satisfier than a differentiator. Unless you get it wrong, and then it will differentiate you to hell.

The auto industry has defined quality in a bipolar way. We have wrung our hands for decades over things gone wrong as measured by J.D. Power studies, such as its Consumer Satisfaction

Index (CSI) and Initial Quality Survey (IQS) quality indexes and the industry's own warranty reporting. The auto industry has focused, invested, and come a long way on quality. Across the board, it deserves a "well done."

Another way we think of quality is things gone right—what customers really like about your car—J.D. Power measures this with its APPEAL study. This reveals how well or how poorly your products differentiate you. It is one of the best ways to find out what owners really like about your design and where you are falling short.

Remember PALS as used by Mazda? You want the APPEAL research to validate your design's performance as *perceived* by your customers. If you wanted to win on fuel economy but get only slightly above-average marks, no matter what the actual fuel economy figures say, you are not living up the customer's expectation. Conversely if you do poorly on economy but great on acceleration (where you wanted to do well), you have won that priority.

Your quality, like everything about you, must be fit for its purpose. That purpose is to please your customers, and getting it right is necessary and expected.

There is one more aspect to quality: the quality of your timing. Every market has its own cadence and rhythm. A critical component to being ahead of the competition is to be at the leading edge of the cadence and on beat with the market rhythm. In the car business, products have life cycles. Allow your products to get too old and you die. So does your brand image.

Many hide behind quality, saying that we will bring our new product to market only when it is ready. It sounds logical, but wait. Being on time is part of the quality story. If it is late you have missed one of your quality targets, and it will cost you as dearly in the marketplace as any other quality glitch.

There is a right time and a wrong time to introduce a new model. Cars have a model year birthday in September, and the best time to launch a new car is either in September or October or in the spring selling season. Getting and staying in sync with market timing is challenging for any technical group, but being out of step is an expensive mistake and gives your competition a leg up.

The Voice of the Customer

New products in the car business are billion-dollar bets, and no one wants to lose that kind of money. Which is why consumer research exists.

Yet as reasonable as it sounds, the industry seems to have applied research as Novocain to ease the pain of judging creativity. We don't trust our own people to know what our customers want, so we will keep asking the customer until all originality is erased. Your authors are not researchophobes, but we are disheartened by how often research is used to replace judgment instead of to augment it.

Research can be extremely useful in giving you an unalloyed view of how your current products are doing in the marketplace against your real competition. In the car industry, syndicated research will give you a valid report card for both current product quality and product performance versus your competition.

This is critical input as you define future product programs, and it is used in conjunction with research on prototypes of future products, often at a car clinic. Car clinics are the biggest punching bag in the industry. They are a research process in which you invite prospective buyers to see and critique future products now in the development stage. Often they are compared with current competitive products.

They are expensive and fallible. As GM can attest, you can still end up with a car like the Pontiac Aztek, something so ugly it became a national joke. But if you think GM has cornered the market for clinic mistakes, remember that Ford took years to get to market with a minivan that had rear doors on both sides of the vehicle. Minivans first came to market with only one sliding rear door on the passenger side of the vehicle. Once Chrysler introduced a sliding door on both sides, the market cheered. Did Ford clinics say that the market wanted one-rear-door minivans?

Two fundamental issues affect clinics' usefulness: the respondents to whom you listen and the ability of all respondents to see into the future.

The first issue is that the car industry too often sees itself as a mass-marketing business, so it concentrates on segments within the auto market. This is especially true at companies which have failed to explicitly define their target customer.

Imagine you are Mazda and are bringing out the new midsize Mazda6, which you want to "clinic" against its competition—chiefly the Toyota Camry and Honda Accord. You will test your prototype new car against your prime competitor's current products. Most companies will conduct this product comparison among customers who intend to buy a midsize car when next in the market.

The recruiting is usually done by segment on a sales-weighted basis with some oversampling from your own owner body. Using the midsize car segment as an example, there will be more Toyota Camry and Honda Accord buyers than other brands. And what will these owners tell you? "Be more like Toyota and Honda." They'll say, "Don't be different, be like them." Look like them, have engines and model lineups like them. Of course, don't price like them, because in their eyes, your car isn't as good. What is the real message here? Easy. The vast majority of buyers aren't your target audience—and they shouldn't be. Listening to them is nuts.

At Mazda, researchers divided the sample into two groups: midsize intenders who fell into Mazda's target market and those who fell outside. Many in the latter group owned Camrys and Accords. Mazda wanted to see how well it did among its target market—the 25 percent of the market with a predisposition toward Mazda.

They were also interested in how the non-target group reacted to the new product. Frankly, Mazda was looking for the biggest variance possible between the two groups. It wasn't that they wanted to alienate the non-target group, just that they'd learned over time that their audience wanted something more than the white bread Toyota and Honda were serving up. The more the car attracted Mazda's target, the less it appealed to the general group. Had Mazda listened to a sales-weighted sample, they would have rushed to be mere imitations of the segment leaders.

The second big issue is asking respondents to stand in the future—without all the opinion-changing experiences they will have gone through to get there.

When Charlie Hughes headed marketing for Porsche/Audi in the early 1980s, he had the opportunity to work with the outspoken and eccentric Tony Lapine, then in charge of Porsche design. Charlie was trying gently to coach Tony about why the Nissan Z was more popular in the US market than the Porsche 924. It was Charlie's none-to-subtle way of telling Tony what to address in future designs.

Tony listened patiently, much as a patient teacher listens to an earnest but errant student, and retorted. "You are telling me how to build today's car, but my job is to build a car that will be a success in five years. That car will not look like today's Z. Neither you nor your customers know what that car should look like because you see everything through today's eyes. I get paid to see what is not so obvious." Well, that put the student in his place, and it was a lesson well learned and well remembered.

Research is only a part of the way you stay close to the customers as you polish your product act.

Never-ending Questions

Businesses are unexcelled at holding executive retreats, producing pithy strategic papers, and writing brand-positioning documents, but they forever come up woefully short in tangibles such as product. That's odd, because product is literally where the rubber meets the road. Then again, maybe it's not so odd. After all, strong words and empty promises incur little risk. The risk exposure comes when you design a product and take it to market where it must face the acid test of public scrutiny. So we ask you . . .

Do you really want to set yourself apart?

Do you want to make a clear promise?

Do you have the skills to execute your promise?

Do you really know your customers?

Do you have your backbone in place?

Don't tell us. Show us with your product.

Conspiracy

"Most teams aren't teams at all but merely collections of individual relationships with the boss. Each individual vying with the others for power, prestige and position."

Douglas McGregor (1906–1964), author,
The Human Side of Enterprise

The Test of Inclusion

Once again dumping on conventional wisdom, we say you must suck it up and substitute conspiracy for teamwork. Remember that the last-place finisher in every league is a team.

Too many companies think their teams consist only of the people on their payrolls—only the employees charged directly with making Ajax Motors a success. They're wrong; their team is much larger than that.

Anyone with the capacity to influence your company's fate in the market needs to be a part of your team: that is the test of inclusion. Suppliers, retailers, customers, analysts, even the press—

anyone who can help you lead the charge must be a part of your conspiracy.

How do you achieve this? You invite them into your conspiracy—a conspiracy dedicated to building something great, something worthy of their time and interest. And you let them know that you need them.

Time and again when we bring up conspiracy, people ask if we don't mean collaboration. No, we mean conspiracy. Conspiracies naturally pique your interest. They're juicy, full of intrigue, and they have insiders and outsiders. Besides, they're more fun. Wouldn't *you* rather be on the inside of an exciting conspiracy than part of some mild-mannered collaboration?

What does this have to do with building great brands? A hell of a lot. Great brands are the result of hitting a critical mass—an inspired ensemble effort by folks working inside and outside the company to generate a convergence of events that can bring a brand to life.

The conspiracy's leader must have the guts and gumption to wear the company's vision on *both* sleeves—and the ability to choose whom to invite along as respected and necessary members of the adventure—*inside* members. He must appeal to a person's instinctive desire to be part of a success story. And he must capture their imagination and welcome their input.

The Land Rover Centre Conspiracy

To learn how powerful a conspiracy can be, hear it from an insider. Charlie Hughes conducted a number of successful conspiracies during his Land Rover days, none more important than a landmark retailing concept called Land Rover Centres. Other conspiracies preceded the development of the Centres, but the Centres provide a clear example of our theory.

> From the first, the management team at Range Rover of North America (RRNA)—later to become Land Rover North America (LRNA)—understood

that we needed help. We needed people's best work, best thinking, and best effort. Yet we recognized that we would not be the biggest date on most dealers' or suppliers' calendars. We could, however, be the most interesting, the most fun, and, ironically, the most demanding. We demanded great work—work that became a showcase and that made people proud of being a part of the Land Rover team. This required that we conspire with both our own people *and* with outside suppliers. Just paying for services would not generate the level of excitement and commitment we sought.

How we attracted a great advertising agency is a perfect example. The Grace & Rothschild agency was new and had no clients at the time we selected it. But they did have two of the most creative people in all of advertising: Roy Grace and Diane Rothschild, whose combined awards would have ranked them fifth among US agencies at that time. Both had worked at Doyle Dane Bernbach during the days of DDB's standout creative work. I had worked at DDB and knew both of them, though I had worked only with Diane.

G&R quickly gained a grasp of what the team wanted to do with Range Rover. They understood who the target market was, and they knew how to get its attention and appeal to it. The night I told Roy that G&R had won the account, I asked him to join us on a journey to build a unique car company: "Roy, I need your best creative thinking . . . not just for the advertising. I want you involved up to your eyeballs in everything we do where you feel you can make a difference."

Roy accepted the invitation and over the next 14 years produced some of the best automotive advertising ever done. Roy and the agency contributed in material ways on issues far afield from advertising—one of the great side-effects of a conspiracy. And we drew in other key suppliers, such as SBS Software and Caterpillar—sometimes with off-road events for their staff but always with an invitation to be on the inside of building Range Rover in the US.

Dealers were the most challenging. Dealers can be friends, foes, disinterested, uninterested, antagonists, or partners. We wanted them to be insiders, co-conspirators. Beginning with the dealer selection process, we cultivated a close relationship with each of them. Still and all, our conspiracy felt the need for some dealers to work with us from the inside. Without dealers as involved co-conspirators, where would an automaker be?

I invited five dealers to counsel us on a confidential basis. We wanted their retail expertise and their knowledge of what worked for other automakers they represented. Thus we created the President's Cabinet, resisting the impulse to call it the President's Conspiracy.

This insider group shared everything of importance, including virtually all of the company's financial information. If an issue was important to Land Rover's success, the Cabinet discussed it to closure. The group traveled together to some exotic places, nicknaming itself The Death March and Gourmet Eating Society. Were there disagreements? No more than a few hundred, but even when things got tense the Cabinet members always believed they were conspiring to build something special. The special bond we shared with dealers who served on the Cabinet laid the groundwork for radical change.

A shining example of radical change was stand-alone Land Rover Centres. Born against all odds, the Land Rover Centre was a breakthrough

in automotive retailing and has since been imi-
tated by other automakers. Like most conspiracies, it was born from a dream. The dream first
took shape at an executive retreat held in July,
1990, a meeting aimed at deciding what RRNA
wanted to be when it grew up. Three years after
introducing Range Rover to the American consumer, the leadership team was hankering for
another rush of start-up adrenalin. The dream
was to transform RRNA into Land Rover North
America and dramatically grow the business.

That dream was formless until the group met
that July and began articulating their boldest aspirations for the company they had started four years
earlier. We dreamed of an expanded product line
that would include the new Discovery, launched the
year before in the UK and Europe. To help market
us through the name change, we would bring a limited edition of the Land Rover 110 to the US. The
110, renamed Defender to alliterate with Discovery,
answered the need to badge more than one model
as a Land Rover. We built 500 consecutively num-
bered Land Rover 110s. Today, a Defender in good
shape brings more than its original price.

An ambitious goal of the group's dream was
to rewrite the way cars were retailed. Range
Rovers had been sold in dual dealerships, primarily in Jaguar, BMW, and Mercedes-Benz stores.
Expanding the product range allowed us to explore setting up Land Rover stores that sold only
Land Rover products.

In the UK Land Rover stores, more often than
not, had been tractor sheds behind small British
car dealerships. The introduction of Discovery in
1989 added a third product, increased volume,
and thereby provided the opportunity to push UK
dealers into building a proper store. While traditionally operated, the new stores looked Land
Roverish in a very British way.

But the team wanted to go further, to extend the brand into the retail experience. Saturn and Lexus had changed the face of automotive retailing in the late 1980s by attacking head-on the issue of customer dissatisfaction with the total dealer experience. Land Rover wanted to communicate the essence of the Land Rover brand and its attendant lifestyle at the point of retail. Land Rover Centres, in their final form, were an early example of retail as entertainment.

But the dream needed to evolve into a vision, something tangible that could be shared with others. In the early going we knew a few hard points: early Range Rover owners loved the lifestyle we introduced them to; they hated the traditional new car buying experience; and our dealers appreciated us. (We stood number one in the 1989 J.D. Power Dealer Satisfaction Index.) Yet many of our dealers still viewed Land Rover as the little truck in the corner of the showroom.

Two challenges were obvious. We needed to create a groundbreaking retail concept, and we had to persuade our dealers to invest millions of dollars in it. We would have no UK funding for either; our source for funds was the dealers' checkbooks. Minus the conspiracy approach, we'd never have managed it.

Our team spent the next 10 months persuading the Brits to embrace the concept of RRNA expanding into LRNA. When they said yes, my boss, Chris Woodwark, immediately became a co-conspirator in the warmest way. He subscribed totally to our desire to take US Land Rover retailing far beyond what the parent company had done in the UK.

We could now think seriously about who we needed inside the tent. Beyond the leadership team at Land Rover UK, we needed our own employees, some of our current suppliers, and some suppliers with whom we had never worked but who had skills we needed. We put David Schworm, head of service, in charge of the project—another illustration of what good conspiracies can do. Small companies provide diverse opportunities for employees, and that's what happened with Dave. He excelled in a job that under normal circumstances would have gone to a sales executive.

Meanwhile, we needed to keep our eye on selling Range Rovers. Sales success was the price of entry to making our transition to Land Rover North America, so we deliberately parceled out work between people concentrating on the future and people working on the present.

At first, our dealers did not react altogether positively to being asked to build costly, odd-looking facilities entirely at their own expense. While we had sought counsel initially from a few leading dealers, we eventually wanted them all on board. We would have to convince them that the concept would work and make money—lots of money.

By mid-1991 we were in full song, analyzing the entire retail cost structure to determine how to make stand-alone Land Rover stores work financially. In early 1992 we started working on the creative aspects. At the annual National Automobile Dealer Association (NADA) convention, we met some folks with impressive retail design credentials. The company was Design Forum, led by Lee Carpenter, and it immediately bought into our retail scheme. They were brand savvy, had broad retail design credentials, and had done work in the car business for Saturn. Best of all, they were excited about the Centre concept.

Design Forum staffers did a background review, gathering information from Land Rover UK, key Land Rover North America employees, and US Land Rover dealers. From this review they produced a carding exercise that used drawings and words on 3″ × 5″ cards to reveal what they had learned and what we all should consider. This seminal event focused our thinking and encouraged our risk taking.

At an early meeting with a couple of dealers, Mark Hennessy, our dealer in Atlanta, verbalized the concept. He suggested making the dealership a Hollywood set and our employees the actors and actresses. The processes we used would be our scripts.

From the beginning, we knew we wanted the stores to look more like a hunting lodge or garden center. We wanted outdoor displays and landscaping, not asphalt parking lots, to dominate the look. Taking this into account, Design Forum generated a variety of designs to consider.

Working with Jim Bernthal, we considered how we wanted the people in the stores to act. How would the processes in this store differ from those of the traditional dealer? Virtually all of these stores would be new and would mix current dealer Land Rover staff with new employees in an all-new retail concept. They would have to form a new team while they built a new business. We decided to get into heretofore taboo subjects such as how the retail team should be paid.

If the stores were to look like hunting lodges, how should the employees dress? To answer that question, Land Rover decided to create its own line of clothing. We enlisted Terry Drake, an expert in retail clothing who understood both the British and Safari looks. We named the clothing Land Rover Gear, and it was worn by retail and LRNA employees. We also sold it in Land Rover Centres, where it became quite popular with customers.

As our thinking and work progressed, we constantly reviewed it with the President's Cabinet. They proved to be great coaches. As conspirators, they enjoyed working on a new retail concept while never underestimating the resistance we would surely face from many of our dealers.

Earlier in 1990, under the tutelage of the Cabinet, we instituted a program called Business Builder that paid dealers substantial money to improve customer satisfaction. Because we expected Business Builder to play a big role in selling the Centre concept, we worked with the Cabinet to modify it to reward dealers who built Centres. The program eventually overcame our inability to provide subsidizing funds for the Centres.

It's never a good idea to surprise your business partners, and nowhere is that truer than when dealing with dealers. In 1990, before Rover Group had approved our move to become Land Rover North America, we shared our dream with our dealers during a dealer meeting at Canada's Lake Louise. Discussed only in general terms, the concept of an expanded LRNA intrigued them.

A year later, at the dealer meeting held in Scottsdale, Arizona, we told our dealers that we wanted them to consider building exclusive Land Rover stores. We hit them with this idea smack in the middle of the worst automotive recession in memory. As Charlie described his dream of stand-alone Land Rover stores, the audience stared in stunned silence. On the other hand, they loved the idea of bringing in more Land Rover models. It was the opening salvo in our campaign to build Land Rover Centres.

The next year, 1992, we took the dealers to the UK to visit Land Rover Centres done the British way. While less controversial than what we were about to do, it let them know that others had blazed this trail. The enthusiasm that the British dealers displayed for Land Rover and their new stores impressed our fact finders. We could sense excitement building.

Softening up the dealers and developing the Land Rover Centre concept came together in 1993. We met twice that year in a two-part meeting called "Find your way to the Centre." The meetings were designed to be highly engaging, and the first meeting was held in May at Beaver Creek, Colorado. The meeting explored how Centres would work as a business. We let dealers discover this for themselves by working in small teams that competed for a $1,000 prize. We explained the new Business Builder Program, floated the notion of exclusive sales territories, and then turned them loose in a realistic business simulation.

To encourage their thinking to go beyond building only one Centre—and to give them a feel for the exclusive territory philosophy—the simulation asked them to develop as much or as little of the State of Georgia as they wanted. We selected Georgia because it had only one big market, Atlanta, and because it had a number of smaller markets with Centre potential. Part of the message was grab, develop, and protect sales territories before someone else did.

As part of the competition, the dealer teams generated Balance Sheets and Profit and Loss figures based on their assumptions. We knew, and they learned, that the Centre concept was financially viable. It was a fast and exciting three days and demonstrated once again the entrepreneurial spirit of US car dealers.

Design Forum presented the design for a Land Rover Centre to the dealers. It included an off-road demonstration track right on the dealership property. To say the entire concept raised eyebrows is to understate the reaction. We received valuable feedback and the expected resistance.

The second meeting, in August, we held in Aspen, Colorado. We presented a revised facility plan that incorporated the dealers' better advice as well as some fresh thinking from us. By then the shock had worn off and the dealers were becoming more positive. We shared with them our thinking on staffing. Discussions included Land Rover Gear, pay and bonuses, initial training, and how the employees would work together. Heated discussions followed over the next two days as we off-roaded with dealers on some spectacular Rocky Mountain trails.

We exposed them to one more conspirator, Watts Wacker, a futurist with an attitude. We had sought his views regarding the Centre concept and how it matched up with what consumers would be looking for in a retail experience. His speech was funny, riveting, and convincing. He told the dealers that Land Rover Centres was the hottest retail concept he had been exposed to and was aimed squarely at where consumers wanted retailing to go.

Most dealers left the second meeting both intrigued and overwhelmed. As one said to us, "I don't always agree with you, but you guys make me think more about this business and where it's going than anyone else." The conspiracy was working.

Mark Hennessy, one of our key conspirators, opened the first Centre in Alpharetta, Georgia, an Atlanta suburb, and within three months more than half of our dealers had visited him. Mark and his team's overt enthusiasm for the concept inspired many other dealers to build Centres.

Like all conspiracies, this one was founded on a big idea, an alluring idea that at first seemed impossible. Far more people than we can mention here played important roles. And they all knew that they had been on the inside of a wild and imaginative ride. These conspirators included our suppliers.

Land Rover Centres were an immediate hit with customers, who found the seamless transition from outside to inside inviting. Outside the cars were on display climbing rock piles and negotiating the tough 110-foot track that demonstrated Land Rover's off-road prowess. Attractive landscaping covered the property. The Centre interior looked like a hunting lodge replete with outdoor paraphernalia. Cars were displayed on a compass rose with the store's correct longitude and latitude. Employees wore Land Rover Gear, and the same gear—along with adventure books and tapes—was on display for sale to customers.

All told, we created an adventuresome, outdoorsy atmosphere that had a distinct, magical feeling—which had been our goal. Many of those who were directly involved, within and without the company, continue to brag about their participation in the Land Rover Centres conspiracy—well over a decade after the fact.

Conventional Wisdom

This is a dog-eat-dog world, and we must own the important core competencies of our business and farm out the rest. This raises interesting questions: what is core to our business and what, if any, competencies must be proprietary? And how important is what we farm out? For instance, every car company has an advertising agency do its creative work.

To some it is heresy to even ask these questions. We want to believe that so much of what we do is special, special to us and different from what so many other folks do. Really? Could it be that what we should see as special is our brand promise and our customers? As we design the experience for our customers, what parts of that experience must fall to us?

It depends on the promise, doesn't it? For Toyota, with its promise of quality and value, it makes sense to own manufacturing and engineering. Yet Toyota buys sub-assemblies for its cars and allows suppliers to do some of the engineering. DaimlerChrysler is happy to allow others, such as Mitsubishi and Magna Steyr, to build entire cars for them.

For decades, car companies believed that they had to do the majority of the engineering of a new car in house. Chrysler in the early 1990s stood that notion on its ear when it created a software system that allowed a diverse group of suppliers to work simultaneously on the design of a particular car. Leadership and an opening of minds led Chrysler to an industry-changing move.

An example of how this worked would be Chrysler brake design. In the past, Chrysler would design the system and send out the specifications for quotes. Was Chrysler the expert in the industry on brakes? No, the larger brake suppliers actually knew more—and had a far better handle on not only current design but also what the future held.

The change was simple. Chrysler selected suppliers based on experience and sent out performance specs for their brakes, including estimating costs. The brake supplier would design the system to meet the specs. Every day the team, using the shared software, could see where all suppliers stood on a given project. As you can see, trust formed a big part of this new way of doing business.

It was a hit with suppliers and Chrysler. Time required to develop a new car dropped, and the quality of engineering went up as costs came down. At one point this led to Chrysler achieving a nearly $1,000 cost advantage per car over its domestic rivals. In survey after survey among parts suppliers, Chrysler came out on top, way above Ford and GM. Those two companies felt that beating on suppliers for arbitrary cost reductions was the best way to do business. Based on recent *Automotive News* headlines, not much has changed.

Trends

There are forces at work that make the notion of conspiracy a no-brainer. Yet depending on whose eyes you look through, some of these trends can either encourage conspiratorial relationships or become roadblocks. The laws of economics argue that a task will move toward the lowest-cost solution. The need to both differentiate a product and to lower costs will drive some to seek active conspiracies that work simultaneously to achieve both.

Downsizing, Outsourcing, and Insourcing

These trends, which move work outside a company, can represent real opportunity on many fronts. The difficulty is harnessing this movement to further your differentiation, which is where the power of conspiracy comes into play.

It is a matter of attitude. Are we, in the cause of cutting costs, simply farming out work we once did, or are we recruiting new team members who bring with them fresh thinking? How do we win them over to our team, our vision, and unlock their talents? How do we entice them to work within our conspiracy?

If you only use outsourcing to lower costs, you could miss a big opportunity.

Proliferation and Fragmentation

As more and more products become alike, it is tempting to say that placing so much work with outsiders is having a homogenizing effect. If you are afraid that this is happening to your business, then we would have to ask, who is leading your business? We're talking about building a conspiracy, not fomenting a jail break where the inmates run wild.

To change for the better requires sustained creativity—not to change the *promise* but to evolve the *experience*. Creativity can come from many sources, and so can homogenization. The company must provide the vision and the backbone to generate creative improvement, and it must have the courage to enlist others to make this happen.

The Work Treadmill

Many of today's executives feel trapped on a treadmill of rising expectations and increasing workloads with no fun in sight. We have seen this first hand and can tell you that trapped executives never saved a company. We can also say that the application of a good healthy conspiracy can raise everyone's spirits.

As we've discussed, a lot of sagging spirits can be traced directly to unrealistic targets and missed goals. Let the beatings begin. This trend, as much as any other, raises the question, "What does it take to get folks engaged?" And which folks should we be getting engaged?

Farming accounting out to Bangalore will depress your accounting department if you let it. Yet it brings the opportunity to meet new people, tap new minds, and hear fresh thinking from the company you hire to do the accounting. How you engage and approach them is critical. Do you say, "We want you for your cheap labor," or, "We want you for your intelligence and fresh thinking"? Do you introduce them to your brand promise and ask, "How can you help us deliver a better experience?"

Virtually all of the trends we see cry out for a good conspiracy. Are you up for it? Can you understand that conspiracies are not devious acts, but an activity that demands visionary leadership and trust?

Building a Conspiracy—Who's On Your Team?

When you build a company from scratch, you learn the simple ways of the self-reliant. Even large corporations driving for the leanest team possible are learning to rely more and more on people who "don't work for the company."

You may be thinking that your company is boring or straightforward and just not fertile ground for a conspiracy. Pity. You'll never set yourself apart in the marketplace if people already on the inside feel this way. All interested employees should be at least partially on the inside, but in most companies they are not. Why?

That's an important question you have to answer. What or who is getting in the way? Start by looking in the mirror, at your leadership. Ask yourself the hard question: do you really want a diverse group of people helping you build the business? If so, what authority are you willing to cede to them?

Then ask yourself who you want on your insider's team?

All companies have numerous constituencies and your merry band of conspirators should draw from all of them. You need customers, investors, retailers, salespersons, suppliers, analysts, the press, and your own employees to be on the conspiracy bus. Form a mental picture of your ideal conspiracy. Some you will have to recruit, some you conscript, and some will surprise you by signing up voluntarily.

Most conspiracies start with the leadership team. If the leaders believe they're on the inside of a great conspiracy, then one exists *de facto*. Remember when you were a child? Every time a group—a conspiracy—of any kind began forming, didn't you want to know more about it? From the inside? Of course you did. We are a nation of insider wannabes. We just want to be wanted, to be in the know, particularly on subjects that intrigue us. With luck, one of those intriguing subjects will be your brand—and your career.

Your key suppliers should feel a part of the inner circle. And they need to think like an insider. You want their best thinking on how to make your vision and your promise a reality. You must lead them to think "our" vision and "our" promise. Just as you strive to have your company's best minds on your insider team, you must also see to it that your suppliers' best people are working on your business.

Neither suppliers nor the talent within those suppliers are all alike. They are not a commodity; they are a talent pool, and you want that pool's best and brightest as fellow conspirators.

The Power of Respect

The desire to join a conspiracy starts with respect. Potential conspirators must respect and, one hopes, admire what you are about. And you must reciprocate. Follow respect with a personal invitation. I want *you* to be a part of this adventure. Here's what we're going to build together, what do you think?

You get commitment by putting ideas—yours and those of others—at risk and letting others build on these thoughts, which must start with the core vision. While we love the democratic system, that is not what we are suggesting. Co-authoring can be an important aspect of vision, yet at some point the top leader—the person who has the final say—must crystallize and own the core vision. This is a contentious point; yet without the deepest commitment at the top, visions rarely come alive.

You must of course lead from the front and find a way to inspire those who follow you. But you must also have the confidence to listen to feedback on your thinking and to welcome fresh—and perhaps contrarian—ideas. At the risk of over-simplifying, keep an open mind. In the end, you must bring these discussions to closure and have the courage to modify where necessary and to stick to your guns where your gut tells you not to compromise.

From your core vision you will derive the brand promise. The brand promise must be championed by the leader because the promise drives the progress of the company. Subsequent leaders must feel as if the promise originated with them. The leader must resist—to the point of being willing to quit—any attempt to change the promise in a damaging way. The experience you wrap the promise in is an area ripe for conspiratorial progress. The experience must evolve to meet ever-rising customer expectations.

Vision, communication, and open participation are critical to a conspiracy, but they are not enough. At every reasonable opportunity, you must also pile sincere recognition on the heads of your fellow conspirators. Recognition is more than the payoff for a job well done; it is an opportunity for the entire team to celebrate your progress. Momentum is paramount, and momentum builds every time you celebrate a victory.

Recognition must be earned, it must be sincere, it must be public, it must be impartial, it must be handed out consistently, and it must be done immediately. To the "work hard, play hard" mantra, we urge you to add "praise hard." Once your team members know that their efforts will be noticed and recognized publicly, hold on to the reins—you're about to go for a wild ride.

Make your recognitions fit the circumstances and individuals involved. For instance, the Land Rover dealers in our conspiracy were not in it for short-term financial gain, they wanted the opportunity to apply their considerable business acumen—and the respect and recognition that went with their contribution. We recognized dealer contributions every time we brought the dealers together.

As you might expect, our Land Rover staff responded to our spot bonus program, but they also responded favorably to being invited to be hosts at our off-road adventures. A number of our extended family providers—the name we used for suppliers— loved the public recognition we gave them in the business press for their role in building Land Rover. We also recognized good work and contributions from all quarters in the "family" meetings we held two or three times a month.

We know you can think of a hundred ways to say thank you, but the important thing is to do it. Make plenty of room for all those who have earned a place in your spotlight. If you lust after self-recognition, remember that the surest way to get credit is to give it.

The Conflict of Interests

Remember shirts and skins from your childhood? That was the easiest way to differentiate between two teams. This concept, unfortunately, has spilled over into our adult lives. We work for the company owned by one set of shareholders, and *you* work for another company owned by a different set of shareholders. Too many believe that doing business with each other is a zero sum game. We say that both parties can win.

Obviously there will be conflicts of interest among different business concerns seeking to profit from each other. These should be dealt with openly and effectively, seeking mutually profitable middle ground. All too often, however, they're dealt with in suicidal ways that destroy relationships that have succeeded for decades.

Is it important to you that your suppliers and retailers be profitable? It had better be—because your conspiracy wants to attract the best and the brightest suppliers and the best and brightest people within those suppliers. This does not mean being overly generous—after all, if they are not smart enough to run their own business at a profit, do you really think they're perfect for you? But too often a business places reducing costs over great productive relationships. Somewhere, there doubtless are competent discount doctors and dentists. Would you go to one of them, or would you remain with the doctors who understand you, your problems, and your goals?

Smart buying requires that you know which purchases are commodities to your business and which purchases are made valuable by talent—a great advertising agency, for example. If talent drives the effectiveness of a supplier, deal with the fact that you want the best talent working on *your* business. And pay for it. Constantly grinding on partners for more cost reductions is not a relationship builder. It sends a clear—and ugly—communication: I want to let you in on a secret about doing business with me. It's my job to win and your job to lose. Who in possession of their faculties would join that kind of conspiracy?

The market demands that you continuously, methodically, and professionally work together to reduce costs. But sudden panic over the next quarter's financial results and consequent demands to drop prices and halt projects takes the life out of a conspiratorial relationship.

Constantly asking multiple firms to bid for your business assures a lowest common denominator attitude and effort. What is a supplier's having done good work for you—and understanding your business—worth? And remember that there are real costs associated with bringing new suppliers up to speed. If the winning low bid includes a loss of expertise and commitment to your business, you've only shown that you have the dubious ability to find and engage second rate talent.

How Not to Build a Conspiracy

When Charlie Hughes went to work for Doyle Dane Bernbach on the Volkswagen account, his sense of loyalty led him to ask if VW had a program to help agency people buy and drive a Volkswagen.

The response he got from his client was, "We don't ask you for a discount on your advertising, so don't ask us for a discount on our cars." Makes a feller feel right welcome, don't it? And, wonder of wonders, it later transpired that VW *did* ask for a discount on its advertising.

What stops the building of effective conspiracies every day?

Let's say that you are put in charge of a cross-functional work team. What are some of the more common mistakes that people make that reduce the chances of the work group's becoming a conspiracy for positive change?

Not being selective in the makeup of your work team is the first mistake, one that you rarely recover from.

Should we invite retailers to join the team? No. Let's wait until we've decided what *we* want to do, then we'll sell them on our plan. Or, do we want someone from the home office to participate? No. They don't know this market, speak our language, or understand what we're going through. That's called excluding your way to the poorhouse. To become rich, include all parties that meet the "necessary and sufficient" rule, no more and no fewer.

How to Form a Good Conspiracy

The number of individuals selected and the talent of those selectees are critically important. Be deliberate in your selection and fight for the right mix of talent, drive, experience, viewpoint, and ability to execute.

Once selected, get them engaged. Start by personally inviting them to join. Tell them you want them in your conspiracy, why they are important, and what you hope to achieve that others probably could not. Make the invitation to the team special and intriguing.

Be demanding; let individuals know they are joining a team with both high aspirations and high standards. Make it clear that you expect team members to contribute at a high level, and weed out those who don't measure up before they wreck things. Tough standards and high expectations attract the best conspirators.

While we counsel discrimination in forming the group, once

it's assembled there must be no sense of discrimination within the group. But here's what too often happens. Don't do it:

> "You have all been invited to be part of this proj-
> ect, and we want to hear from each and every
> one of you." (Except for those of you who I don't
> think know much about this subject or those of
> you who don't get a vote because you don't work
> for the company.)

> "We will make the important decisions together."
> (As long as you agree with me, or else I will find
> a way to win my point.)

Other conspiracy killers include failing to listen to under-currents that could lead to a conspiracy within a conspiracy—against the one you're leading, finding excuses not to celebrate progress, forgetting to recognize and reward, and failing to find the right balance between today's business reality and your vision for the future.

The Power of Zealotry

The simple goal here is to create a broad-based team—a conspiracy—that is more involved, more committed and more talented than the competition. The first step is herding them to the inside. Invite your co-conspirators personally to be part of a team that is driven to create something magical together. Don't be surprised if you get more help than you planned, but leading this help is half the fun, and you will feel a powerful sense of energy.

You must channel this energy into a common cause. That common cause becomes the unwritten contract that keeps everyone pulling together—a common cause that appeals to emotions and egos usually attracts the widest array of revolutionaries, eccentrics, and just plain wackos. This, in an odd way, is a good thing. It was original thinking and boundless energy that you were after to begin with, wasn't it?

Few things are more powerful than zealots on a mission. You achieve that kind of power when you have an engaged, branded culture and a conspiracy among all your key players. All of this will resonate with some of you, and some of you may say what a load of manure. The latter crowd better get used to the smell of defeat.

7

Consistency

> "We would make the biggest error of all if we hired a new v.p. of marketing and let that person change the [ad tag] line to something like 'Spirit of life.' . . . There is a basic trust created in consistent marketing, and if you keep changing, people don't know who you are."
>
> —*Tom Purves, CEO of BMW North America*
> *quoted in the* Wall Street Journal

The Test of Will

If there's one thing worse than fear of change, it's fear of doing what's necessary to remain the kind of company that your customers expect and demand. We will examine how cowards mistake change for progress—and how to tell the difference.

Being the cowboys that Americans so love to be, the word *consistency* sounds boring and makes you feel hog-tied. We want our options open, and we pride ourselves on maintaining the right to change our minds. We'd prefer an open range to fences.

All of which is dodgy if you believe, as we do, that a brand is a promise wrapped in an experience—a consistent promise wrapped in a consistent experience.

Building a class-beating brand comes down to how badly you want to be who you want to be. The test of will tests your grit, your determination to bring your vision to fruition. And not surprisingly, if you are inconsistent over operational areas you have failed the test of will. This is no easy test. Between changes in the market and the maverick nature of most American staffs, you will surely be tested. Without achieving consistency, you will struggle to rise above the ordinary.

As we've said, the clarity of your promise brings great strength and separation in the marketplace, but only if you communicate it properly. The experience in which you wrap your promise is the acid test of your commitment to that promise. And the experience encompasses everything you do.

Not just the big things like product, advertising, public relations or the retail sales experience, but all the small things as well. Things such as how you answer the phone in customer service, what experience you give your associates in training sessions, what your letterhead and business cards look like. Consumers receive messages from each and every exposure they have to your company. To dazzle customers, every scrap of communication must consistently communicate your commitment to delivering your promise. The experience enables the customer to believe your promise.

The Inconsistency of Jaguar

Throughout this book, we have bludgeoned you with the importance of standing for something, setting yourself apart, making a promise and delivering it in a well-designed experience. If somehow you have not tumbled to the message, you can skip this chapter. Why? Well, you can be consistently bad, consistently boring, and consistently inconsistent without even trying.

But you can only be consistently you when there is a real you to begin with.

Jaguar provides an interesting example. Jaguar is a storied British brand whose primary competition is BMW and Mercedes-Benz. There is no doubt that Jaguar is different from its German competition. For one, it has been owned by Ford since 1989. Ford has invested heavily in Jaguar and has improved its quality. But during its reign, Ford has somehow failed to define satisfactorily the reason why someone should choose a Jaguar over a BMW or Mercedes-Benz. What is Jaguar promising its customers that it will do better than its competitors? Once it was British stylishness. Today the answer is not clear.

Jaguars are now derived from a "clever" strategy that shares platforms with other Ford products. The Jaguar lineup for 2006 included an X-type, an S-type, an XK, and an XJ. The X-type uses the European Ford Mondeo front-wheel-drive platform; the S-type shares a platform with the Lincoln LS; XK is an evolved Jaguar platform shared with Aston Martin, and the XJ is an all-new aluminum Jaguar-only platform. One can fairly ask, what exactly is a Jaguar?

Do potential Jaguar customers know the finer points of the shared platform strategy? Most don't, though they've been well publicized by the enthusiast press. But they do hear what is *not* being said. What are the shared features of all Jaguars that set them apart from the luxury herd? What do they all share that makes them a Jaguar and better than the competition? What am I getting for my money when I buy a Jaguar that makes me feel smart? They don't hear it because, save for retro styling and British origin, it doesn't exist. Thus, the marketing sounds hollow and lacks a clear point of view.

Even the retro styling is problematic, because Jaguar management has yet to settle on the period of retro styling from Jaguar's history they want to bring into the present. Jaguar's current lineup mimics old Jaguars from several different eras, which just adds further confusion about what Jaguar wants to be.

Jaguar seems determined to become a pale copy of itself. The current technically brilliant XJ feels more like a copy than an original. Its timid, creatively bankrupt design is virtually indistinguishable from the last generation XJ.

A tired design tells the market that your new car is no different from your previous model—which is especially foolish because in fact the car is all new and arguably the best Jaguar ever. Do buyers want it to look like a Jaguar? Yes they do. But they want it to look like a *new* Jaguar, fresh and better looking than the model it replaces. They want to demonstrate that they're smart enough to buy the hot new thing, not some warmed over has-been. Jaguar, a brand that has generated passion for decades, feels suddenly passionless.

In 2006, Jaguar introduced a new Jaguar XK sports car in both coupe and convertible versions. Is it good looking? Yes it is, but in an unfortunately familiar way. Some journalists feel that it looks too much like some Aston Martin models that were designed by the same designer, Ian Callum.

Automotive News, on October 6, 2005, headlined an article discussing the new XK with the headline "Callum defends XK's look." The subhead went on to say "Top Jaguar designer blames EU, US rules for lines of car's hood." If this weren't so desperately sad, it would be laughable. But the article goes on with a discussion of the oval grille:

> Then there are the design cues such as the oval grille. In the US the most frequent critical comment is that the XK's oval grille looks similar to the grille on the US-market Ford Taurus sedan. Callum says through gritted teeth: "It's a Jaguar grille. BMW has its kidney grille. Mercedes has its grille. And Jaguar has its oval grille." Jaguar has used oval grilles on the D-Type, E-Type, XJ220 and XJ13 vehicles, Callum said. He is studying how to incorporate oval grilles in every Jaguar in the future lineup.

So it's the oval grille that makes a Jag a Jag?

The next car to be replaced will be the Jaguar S-type. Here is what J Mays had to say in *Automotive News* on November 7, 2005:

> "Wait until you see the next S-Type," J Mays, vice president of design at Ford Motor Co., told *Automotive News Europe*, a sister publication to *Automotive News*: "It will express Jaguar's daring design spirit again."

Does this sound like a team on the same page? Again, if you don't know who you are, consistency is a moot point.

Then there is the matter of technology. The current XJ and new XK are built on a high-tech aluminum platform. As for the new S-type, will it be built on the same platform using the same technology—something Jaguar could promote as a unique selling proposition? Well no, it will use some aluminum but will be based on the old steel platform. Why? Because it is cheaper to design and build it that way. Where is the strong technical point of view on what makes a Jaguar a Jaguar?

It no longer feels as if Jaguars are designed by people who see every Jaguar as a monument to Jaguar's vision of British sports and luxury cars—or who share a common vision of any kind.

Worse yet, Jaguar has depended on distress leasing to generate sales. And all savvy customers know that high-line brands that live on deals haven't quite arrived, have they?

The confusion affects Jaguar's image of itself and all of its communications. For instance, Jaguar has avoided entry into the SUV market. With Land Rover as a cousin you might say this makes sense. Yet BMW managed to build a crossover SUV, two in fact, that are real BMWs. Mercedes has managed this as well. Wouldn't the world warm up to a beautiful on-road Jaguar crossover SUV built on the high tech XJ platform? One would think so, but the conflict within Ford's brand portfolio prevents this.

How do you market a Jaguar that appears so lost? What do you say? In the fall of 2005, Jaguar launched what it termed a "fashion campaign." In interviews Jaguar officials said that they no longer want to be perceived as a car brand but instead as a luxury item. Should someone introduce these folks to the concept of durable goods? Borrowing heavily from the world of perfume advertising, the word "Gorgeous" was repeated throughout the television executions.

All of this has taken its toll on Jaguar. Sales have been declining for three years, and Ford has lost hundreds of millions of dollars each year during this period. Rumors persist that Ford would entertain selling Jaguar. A truly sad state of affairs.

What you say and what you don't or can't say about yourself sends far clearer signals to the market than most auto executives perceive. It is imperative that you understand how your message is heard. A great way to bring clarity to your communication is to start with a promise that permeates every last thing that you do.

Conventional Wisdom

"We brand our products with marketing, because what we say about ourselves is what drives consumers' perception of our brand." Let's see if we understand that: your competition is doing 90 percent of everything very well, but all you have to get right is the *marketing*?

Both authors come from marketing backgrounds, and it is a discipline we love and respect. Too many times, we've heard the notion that marketing can fix whatever ails a company. This is said most often by people who are not marketing experts, but who feel that marketing is not a difficult discipline.

When things are not going your way, is marketing the area to change? Well, it's easy, handy, quick, and makes you feel as if you are proactively attacking the problem. And it is precisely what gets so many brands in trouble.

We believe in Marketing with a capital M—the overarching strategy you devise to take your product to market. Branding is one part of that strategy, one you can either support or destroy with your tactical marketing approach. If your marketing plans peter out after 90 days, if you are changing ad agencies every three to four years, it is a safe assumption that you are undermining your stated goal of building a strong brand.

We are mesmerized by speed and don't always accept that speed is a measure of time, not of goodness. We tell ourselves, "Surely there must be some shortcut to building a successful brand that doesn't take so much . . . umm . . . time."

In our eternal quest to do things faster, is there a way to speed up this whole brand development process? Research tells us that it takes five to ten years to change consumer perceptions of brands. This sounds like an eternity in most contexts, but let's take an optimist's approach and say that we might do it in five years, which is far qucker than ten.

So how do you speed up a brand-building effort? Simple, you must be ruthlessly consistent. That's right, *ruthlessly* consistent. Why? For two reasons. First, to stand out, you must carve out a place in the market, and you won't do that if you're spewing inconsistent, ever changing, all-over-the-lot messages. You will just get lost in the clutter.

Second, after you carve out your space, you must prove— *prove*—to your customers that you deliver what you promise. Inconsistency in any form of communication creates doubt that may cause them to believe otherwise. Believe us, American consumers have a fine nose for the smell of inconsistency.

Trends

Our fast-moving world is not infatuated with consistency. We are drawn to change. Here are three trends that—if you read between the lines—show how powerful consistency can be.

Management Turnover

Management turnover is accelerating. On December 13, 2005, *CNNMoney* wrote that, "Overall, CEO departures have doubled in 2005, according to the Challenger survey, with 1,228 departures recorded from the beginning of 2005 through November, up

102 percent from the same period in 2004." CEOs are lucky to get two to three years to leave their mark.

Unfortunately, with so many CEOs on the bubble, the incumbent CEO frequently decides that he or she must "shake things up" in an attempt to be a leader of action and thereby stave off being fired or forced to resign.

Incoming CEOs are also known to shake things, frequently their fist. When the CEO changes, so do a lot of other folks. New CEOs generally want to bring along some of their own people. The mere fact that a new CEO is required says that much needs to change. Even if the basic positioning of the company is safe, often little else is. An organization can become dizzy and disoriented from all this shaking.

Rick Wagoner, Chairman of General Motors, was under tremendous pressure throughout 2005 for the poor performance of the company. When asked in December about the possibility of being replaced, he said, "A management shakeup might slow down GM's turnaround. When you bring in a lot of new people, you bring in a lot of change and people just sort of sit there and try to figure out what to do."

The churn within executive ranks often says more about our impatience than about the capability of management. Brands grow best under the steady leadership of a team that knows its course and is backed by a board that also knows. Management teams should be judged on the viability of their strategy and the progress they make in the marketplace. Impatience and great brands make poor companions.

Too Much Choice

One of the trends we keep coming back to is too much choice. Obfuscation by choice might be more like it. Most marketers, even as they lament the depth and breadth of competition, just keep piling on the choices. They are missing an enormous opportunity, the opportunity to simplify people's lives.

Let's look at Jaguar's top of the line XJ models as an example. In 2005 they sold 8,304 units. To do this, they felt that they needed five models: the XJ8, XJ8L, Vanden Plas, XJR, and Super V8. Really? What is this nonsense all about? The XJ comes in two different wheelbases. There are two available engines, with the more powerful one being supercharged. And they have two different trim levels, with the more luxurious one only being offered on the long wheelbase model. Does all that make you feel proud to buy the "base" model for a mere $61,000?

Confusion is not a sound marketing platform. Complexity in all forms slows down communication. Your goal is to sell your products' intrinsic value. If it takes more than a few words or phases to describe your model lineup, you have made it unnecessarily complicated. Make it easy and simple for the customer to say yes.

There is another dark side to too much choice. Marketing budgets are finite. Most companies offer more choice than they are able to support with any meaningful level of advertising. An un-marketed overblown lineup sounds, well, awful. Yet it is more common than uncommon. Do you see the opportunity?

Too Much Noise

We have combined too much choice with too many messages. We live in a world of magpie marketing. We hear lots of noise, but nobody's saying much. Traditional advertising has just about worn out all our senses. Interactive marketing is the brave new frontier that we will all learn to navigate, helped along by our customers. One-on-one marketing gives us the chance to listen to what our customers really want from us.

Make no mistake, as technology creates more ways to reach our customers, the fatigue with it all will only grow. One-on-one marketing will only increase the need to project a consistent message. We should remember the goal: earn a spot on people's shopping lists and then fight to stay on it.

Raising the volume on your commercials does not make them more attractive or understandable, just more irritating. Parroting the same tired words—value, well-equipped, fun to drive—wastes precious money, your money. And as an industry we've almost killed the Hope Diamond of marketing speak: all new.

How can you stand out in a crowded room full of shouting loudmouths? The odds are against your being able to out-shout them. Start by understanding that your customers are faced with a ton of choice and two tons of noise.

The Power of Consistency

The clarity of your promise can produce great strength and separation in the marketplace, but only if you communicate consistently. Consistency runs contrary to our impulses. You have to laugh at the thought of a company that combines impatience with inconsistency, yet the market is awash with examples of just that. Why?

We think there are two main culprits, and they usually travel together. The first is a lack of commitment to a specific strategy of differentiation. No vision, no promise, no commitment. We seem to enjoy being all things to all people—the flavor of the month.

The second malefactor is impatience. Standing for little and expecting much in the way of sales sets you on a fast follower's course. You are constantly trying to catch up to someone.

Given the mindset of this business environment, do you see the power of consistency? When you consider the overwhelming choices a customer faces, consistency—standing for one important thing over time—should be a no-brainer. Obviously it isn't.

The key ingredient is a compelling brand promise. Compelling to everyone involved. Once you are determined to bring that promise to life in your brand, consistency becomes the obvious and most expedient route.   And the most effective.

Designing the Experience. All of It.

Consistency is not the outcome of an email memo demanding its implementation. Consistency is part and parcel of a well developed plan for the ownership experience, a plan that you and your team labor over as you fight for every competitive advantage you can build into your owners' experience—a creatively crafted experience that truly sets you apart.

You gain consistency in the design of your owner's experience by embracing these statements:

1. The experience you are designing is for *your* customers, not the general market or a segment. This requires that you know them intimately and have firm opinions about how you can excel with them based on your observations. You are, after all, designing the experience for them, and in the end you want them to give you a standing ovation.
2. Consistency is directly connected to the clarity of your promise.
3. You communicate something about you in all that you do.
4. The experience makes a statement about your knowledge of your customers and how important they are to you.

As you set about designing the ownership experience, you will quickly learn how clear—or cloudy—your promise is in your own company's collective mind. Designing the experience is a complex task that often requires subtlety. You want a number of people involved initially and a process for regular review. What you want to avoid is public relations designing the tone of its press programs, marketing doing the advertising in one group and the Web site in another, and sales designing the "store"—all building individual fiefdoms or silos. Or, worse yet, creating their own mini brand.

All facets of the experience must tell the same story. This means they should be designed against the brand promise, knowledge about the consumers, and the way we want to make our statement. That requires that all hands design the experience together. Trust us, it is a cathartic rite of passage filled with emotion. It is also a quick way to bond a team and identify those players who get it and those who don't.

You can use the Brand Triangle to design an experience that will deliver on your promise. You need to know what the customer is looking for and have a clearly recognizable way to address those expectations. You need to answer the following questions:

- Which component of the Triangle will drive the experience?
- Will it be brand, product, retail or culture?
- What is next most important?
- As you work your way around the triangle, how do you weave a desirable and consistent experience?

Brand

First, we will assume that your brand promise is clear and compelling and that you are irrevocably committed to it.

If commodity + experience = price/value, what are the value-added parts of our experience? Again, will this experience be brand, product, retail, or culture centric? Where does the magic lie, and how do the other components reinforce it? Which parts of the experience will be generic, and which will be the distinct elements attractive to our target customers? How do all the elements work together?

Following standard industry practices won't do it. Benchmarking and trying to incrementally raise the bar is unlikely to do it either. To stand out means you deliver a memorable experience. And that is our mission, to stand out in a crowded marketplace, to get noticed, and get put on our target market's shopping list. In old speak, you are building awareness and image. The car industry loves the Allison-Fisher Purchase Funnel model. Within this model you are building the upper purchase funnel which includes awareness, familiarity, opinion, and consideration. Whatever marketing model you use, your goal is to raise people's emotional and rational expectation of and attachment to your brand.

Allison-Fisher Incorportated Purchase Funnel

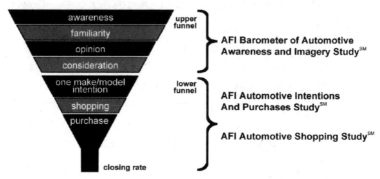

On the emotional side, words such as trust, prestige, heritage, third-party endorsements, and being viewed as a leader in your field become important to the experience you are designing. On the rational side, the market is judging your performance both in terms of your product's performance and the support you put behind those products. The importance of emotional and rational considerations varies by customer and customer group. Where the car business most often gets it wrong is in the errant belief that the brand's performance is not all that important. Hence, so many look-alike products whose real world performance is average at best.

You can find a lot of help with this subject, but it won't be specific to you. That is why you must design the experience and test it in the marketplace as soon as you are comfortable with an order pad.

Culture

To achieve consistency, culture comes right behind differentiation in importance. Many people will have a hand in "marketing" your brand, including all of your employees. Wouldn't it be charming if they all saw the brand the same way? How about paramount?

The challenge of getting all your team members to see your brand the same way is a microcosm of the challenge of getting your buying public to see it the same way. Your team must get it first. Throughout this book we have repeatedly reinforced the need for a clear, compelling brand promise that you and your team are fully committed to.

A company's chances of being consistent in all that it does are closely correlated to how well the culture is branded. And who we are and how we do things in a branded way does not occur accidentally. You brand a culture through leadership, training, and observed behavior. There is a gyroscope effect to branded cultures that always seems to self-correct to the brand promise. Within branded cultures there is peer pressure to be exactly who we say we want to be.

As you design the experience for your customer, you are simultaneously spelling out what you need to instill in your employees. They will find it hard to support an experience they neither understand nor appreciate. Often, to appreciate it they must experience it for themselves. Once they identify with both the customer and experience, you are well on your way to providing a consistent experience.

Orientation and training are the tools with which you communicate to your employees who we are and how we do things. Our promise, our values, and our intended customer experience must be spelled out clearly. The company must not only provide ongoing training, but must set expectations that we will be who we say we are.

Which brings us to observed behavior. Any company lapses will be observed and will undermine your culture. When times get tough, and they always do, branded cultures must mimic the human body, sacrificing limbs or less important programs to maintain the core of the body or essence of the brand promise. Volvo might discount cars and reduce staff if conditions dictated such actions, but it would be unthinkable to make cars that are less safe than their current state of the art.

We also believe that the higher the percentage of your team that can spend time in the marketplace and with customers, the more relevant your branded culture will be. Selling and satisfying customers is virtually impossible if you have no feel for the market and no feel for who your customers are and their expectations. Invent ways to keep actual customers in front of your employees.

Product

Your product must fulfill your promise. Who would argue with that? Yet, in the car business—either because there is no promise or no drive to execute a promise—few deliver. As you design the experience, product obviously must play its role.

In the car business, that role is both rational—0 to 60 mph, fuel economy, trunk size—and emotional—drop-dead good looking, fun to drive, it's been my dream to own one of these. You must design for both considerations, and this is where art comes into play. Your goal is high rational *and* high emotional ratings by your customers.

Your products must be consistent with the brand and with each another. Building an exciting sedan and a boring minivan does not work. Honda, with its last two generations of the Odyssey minivan, has shown how consistent you can be.

Adopting a product development process such as PALS (described in Chapter 5) is a great approach. Getting design to the point where it is attractive and where it becomes your look is essential. If each of your products is striving to be bold and unique—or, more likely, just like everyone else—it will not only be hard to tell your story; it will be hard to pick you out in the everyday world. Brands reinforce themselves publicly with familiar visual brand cues.

We have discussed how the experience must deliver the promise and evolve with the times. Product is an excellent example of how critical and difficult this is to do. You must remain faithful to who you are while being every bit as current as your promise leads customers to expect.

Retail

Retail is exciting, fast paced, and complex. Today, companies go to market in a bewildering number of ways—often simultaneously. We define *retail* as all ways that a company sells to the end customer.

As a footnote, the car industry has puzzled over who is their customer, with far too many believing it is their retail dealer. Merriam-Webster's definition of retail is "to sell in small quantities directly to the ultimate consumer." Let's be clear: Dealers or your distribution chain are partners at best—those whom you select and work with to sell your products to the customer. They are vital to your success; they are decision-makers; and the best way to get them in your corner is to provide them with products your customers want. When you create demand, you'll be surprised by how many people will want to help you sell.

Automotive retailing is a world unto itself. For decades the car dealer was the biggest brand homogenizer in the industry—a three-sided glass showroom in front of a Butler building that sat on a large asphalt parking lot full of cars. The only thing that separated a Dodge store from a Pontiac store was the signage and fascia on the building. In less than a week, you could pull one brand out and slot another one in.

And while dealers pride themselves on being independent businesspeople, from nameplate to nameplate the way their stores were run didn't vary much either. In the mid-1980s, a few brave souls started asking whether the brand experience could be extended right down to retail? As we discussed in Chapter 6, Saturn and Lexus and then Land Rover examined the car-buying experience with an eye toward actually making it attractive to their customers.

As noted, Land Rover Centres charmed customers. How? With their well-landscaped exteriors incorporating an off-road demonstration course and with a hunting-lodge-like interior that featured a compass rose, outdoorsy memorabilia, and Land Rover Gear clothing. The dealerships were actually fun to visit.

The Land Rover Centre concept was a direct outgrowth of the brand's identity and Land Rover's drive to create a unique and consistent ownership experience. The Brand Triangle was used to ensure all aspects of the effort were thought through.

Of course the Internet has changed retailing in a dramatic way. Before the Internet, you had two basic models: direct to consumers through direct marketing (phone, direct mail, TV direct, etc.) or through physical retail outlets, which you might or might not own. With the Internet the model has gotten scrambled. People use the Internet for gathering information and for buying. Yet for expensive or complex purchases such as a car, they are likely to do their homework on the Internet and then buy at a retail location. More than 70 percent of new cars buyers first do research on the Internet, about six hours worth.

This is a situation that the auto industry is still grappling with. Customers have a thoroughly modern experience on the Internet—on their time and their conditions—only to go to a car dealer and be jerked 30 years back in time to an uncomfortable horse-trading affair. In too many instances it is a broken process.

That situation is what Mazda set out to tackle with its Retail Revolution. Mazda's goal was to create a seamless experience from the Web to dealer. The experience at the dealer assumed that customers had done their homework on the Internet, had likely gone to Kelley Blue Book to look up their used car value, and had visited *edmunds.com* to find new-car invoice prices. With a cyber café within the Mazda store, customers and salespersons could explore those sites together so that they were dealing with the same information. The salesperson could become a partner helping the customer find the right car instead of a confrontational annoyance.

The retail experience at a Retail Revolution store concentrated on what customers wanted out of the experience: to drive the car of their choice, talk to an expert about it, negotiate to get the best price, and to enjoy the visit. The retail experience became an extension of Mazda's promise, "always the soul of a sports car," and was designed to suit the times and customers' expectations. The vision was simple. Sports cars are fast, fun, and cool, and to be consistent, the retail experience should be fast, fun, and cool as well.

The strength of the Brand Triangle[sm] methodology is the very conversation it stimulates. Conversations debating the many aspects of ownership, searching for where and how you will beat the competition. Many people will create and develop different parts of the experience—and will own the result. Seeing all this through the eyes of your customers helps you achieve consistency.

Necessary Constants: Vision and Leadership

Like so many things, consistency starts at the top. It begins with an enduring vision. Enduring in terms of time and leadership. Human resource experts say that it takes a CEO two years to form a team and learn from a few initial mistakes. CEOs then start to hit their prime in the fifth year and continue to produce through the tenth year. That means that our current CEO run of two to three years incorporates the formation and error periods and never reaches the prime period.

Continuous change at the top invariably means changes throughout an organization: people getting to know each other, people getting to know the brand and the customers, people doing a lot of things for the first time—with many of them determined to leave their mark by reinventing the wheel. It is not a winning strategy, but we watch it played out every day.

The strongest brands demonstrate remarkable stability in their US operations. In the 1970s Jack Cook led BMW from its humble beginnings at a New York car dealer's warehouse to sales of 60,000 units a year and recognition as an up-and-coming brand. In the 1980s, Bob Sinclair resurrected Saab in the US. In one period during his 10 years at the helm, Sinclair led Saab through 61 consecutive months of sales growth. Starting in the 1990s Charlie Hughes led Land Rover for over 13 years and turned an investment of a few million dollars into a desirable brand with revenues well over a billion dollars.

In the twenty-first century, these winning brands are showing a consistency of leadership, rarely making top-level changes. An example is Charlie's old boss, Tom Purves, at BMW. At Chrysler, Dieter Zetsche took from November 2000 to September 2005 to get things going. You need only look at all the churn at GM and Ford to understand how damaging constant change in the top management ranks can be. We link consistency of leadership with vision, and both need to be in place to drive consistency.

Transparency of Communication

In our choice-filled world full of noise and nonsense, the best way to make yourself important is to say something important and say it well. Reduce what you want to say to its essence. Let that essence shine throughout all your work. Simplify everything that gets in the way of clarity. Let your competitors be the ones hamstrung by needless complexity.

Conversely, if you stand for nothing, bold statements are worthless. If there is nothing remarkable about you, what can you say? Believing that one needs no substance behind the message is delusional. You say something about yourself in everything you do. And folks who don't know who they are communicate that fact as clearly as folks who actually have something to say.

It does not matter if you are smart or dumb, confident or scared. It will be apparent to the onlooker. And why wouldn't it? Want to be just like Honda? You will communicate that you are an imitation. Want to charge more for your cars than both you and your customers know they're worth? You'll sound out of touch. Have nothing to say, and you will appear lost. Have nothing to say and saying it loudly will make you sound shrill.

We would say this is obvious, but the car business proves otherwise. It is a revelation to many executives. Mitsubishi, trying to save itself in 2004, did "hard-hitting" comparison advertising with the implicit message being, "We're as good as or better than Honda." Right. And Pope Benedict goes snowboarding. Credible? No. Effective? No. Did people flock to Mitsubishi showrooms to buy their cars based on this revelation? No. What did they communicate? This: we don't know our place, we are in trouble and we're selective with the truth.

Accept that the American consumer has a keen nose for panic. GM has all but killed its brands with excessive discounting—spreading an atmosphere of panic across all its car lines. When you are missing sales targets and running scared (as GM did throughout 2001–2005), the consumer quickly catches on.

The flexibility enthusiasts should keep this in mind: most people want to deal with companies they know and trust, and schizophrenia rarely generates trust. So as you wrestle with the transparency of communication, remember that the basis of effective communication is confidence in who you are and what you stand for.

Your Personality and Your Tone of Voice

It is easy to make a big splash once, but that is hardly what building a world-class brand is about. We're looking for a run of years and decades. Do that, and customers actually start to seek you out. You want to make it simple for them to recognize you. That's why companies strive so hard to develop easily recognized names and logos. They then create elaborate safeguards against misusing them.

Yet that is just scratching the surface. To be recognizable, you must have character and a personality that makes you easy to pick out of a crowd. Just like the ability to recognize a friend's voice in one or two words on the telephone. You want a distinct tone of voice, one that customers instantly recognize as yours. This is tough to do, but some notable brands have achieved it. Some have achieved it—Chevy Truck's "Like a Rock" comes to mind—only to walk away from it. A familiar tone of voice is reassuring to customers. It conveys that you are the same you. It aids loyalty, a subject unto itself. It can also help define and clarify your promise. The right tone of voice puts the personality in who you are.

Tone of voice was one of the important must-get-right tasks Land Rover North America set for itself in the early days. Advertising, the team felt, was a good starting place. Tone of voice became an emotional issue that sparked long hours of discussion and debate. At product clinics, Land Rover exposed potential customers to positioning statements embodied in a range of creative work. More debate followed. The result was a tone of voice that permeated not only the advertising but all communication for 14 years. Using the same suppliers for all those years helped immeasurably. The main ingredients to Land Rover's tone of voice were:

> Confident not arrogant
> Smart
> Rugged
> Wry humor
> British with a small "b"
> Global—seen in and relied on throughout the world
> Adventure—the vehicle of choice for expeditions

Of course there was no cookbook detailing how much of each ingredient needed to appear when. That varied by time and need. Yet, within a year, the Land Rover staff started to develop a fine ear for the Land Rover tone of voice.

Crafting your persona takes years and brilliant creative people both inside and outside the company. It takes great care in selecting and indoctrinating suppliers who create most of this work. You must clearly "hear" the brand the same way and not get easily bored with it. One of the reasons that VW, Mercedes-Benz, Volvo, and BMW became such strong brands in the US in their early years is that they selected talented ad agencies, worked together to set the tone, and then stayed with the same agencies for years. You can say the same about Honda, which has been at RubinPostaer (now RPA) since the disappearance of the wooly mammoth.

Price vs. Value

Why do we mention price vs. value in a chapter devoted to consistency? It should be obvious. Pricing actions either support the value you are projecting with your brand or contradict it. Constant discounting totally undermines any long-term strategy for building brand value. Yet price is a mighty lever in America. We live in a mature market where supply seems always to outstrip demand. Branding is the art of adding value to people's lives and being remembered and rewarded for it.

Discounting is about cutting prices, period. Americans are inveterate shoppers, and because we already own so much stuff, the "deal" has become a powerful inducer. It provides the rationale for buying things we don't need, marginally need, or don't need right this minute. A deal makes you feel smart instead of gluttonous. Discounting is a drug, and both the buyer and the seller are users.

In 2001, the 9/11 tragedy brought this country to a halt. We were afraid to get on with our lives. Economists were concerned that the greatest impact of this terrorist act would be to derail our economy. People would just stop buying and postpone any purchase that was not absolutely necessary. Of course, durable goods such as cars would be hurt first. Then, as previously discussed, General Motors took bold action that in hindsight prevented the economy from stalling. They launched a zero-percent interest plan across all brands and all models, something unheard of before. You could finance the purchase of a car and pay no interest during the life of the loan. It dramatically lowered monthly payments and felt like the deal of a lifetime. Did Americans unsure of the future respond? Yes they did, in droves. That is how ingrained and powerful our desire for a deal is.

Contending with discounting is a fact of life. How does this news translate into our quest to build a world-class brand? Throughout this book, we have argued that to set yourself apart most often requires doing something much better than the competition. If you are no more than comparable to the competition, then the stage is set for competing on price.

It takes true grit to say you are going to be better than the competition, even with pricing. Competing primarily on price takes a determination to be the lowest-cost provider, or you will simply go bankrupt giving your goods away. Either way, you're back to having to be the best at something. If it is not the most efficient, you'd better find a way to add tangible value somewhere.

Price is what you pay, and value is what you think you get.

And if you lean on heavy, chronic discounting, what does that say about the value of your products? More important, what is the *market* saying about the value of your products? Your worth in the marketplace is the sum total value of all you do in comparison to your competitors. General Motors is a sad example of what happens when you fail to put enough value into the equation and instead sell constantly on price. At some point, a discounted price becomes the only way to get someone to buy.

The greatest tragedy of relying on discounting is that deals require promoting. There is no point in offering a deal if you don't tell someone about it. Otherwise, you just lower the revenue on the same amount of unit sales—truly dumb but done all the time. Every dollar you spend on marketing the deal is one dollar less you can spend on marketing your story, your strong attributes, and your value.

Hyundai is an interesting example of a company getting off this treadmill. In the late 1990s, Hyundai's sales were in a state of decline. It kept going to market with ever-increasing discounts. Hyundai had a terrible image caused by marginal quality, and discounting did nothing to improve it. Hyundai decided in 1998 that its very survival demanded drastic changes.

The company launched an unheard-of 10-year/100,000 mile warranty, a move widely credited with turning the company around. It certainly hit its biggest image problem head on. Yet it was something else Hyundai did that made its warranty work. It changed its pricing strategy from heavy discounting to what it called transaction pricing. Hyundai priced its cars close to what people had actually been paying after taking into account all the manufacturer and dealer discounts. Hyundai reallocated the discount budget to cutting its prices.

Hyundai's move did not lend itself to advertising. "Hey, we've cut our prices to what you have already been paying," might not resonate with the consumer. Yet from a marketing viewpoint it was sheer genius. The new prices on their cars looked extremely attractive, and they were far below the competition's prices. More important, with no discounts, there were no discounts to advertise. All of

Hyundai's marketing funds could be applied to selling Hyundai, its products and its new warranty—all substantive, competitive, product-based benefits of genuine interest to customers. In seven years, Hyundai sales have gone up 504 percent—helped along, we should add, by an astounding improvement in product quality (Hyundai stood third in the 2006 IQS sweepstakes).

Pricing will always play a role, but if you live on price, you will fast become a generic that can easily be substituted for a lower-price alternative. Yes, great brands use discounts and have sales, but "always on sale" says something else. Relying too heavily on price erodes brand equity as GM has proved. The history of the car business shows all too clearly that, in the long run, constant discounting will reduce sales. Adding value, as Toyota has done, increases sales.

Underlying your promise is a statement of value. Don't get caught in the trap of saying you are worth something only to constantly interrupt yourself with a fire sale.

Creative Consistency

We stated at the beginning of this chapter that consistency is a test of will. Consistency tests your resolve to be who you say you want to be in *everything* you do. It is not a contract to be boring or one-dimensional. It is, rather, a contract to bring yourself to life—creatively—in the mind and heart of the consumer.

The salient thought here is to bring *you* to life. That thought assumes that you have an identity and purpose that you want to promote. When your identity runs right to your core, it gives you a license to be very creative.

In the age of the chief marketing officer, we have ratcheted up our use of technobabble. Phrases such as "data and channel integration," "ROI-driven marketing programs" and the buzz for "interactive" marketing have blurred what we are trying to accomplish—the location of potential customers, identification of their needs and wants, and the sale of our product to those customers.

Creativity presupposes originality. But remember: as you

concentrate on breaking out, creativity must be appropriate to you, your market, and your customers. Contrast creatively consistent with consistently creative. Your brand promise comes first, followed by creative execution. Too often, companies get bored with who they are and look for "big" ideas to spark interest. Remember: the big idea is who you are and what you stand for—and this must remain constant over time.

The experience you provide will, one hopes, evolve with changing times, and the way you tell your story will evolve as well—yet your personality and your character are the bedrock of your identity. Companies that constantly bounce from big new idea to big new idea, or spin through new ad campaigns, are displaying a consistency of indecision.

Those who promote themselves and their brand by being ruthlessly consistent are seen as decisive and desirable, and they will gain consideration by the customer.

Passion

> "We didn't just want to put our colors on somebody else's car; we wanted to be owners. It's not just about promotion. It's about passion—about putting our soul into racing and taking responsibility for what happens."
>
> *Dan Ginsberg, CEO Red Bull N.A.*
> Automobile Magazine, *June 2006*

The Test of Emotion

If you aren't ambitious enough to operate on a take-no-prisoners basis, you don't care about your product, your company, or yourself. Take up meditation. Or knitting.

Doesn't every company dream of having passionate customers—customers who so love its products that they become its best salespersons? Of course—because customers who are believers sell with conviction and credibility. They become emotionally attached to your brand.

Passion is not irrational, unstable, or characterized by emotional outbursts. Passion means bringing enthusiasm for what the company is doing, together with energy, to the game each and every day. Passion is the test of emotion, in the sense of having strong positive emotional involvement in what's being done as a team—emotional involvement that you can see and feel. Emotional involvement fueled by energy, enthusiasm, and expertise.

And doesn't it make sense that the customer's passion must spring from yours? Sure it does. A company must be passionate first, after which it can worry about attracting customers who mirror its passion. Creating a passionate team is the test of emotion.

The Story of Helmut Bott

A handful of storied automotive brands define the word passion, perhaps none more so than Porsche. Charlie Hughes had the chance to experience the Porsche passion first hand when he was head of marketing for Porsche+Audi in the US. Passion was everywhere,and perhaps one of the most telling examples of this passion occurred at Le Mans.

In the mid-1970s Porsche developed two front-engine, rear-wheel-drive cars, the 924 and the 928. In spite of some nifty new technology, most of the Porsche faithful rejected these cars with the belief that they were not real Porsches. Proper Porsches had air-cooled opposed-cylinder "boxer" engines in the back.

Despite a lukewarm reception, Porsche continued to develop the 924 into what became the 944 as it addressed the car's glaring shortcomings. The designers restyled the car so it looked more masculine. The engineers created a 4-cylinder engine derived from half of the Porsche V-8 engine designed for the Porsche 928. It produced far more power than the original 924 engine and allowed the 944 to claim it had a real Porsche engine. The 928's high performance profile provided the 944 with a degree of Porsche pedigree.

Before Porsche launched the 944, Helmut Bott, who was

Porsche's head of engineering and a true engineering genius, received permission to enter a pair of 944s at the 24 Hours of Le Mans, the world's most famous endurance race. For a company passionate about performance, taking its new car to the French event was a natural move. Because they were not yet on sale, the cars had to run in a prototype class, which meant they would run against larger, more powerful cars. However, the race would give Porsche hands-on experience with the 944 and would buttress the claim that they were "real" Porsches. "Hey, look! They've been raced at Le Mans," would send as important a message inside the company as outside.

The marketplace did not yet know that the 944 was coming, and the team kept its engine under wraps throughout the race. The engine was the 4-cylinder that became the power plant for the 944, but it had been turbocharged to give the car a performance boost for the race.

Hughes was at Le Mans that year, and as the race went into the evening, one of the 944 prototypes fetched up with engine problems. The team called it into the pits, and the first person over the pit wall was Helmut Bott. Helmut, then a spry 57 and surrounded by a contingent of far younger technicians. Bott popped open the hood, surveyed what was going on, and determined that they had to replace the turbocharger—which at that point had cooled to about 400 degrees Fahrenheit. The crew worked to disconnect it, and when they had finally undone all the fasteners, Helmut held up his hands, surgeon-like, and immediately two of the young technicians fitted asbestos mittens over them. He plunged his hands under the hood, grabbed the turbocharger, pulled it out and threw it over the wall.

Here was one of the most influential engineers in the world—a leader who, with a pointing finger, could have sent a platoon of technicians scurrying to do his bidding. Instead, he personified the Porsche culture, which was a passionate and talented bunch of engineers who loved what they were doing—and doing it hands-on. It was one of those sights that stay with you forever. And you just know that this story was told and retold numerous times at Weissach, Porsche's engineering center.

Conventional Wisdom

Conventional wisdom says you must never let them see you sweat. You must be every inch the level-headed professional business person. Getting emotionally charged works okay for sports, but in business we must remain calm.

Bull.

Every marketplace is crowded to the fence rails with competition, and winning takes many things, not the least of which is passion. We define passion as energy, enthusiasm, and expertise. Clearly, the first two can be dangerous without the third, yet one boss of ours loved saying that a committed fool will always beat an uncommitted genius.

During the tech boom of the 1990s, extremely passionate people created whole industries. These hard chargers worked long hours and battled even longer odds to launch successful enterprises. Their passion led to the expression 24/7, which not only had to do with hours of operation but also connoted a culture that believed in doing anything to make things work for themselves and for the customer.

That kind of dedication requires a real love for what you do and what you're about—the level of passion we admire every day in winning sports teams. Passion is also a critical component of winning companies. This is not a matter of putting in long hours because someone is looking or short hours because they are not. It's putting in long hours because you love it, because you're driven, and because you have a fanatical zeal for what your company has promised the world.

Most companies have at least a few passionate souls; the trick is to have an entire team passionately pursuing the company's vision. Combine that with the right level of skills and you have a team that is going to be tough to take down in the marketplace. Why? Because their shared passion to succeed will drive them to win—as a team and without regard to how difficult a task might be. That kind of chemistry is contagious. People naturally like doing business with folks who are enthused about what they do.

Passion is important because logic will only take you so far. The world is tough and unpredictable, and it requires strong positive emotions to overcome all the problems the business world throws at you. Passion brings businesses to life, and while is it not sufficient in and of itself to ensure success, it is an *essential* ingredient.

So what is the hangup? If passion is so important, what stops everyone from having it?

Trends

Assuming you—and your company—have made the commitment to stimulate passion, you still can't relax. A number of trends, some positive, most negative, will combine to shape your business environment.

Consolidation and Culture Takeovers

Over the past 15 years, the car business has experienced dramatic consolidation. Ford now owns Jaguar, Aston Martin, Volvo, and Land Rover—in addition to the three brands of Ford, Mercury, and Lincoln that it already had. Ford also owns a controlling interest in Mazda. GM has acquired Saab and Hummer and experimented with partial ownership of Suzuki, Subaru, and Isuzu. GM narrowly avoided self-immolation when its agreement to buy a huge interest in Fiat came apart.

The consolidation trend is global. At the smaller end of the spectrum, BMW tried its hand with Rover Group, eventually selling off everything but Mini, and then buying Rolls-Royce. Daimler-Benz, the parent of Mercedes-Benz, acquired Chrysler in the so-called "merger of equals that created DaimlerChrysler." Hyundai bought out Kia, and a Chinese company has purchased a controlling interest in Sangyong, a Korean carbuilder. Even the

French have made their own play with Renault's purchase of a controlling interest in Nissan.

Remember the lessons learned about culture in Chapter 4? If culture is who we are and how we do things, when you combine companies you also combine cultures. Most people resist changing their perception of "who we are and how we do things." The stronger the culture, the greater the resistance. When you buy a company, you may be buying many strengths. You would hope that part of these strengths would be its intellectual capital and a team that has its own identity. And that the company is living a viable brand promise and has grown a culture to support it.

The purchasing company probably paid a ton of money for the value of the brand it bought. But in most mergers and acquisitions, here's what happens. First comes the search for "efficiencies." We "help" the company learn how to do things our way. If it has pride and a history, its people will resist. Does this sound familiar? Or efficient? Does this sound like a situation in which passion will thrive?

No, it is an environment of uncertainty and often uncharted and unintended change. Passion comes from believing in what you are doing in the marketplace, not what you're doing to absorb a company. Consolidation is inwardly focused and, left unmanaged, will defuse passion. When the enemy becomes the company that has purchased you, little good will come from your newly acquired culture and its passion.

Death of the Entrepreneurial Spirit

People often reminisce wistfully about start-up endeavors in their careers. "I never worked so hard in my life, nor had so much fun doing it," they will say. Both authors of this book have started companies from scratch and share this enthusiasm. Being on the inside as you bring a new company to life makes you feel alive and empowered. There is action and speed and a true sense of mission. It is a make it or break it time. And of course there's passion.

When Charlie Hughes started Range Rover, a core of about 40 people were working there by the time it launched its first vehicle.

About a year later there were 65. One of the field managers walked into Charlie's office about that time and said, "It's not the same here any more. There are too many people, and everything takes too long to do." Range Rover was hardly overstaffed at that moment; the manager just missed the adrenalin rush of a start-up.

Yet the point is well taken. As companies grow, they add more internal drag and show less entrepreneurial spirit. When you start a company, failure is a real possibility. This means you attract risk-takers. Mature companies generate more conservative groups, and this has a way of dampening passion.

Passion goes hand-in-glove with a sense of team and purpose. Many large companies have pockets of extremely passionate people. No one would describe GM as a passionate workplace. The leadership there has come primarily from the finance community, which understands conviction but is not a hotbed of passion.

That said, there are teams at General Motors that are extraordinarily passionate. One is the Corvette team. With the C-5 generation platform, now followed by the improved C-6 version, they are building world-class cars and are justifiably proud of it. They have successfully competed at the 24 Hours of Le Mans, and they have a winning, positive attitude. They also embody an entrepreneurial spirit and are, in effect, running a small business that works.

Growth Mania . . .

Ambition can be a fine thing; setting unrealistic growth targets is an awful thing. Businesses need to grow, but the growth needs to measured, planned, and *earned*. Just putting pie-in-the-sky numbers on a business plan doesn't count.

We are all for stretch targets, because they bring a team to life. Winning also brings a team to life. You know you've stretched too far, however, when the outside world thinks you're doing a great job, but everyone on the inside is getting blamed for continually missing targets. As we discussed earlier, this is a common occurrence in the car business today. It is happening at car companies that are hot, car companies that are growing nicely, and car companies that are holding their own in spite of severe handicaps such as old or poor products.

It is hard for folks to maintain their passion when they are constantly being criticized for their results—no matter how good those results may be. Too strong a focus on hitting short-term goals, and the attendant pressure that puts on the entire organization, makes everyone feel as if they're on a treadmill to nowhere.

Missed short-term goals often lead to endless price discounting, a trap GM has been caught in for years. It is hard to sustain passion when the only thing that excites the customer is the deal. It starts to feel something like prostitution.

Risk Aversion . . .

We have cataloged the problems associated with platform sharing and Me-Too design. Add one more: loss of passion. If the products are bland and boring, the troops will feel bland and boring. Passion springs from feeling special about what you're producing. How do you wind up with bland and boring products? Largely by being averse to risk in all its forms.

Ask any mid-level Detroit executive, and most of the import executives as well, to tell you about the last time he or she stood up at a meeting and ventured a negative opinion about the company product. You won't hear much.

Demographics . . .

They say passion is the province of the young. That shouldn't be so, but maybe it is these days. The graying of the Baby Boomer generation is adversely affecting corporate America, and not just in health care costs. Senior workers tend to suffer from enthusiasm dysfunction and become cynical over time. Many have careers that have topped out, and their hearts are no longer in the game. But having achieved heavy-duty salaries and benefits, they don't want to retire just yet.

We realize that this paints Boomers with a broad brush. A great many executives never lose their passion. They live to work because that is their nature. They are enthusiastic about their work and bring passion to their job and team every day. Unfortunately, in companies that we have worked for or consulted with there always seems to be a sense of fatigue as the company and its employees age.

Globalization . . . New Entrepreneurs, New Workers

It may be bad news for the US, but whole generations of young Indians, Chinese, Russians, and others are willing to give their passionate all for a chance of success in business. And they are increasingly getting that chance in our globally connected world. Our country has its own entrepreneurial class that by and large shuns big business. Why? Because big business is too slow to act, too slow to give real responsibility, requires too much capital, and is not willing to pay what entrepreneurs might make by starting their own businesses.

The best car dealers will amass far more wealth over their careers than all but a handful of automotive industry executives. Both occupations attract different personality types. Guess where the risk-takers go.

In the car business, Chinese brands will soon come to America at prices not seen for years. Some analysts fear that the pricing will be so low as to change the dynamics of pricing in the US,which means even more pressure on the domestic companies. For the domestics to survive, they will need far more passion and entrepreneurial spirit than they now have.

Now You See It . . . Now You Don't . . . .

Why do some companies have palpable passion and others seem asleep at the wheel? Why do German companies seem to have more passion than American and Japanese companies? While we can agree that leadership is critical, what is it about those Germans? They just seem to have a clearer view of who they are, who they want to appeal to, and what constitutes their role in the market.

But you must be ever vigilant, for even the Germans have momentary lapses. For example, Mercedes-Benz recently badly lost its way. BMW, in advertising introduced in 2006, seems reluctant to show its Ultimate Driving Machines. That said, over the years the Germans have demonstrated a passion for cars and driving that's mostly missing in our domestic companies.

With one exception. Chrysler has been on a roll with cars such as the Chrysler 300, Dodge Magnum and Charger, and the resurrected Hemi V-8. Is it significant that those cars have come to life under a German leadership team? The leaders at Chrysler appear to have better understood the essence of the American car and what it could be than did their competitors across town.

Chrysler built a large, rear-drive car with a thumping big V-8 and styling that was unmistakably American. The Chevrolet Impala and Ford Five Hundred, meanwhile, blend all sorts of influences and are bland. It is sad when Ford brings out a car like the Five Hundred, builds it off a Volvo platform, styles it like a VW Passat, and installs a 3.0-liter V-6 that wouldn't pull the foam off your latte.

Customers are passionate about the Chryslers—as they should be. The passion of the people who designed them is obvious. But the marketplace never tires of asking, "What have you introduced to me lately?" and the Chrysler 300 has already stayed at the fair long enough to see the discounts begin.

There are other pockets of passion. Contrast the Ford Five Hundred sedan with the Ford F150 pickup truck. Brought to market in 2004 at a time when the Japanese where talking about increasing their truck market—and when General Motors was challenging Ford for pickup sales leadership after 25 years—the F150 is a winner. It is a winner because the Ford truck group believes passionately that they know how to build the best pickups in the world.

Ford Division's advertising for the F150 consistently extolled the technical virtues that make it a better truck. And the differences are real and important to the market. Ford promotes the

F150's stronger frame, stronger fasteners, better suspension, and an upgraded engine. You can feel the passion.

So what goes into building teams that have passion?

How to Generate Energy, Enthusiasm, and Expertise

We see passion in terms of energy, enthusiasm, and expertise—passion that's focused on the differentiation and culture that define who you are, your target customers and the role you want to play in the market. To that, add leaders who lead with clarity and vigor, have the courage to wear their hearts on their sleeves, and who are the first to show their passion.

Let's look first at expertise, because all the energy and enthusiasm in the world won't help you if you don't know what you're doing.

Expertise: The Art of Selection

We have heard how important our people are until we're sick of it. Do most companies live that belief? Apparently not, if the vast number of incompetents and fraidy cats populating most companies is any indication. *Fast Company* once ran a headline that said "Microsoft captures the only market worth having . . . talent." Before you even start to think about passion, take a hard look at the talent pool you have. How many people are there for the wrong reasons? "Tom has been here a long time and has always done a good job." "The dealers like Phil." "Mary has always been a loyal employee."

Please. How talented are they really? How do your team members stack up against their counterparts at the competition? Who is more experienced, better educated, smarter, harder working, more creative, and a better risk-taker? Fundamental to accomplishing every dream you have is the quality of the talent you attract. Quality of talent means more than a few stars; it means quality people throughout the organization. And it starts with functional expertise. You do not want team members having to compensate or cover up for underperforming mates. Passion comes from sharing a vision, confidence, and trust. Talent is critical to confidence and trust. Leaving underperforming people in their jobs is a cancer that eats away at an organization. Find, select, and pay for the best.

In the mid-1990s, when Land Rover was struggling with quality, it was suggested to the new head of manufacturing that he would be well served if he went out and paid each of the top three or four best manufacturing minds in the UK a million pounds a year if they could solve the problems. That was probably five times more than the head of manufacturing was making, but the thought was correct. It would have been cheap money compared to the expense of the quality issues. Of course he didn't follow that advice, preferring to believe that one or two new leaders who had come up through the same Rover Group system could turn things around. That thought was wrong, as it turned out.

Functional expertise lays the groundwork, but what else should you look for in the selection process? We suggest selecting people with a feel for the marketplace, good general business acumen, at least some street smarts, and a love of the game.

Enthusiasm: Selling and Storytelling

The head of one of the large advertising agencies in Detroit was proud of a sign he displayed on his desk. It read: "Come before me fired with enthusiasm, or you soon will be." Silly but insightful. He understood the importance of enthusiasm, just not its source.

Enthusiasm comes from within. In the short run it can be faked, but the passage of time will unmask the pretenders. People are either enthusiastic about what they are doing or they aren't. And what gets them enthusiastic? Not the satisfiers and pacifiers doled out by the HR department. No, it is the sense of mission—where we are taking this business combined with the opportunity to affect the outcome—that lights people up once you've let them in on the destination.

A compelling vision, a call to participate, and some early victories will stimulate enthusiasm. Leaders who are enthusiastic themselves set the tone and example. We realize that enthusiasm is not a perpetual state of mind. We all have our up and down days. Some days the challenges are suffocating, but always—at our core—we remain enthusiastic for what we stand for and where we are headed.

One revealing test of your vision is how often your troops enjoy telling the "story." And how well they describe the journey you are taking together. Enthusiasm manifests itself in selling, first to yourself and then others. It is why successful companies have vast oral histories, tales told and retold as if by a proud tribe squatting around a campfire.

Energy: Environment and Chemistry

It's often said that the devil is in the details. So is success. High energy in your team is not a detail, which is perhaps why so many executives give it so little attention. The work environment, chemistry, pacing, winning, and even everyone's body language all play a role. Because our world works at the speed of electrons, low energy produces low results. Yet in company after company we're involved with, the topic rarely comes up. People will say, "I don't have much energy today," but rarely will a leader say, "What do we have to do to raise our energy level?" Sales, yes. Profit, yes. Energy, no.

If you are even marginally alert, the minute you walk into a building, a hotel, a room or a meeting, you sense its buzz. Or lack of buzz. Energy is palpable, and it is as necessary as oxygen these days. More valuable than money or time. Imagine an entertainer without energy—and to some degree aren't we all entertainers?

You can have expertise and enthusiasm and still have a low level of energy. Energy has less to do with the grand scheme and more to do with the moment. For instance, it is hard to maintain a high level of energy in a three-hour meeting that's become a five-hour meeting.

Can you design an environment for high energy? Yes, and

there are experts who can help you do it. Think about both the physical environment and the mental environment. Let's look at the hallmarks of a high energy physical environment.

The Hawthorne Effect aside, our observations would include lots of light, natural when possible, multimedia meeting rooms where you can make noise, and a group tolerance for lots of activity. Density of people is a balance point as well. People engender energy in each another, so having enough people in an area is important. Go too far, of course, and people feel like inmates of a chicken-raising operation, which doesn't work. Individuals have different energy levels and different tolerances of energy.

Selection of people and where you place them is part of the physical environment. We believe leaders should be with their teammates and not on a Mahogany Row. Leadership works best with visibility that generates a "we're in this together" attitude.

The mental environment is a bit more difficult. But on the list of positives are energetic and energized leaders, rapid communication, high expectations, group excellence standards, and fast decision-making.

Did we say fast decision-making? People who have worked with both authors will correctly say that we have been both fast and slow decision-makers. Fast has inevitably worked better for everyone and almost always led to more effective results. Fast simply takes more confidence.

Good decision-making requires always moving toward your vision, knowing who you are, where you want to go, and what market reality is telling you. You need to understand which few decisions you must positively get right each year and which benefit as much from speed as anything else. People with a sense of history and market perspective know the difference.

When you don't know the difference, too much weight is placed on making the right decision as opposed to making your decision right. Optimizing decisions instead of optimizing execution. And often speed is a key component to optimizing your decision. Speed, quality, and cost all impact results—and our ultimate view of the rightness of a decision. Some strategic decisions deserve a long hard look. Most others benefit from a fast decision and just getting on with making it work. It's like sailing—making way in any direction, even the wrong one, beats stalling the boat. Know that a habitually slow decision-making environment slows everyone down and drains their energy dramatically. Solid expertise, experience, and judgment are prerequisites to good decision-making at any speed, and they become even more important as the pace quickens. Nurture momentum and increase energy, continually emphasizing that we know where we are going, we make decisions quickly, and we are making progress.

Varying the schedule helps too. We believe in the "high school" theory of management. Remember when you were in high school how the schedule was full of different and ever-changing events? Pep rallies, football games, dances, SATs, yearbook pictures, and football, basketball, and baseball seasons. Even your daily schedule moved you from class to class.

Businesses with high energy work the same way. They vary the routine, give people events to look forward to and promote cross-work groups and tight deadlines. Employees need to see activity that accomplishes interesting things. Things that take skill and that are done against real-world pressures. Celebrating victories, achievements, and milestones together will create a sense of momentum that brings its own energy. Even just having a building full of people who walk quickly and with purpose creates energy.

Last, and anything but least, maintain a positive outlook and attitude. Optimism keeps you and your team moving forward. We know there are two types of energy, positive and negative. Negative energy is an organizational killer. Invest the time required to create a work environment that generates positive energy, and then reward those who have that energy.

An Impassioned Conclusion

It is easy to see passion in start-ups and small companies, but all successful companies have it, whatever their size. A company can be cool and passionate at the same time. Consider Porsche, Honda, BMW, and even Mazda. Not all of them have been simultaneously passionate and cool all the time. But when they had a clear-eyed view of their mission and were enjoying carrying it out, they were.

Think of it as putting it all on the line, living up to your promise, and then enjoying your success. Who wouldn't like that?

We have talked about trends that have made life difficult and stressful for a lot of persons who work in the car business. Nothing is easy, yet passion for what you are doing can help get your team past obstacles that buffalo the less passionate. A clear vision allows you to view any challenge, whatever its magnitude, as just one more problem to solve.

We live in a combative world. Do you want to fight or flee? If you decide to fight, do it with passion.

Patience

"The only way to stop [long term damage] is to stop performing unnatural acts in the market. We just have to be patient."

Robert Lutz, GM Vice Chairman
Automotive News *May 22, 2006*

The Test of Conviction

Bob Lutz was speaking about the need for patience, and that need is real. Rome really wasn't built in a day. Neither was BMW or Toyota. A company must fight battles as they occur, not cut and run at the first sign of difficulty.

Patience is different from endurance. Patience is a virtue that makes mothers proud and gives shareholders heartburn. The investment world's motto seems to be "Anything worth doing should be done in one quarter or less." A Super Bowl in one season. Such unrealistic expectations are ridiculous, but a lot of people running companies don't appear to know that.

Building great brands takes time. In a world where new CEOs typically have three years or less to prove themselves, this is upsetting news. With your board of directors clamoring for immediate results, it takes conviction to conduct your business in a way that builds brand equity. This often means putting the good of the brand ahead of even such important considerations as you and your career.

Even though a great many companies have patiently spent decades successfully building up their brand's equity, most executives don't want to hear stories that include the word decades unless they concern their deferred compensation plans. That being the case, perhaps you should listen to how Nissan—by being patient for almost a year—turned itself around.

Nissan—the Irrational Discounter

Throughout most of the 1990s, Nissan muddled about in the market with weak product offerings and constantly changing advertising themes. Dull products and uninspired marketing led to—you guessed it—advertising and selling on price. Not the world's freshest or brightest strategy, but Nissan took it to a whole new level. Rapidly changing and ever-escalating incentive plans earned Nissan the nickname among its West Coast competitors of "the irrational discounters."

Nissan dealers immediately got hooked, even though they had a hard time following some of the logic. Still, they enjoyed playing the "Let's Give Cars Away" game. Many of them added their own insane ingredients to the pricing stew. Nissan's discounting at the time was dizzying, never mind that it would look almost normal today. In its time, however, Nissan's behavior looked radical, particularly when compared with the other big Japanese companies, Toyota and Honda, which did almost no discounting.

Nissan went from being the Japanese brand second only to Toyota to a distant third behind Honda. Proving once again that distress merchandising done long term will lose market share, not gain it.

When Carlos Ghosn, everybody's current candidate for Messiah of the car industry, took over Nissan, it was wobbling on the edge of bankruptcy. During his first visit to the US, Ghosn asked his local executives what would it take to make Nissan profitable in North America? His strategy was to build a profitable business, not to keep plants busy making high-volume money losers. Their answer was new product and a move toward advertising product, not price.

This raised a knotty question: exactly when do you change strategies? Old habits die hard, and if you wait until you have new products, the market—and the dealers—will exert tremendous pressure to continue selling on price. Stop discounting before the new products arrive, and sales will drop like a rock.

The Nissan leadership agreed to dramatically reduce discounting at the beginning of 2001 and suffer a decline in sales prior to the introduction of the first new car. That car, the Altima, would not be introduced until fall. Nissan then took an overdose of courage salts and went on the road to share the new strategy with its dealer body.

The story line was simple: the new strategy would generate more profit for both dealers and Nissan. Rarely is money made giving cars away, and most people attending these meetings knew it. Nissan's team was honest in admitting what would happen before the new Altima arrived. They predicted a sales decline of 12 percent. They also sold the idea that new cars would be more competitive and interesting than the old ones—a promise the new Nissan Altima would make good on. Last, they told the dealers that the new cars alone would not generate more profit—unless the dealers collectively fixed their own behavior.

In the end it worked, but getting there was hell. It tested local management's patience daily, and especially at the end of every month when sales figures were published. The dealers bought off on the strategy, but as the discounting went down, followed quickly by sales, they howled. It was not a happy time to be a

district sales manager calling on increasingly hostile Nissan dealers. To stir the pot, as if it needed it, Nissan mandated that there
would be no discount price advertising for the new Altima when
it came to market. The losing tactic that the dealers had grown to
love was now forbidden.

Nissan withstood the heat for more than a half a year while
sales went down. Happily, the new Altima was everything everyone had hoped it would be. With virtually no incentives, it allowed both the factory and the dealers to concentrate their
marketing money on telling the world what a great car it was.
They launched with a new campaign called "Shift," and it indeed
shifted consumer perception of Nissan.

Nissan had done its product homework: the new Altima was
bigger, good looking, well designed, and offered a V-6 for the first
time. Moreover, its price was $200 below the old Altima, a dated,
unattractive toad of a product. It was thus a relative bargain compared to either a Toyota Camry or a Honda Accord. Incentive
spending plummeted from almost $2,200 a car to $250. With
everyone solidly marketing the same product story, sales took off.
Dealer profitability jumped dramatically, and the dealers became
converts to a strategy that they knew was right but about which
they had complained bitterly during the months before the new
Altima appeared.

Nissan thus turned the corner and went on to introduce a
string of successful new products, all marketed on its corporate vision of offering cars that had a touch more style and performance
than the competition. Smart pricing and small discounts where
market pressures required them have replaced the irrational discounts. And Nissan has become very profitable. A marvelous result
based on Nissan having had the courage of its convictions and the
patience to withstand six months of heat from its dealers.

Conventional Wisdom

Conventional wisdom says our world rewards speed and hard
work. We don't have the luxury of time to make a promise and

then shepherd the owner through the experience of owning our product. After all, customers have become so cynical, chasing one fad after another, that we don't have to worry. We can still rope them in with great marketing, and if that doesn't work, we'll use price—which is what most of them are interested in anyway.

What conventional wisdom doesn't understand is the difference between strategy and execution. We have fallen in love with rapid-fire execution and ignored the importance of having a well-thought-out strategy. We have gone from "ready, aim, fire" to "fire, fire, fire."

Sounds silly to even say it, but examples abound in the car business. One recent hip-shoot involved Lincoln playing the heritage card by naming a new car the Zephyr, a name last used by the brand in the 1940s. Today, with Zephyr advertising still on the air, the company announced a change to the MKZ. That's pronounced Mark Z, if you're wondering.

If you don't have a strategy so captivating that it makes you want to invest the time needed to make it work, look for a new one. Better yet, change your attitude.

Trends

If you were paranoid, you'd think sinister forces are at work pushing us into extremely short-sighted actions. Well, look around, and you'll spot trends that continue to condition many executives' thinking about the value of patience.

Customer Value vs. Shareholder Value

This is a dilemma that management has wrestled with since the first shareholder invested in a company. But the Information Age has accelerated the pressures that push shareholder value ahead of customer value.

In his book, *Authentic Leadership*, Bill George made the point that all companies have at least three constituencies—customers, employees, and shareholders. The companies that perform best for the shareholder over time are the companies that focus their attention on the customer first, the employee second, and the shareholder last. It is called winning in the marketplace with customers.

Our domestic car companies—losing market share because of having lost touch with the market—constantly yap about shareholder value. They talk while the share price falls. It would be fascinating if it were not so sad. A share of General Motors bought forty years ago would be two shares today—and worth about what you paid for the original single share.

We know it is difficult for leaders to stand up to a stream of criticism and second guessing from stock analysts who have instant access to almost as much information as management itself. But we are hard-pressed to think of an example of a successful company that got that way by putting shareholders first and customers second. Well, there's Tony Soprano's Ba Da Bing topless bar, but you get the point.

A slavish focus on short-term business results aimed at impressing the analysts inevitably comes at a cost to your customers. Over time, customers will gravitate to companies that transparently put the customer's interest first. This should not come as a surprise, but to a lot of marketers it does. Analysts will sing your praises if your customers do. It's as simple as that, and it means that you absolutely must concentrate your efforts on inspiring customers to pick you out of the crowd.

Growth vs. Reality

Unrealistic goals create problems throughout your business, and nowhere is that more evident than their effect on sticking to a strategy and plan. We've worked with companies where there was so much time devoted to recovery plans they were called plans *du jour*. It's hard to imagine building anything worthwhile under those conditions.

Automotive market saturation—nearly four dozen brands, more than 300 models, $12 billion in advertising, 21,000 car dealerships—has led to a level of competition undreamed of even

10 years ago. Add to that the availability of more sales and pricing data than ever before—available the day after sales close each month—and the result is a hyper-reactive market.

When J.D. Power and Associates created the Power Information Network (PIN), it changed overnight the way car companies could and did do business. PIN data comes from car dealers' computer systems, and it gives complete and accurate information on daily sales, transaction price, list price, cash rebates, interest rates, lease penetration rates, and dealer gross profits for any manufacturer's cars that you're willing to pay for. At the end of the month you can analyze your sales results using information that was unavailable before PIN. And J.D. Power and Associates is now working on software that can tell you the percentage of your sales generated by each category of sales and marketing expenditure, including advertising.

For people in a rush, this is akin to giving dynamite to your children. The advantage of this data is that it increases knowledge of what's working in the marketplace. The danger is that it encourages those without a solid strategy and who don't have patience and don't like last month's sales results, to react quickly—and differently—12 times a year. This can decrease your reliance on strategic planning and replace it with reactive planning or, worse, over-reactive planning. Constant fine tuning and tinkering with a sales and marketing plan ceases at some point to *be* planning.

Let's be honest: spending an inordinate amount of management time and attention on tactical marketing and pricing will skew a corporate culture's judgment about what's really important. A company will become one-dimensional, and that dimension has nothing to do with long-term success.

The Power of Patience

It's ironic that companies stay up nights looking for the smallest competitive advantage yet often manage to miss the big advantage: the compounding effect of standing for the same important thing, year after year. Look at BMW, Ferrari, and Lexus. Each of them dukes it out in the marketplace each month, but each also has the advantage of having spent years demonstrating who they are and what they stand for.

Unwaveringly.

Patience Means . . .

If great brands are a promise wrapped in an experience, how long do they take to build? Like all serious promises, a brand promise takes trust, and building trust takes time. Trust can be earned or lost through experience. Given the manipulation that goes on in the marketplace, it's amazing that Americans trust anything, but they will. They may be comforted by warranties and guarantees, but they'd rather hear a believable story.

Customers, however, will reserve judgment. As simple as this sounds, your business grows when more and more people try your product and enjoy the experience. People initially attracted by your promise will learn first hand that you deliver a different and better experience. Your hard work and effort have paid off. But there's a catch: it takes time. Although we live in a world of constant, rapid communication and epidemic message overload, consumer perceptions change at glacial speed. This reality can be a good thing if you embrace it—and if you believe that time can be on your side.

The notion that it takes a long time to build a successful brand conflicts with our culture of instant gratification. It is discouraging to those who live in the moment, must succeed in the moment, chase what is hot in the moment, and let the exigencies of the moment control them. How many times have you heard, "We'll really start building our brand as soon as we get rid of this excess inventory?" Or "when we launch the new product," or "after we've fixed our retail problems?" Sound familiar?

We want to win and we want to win now. We are impatient, which works both for and against us. The Pyramids were built by patient people—ruthless, too, of course, but patient. They showed great devotion to the design, for the Pyramids would have never been finished had they changed the design first to a trapezoid and then to a rectangle. No. Stone had to be cut and fit to a meticulous long-range plan.

That still applies. A company must be abuzz with enthusiasm for getting on with what needs to be accomplished, but it must also remain steadfast to its master plan.

Leadership . . . the Courage of Your Convictions

Most pundits agree that it takes a long time to build a successful brand. We say it takes one day—today. Great brands are built by doing the right thing today and every today thereafter. Which sounds easy but isn't. And it takes the courage to be patient.

We have talked about the importance of a branded culture, which means that a company's people are aligned in a cause or a mission that is absolutely clear to them. Now ask yourself, what makes it so clear? Is it flowery words or brave speeches? Hardly. It is joining with others in a steady march toward a shared, inspiring vision. It is demonstrating over and over again that the leadership has the courage of its convictions—that, as problems arise, both expected and unexpected, the company will stay the course. We will keep our promise and find new ways to make that promise valid and enticing to customers.

Being steadfast to your vision, your promise, and to your customers unlocks powerful organizational benefits. Employees are released from the anxiety that plagues many workplaces. They know where "we" are headed, and they know the context for every problem the company will face. They know what they are expected to contribute and how they will be judged. And they see the determination their leaders demonstrate every day, determination that reinforces attitudes and performance.

Too many companies have become job shops, working project by project to hit the numbers. Direction changes and personal work schedules are altered on a dizzying basis. No sane person would argue against the need for flexibility in the workplace, yet what an individual does needs to fit into a picture of company progress. And if it does not, then employee satisfaction goes to hell in a hand basket. An unending series of unexpected changes that lead nowhere will never inspire confidence.

In our superheated market, key competitors are living this nightmare. It is scary to compare General Motors with Toyota. As General Motors scrambled to reverse market share losses, it literally blew one way and another, chasing marketing programs designed and redesigned to sell more cars and trucks. Toyota, meanwhile, just keeps working its plan and growing its business, spending less on incentives than the domestics and bringing desirable innovation such as hybrids to market.

Without the foundation of having the courage of your convictions, employees will judge management instead of the other way around. Once that judgment reversal sets in, getting people engaged takes more time than it should because they spend time weighing what you want them to do. The byword is reaction, which is not what you want. You want a motivated work force collectively judging themselves by their progress in building a great brand as viewed by the marketplace.

Being steadfast by holding to your vision sets the stage for greatness. It naturally directs the vast majority of work in the right direction and gives people confidence. Confidence in leaders who know where "we" are going and have the courage to face down and solve the inevitable problems—not execute knee-jerk and out-of-character reactions that adversely affect morale.

The marketplace continually tests every brand to see if it will remain true to its charter. BMW underwent just such a test during the 1990s as sales of SUVs continued to explode. Its dealer body began agitating for an SUV. The company's dilemma was that SUVs were then built on truck platforms. That meant large heavy frames that ensured off-road capability, but it also meant a very truck-like personality. Doesn't sound much like a BMW, does it?

BMW's first solution was to purchase Land Rover, which gave it a respected, although separate, sport utility brand. The US BMW dealers, however, continued to demand their own SUV because they were losing customers to the competition. At this point, the industry started developing "crossover" vehicles that looked like SUVs but were based on car platforms. Crossovers were ideal for customers whose biggest off-road excursion was a gravel parking lot and who wanted a more car-like feel. Lexus got to market first with the RX300. BMW decided that its dealers were right: a market existed for a BMW SUV.

BMW would design an SUV *its* way—loud on sport and quiet on utility. To deflect criticism that it was not a real SUV, they called it a SAV for Sports Activity Vehicle. Never mind that not one customer is known to have uttered the term SAV out loud, BMW designers and engineers built a genuine BMW clad in SUV clothing. Like all BMWs, its final test was at the Nürburgring, a long and difficult German racetrack. There, the new BMW X5 was held to BMW's "Ultimate Driving Machine" performance standards. It passed.

The company created the X5 only *after* worrying about the implications of building a BMW SUV, buying another brand, and then figuring out that it could do it best by just being BMW. They patiently worked through the issue, taking actions in keeping with their vision of the BMW brand. The market and BMW dealers screamed, "Build an SUV!" BMW screamed back, "Only when it can be a real BMW!"

Time to Make It Work

We are impatient and we enjoy being so. Knowing this, how do we get time to be on our side? How do we give ourselves permission to take the time to make it work? We are tempted to say confidence and faith are the simple answer, but it's being in love with your vision that gets you past the harsh realties of life.

The best companies and the best people are passionately committed. Care in how they see the market, and care in how they express their vision in terms of a promise and the experience fuels that commitment. It's why great brands are a promise wrapped in an experience. Their unabashedly clear promise drives them to be the best. And they worry over all aspects of the customer's experience. Yet a promise wrapped in an experience is both defining and open ended. The promise must be real. It takes time to prove you will deliver, so you must stick with it. Yet as the saying goes, *change* happens.

As the market shifts and your customers' tastes evolve, you must also change. This does not mean changing who you are; it means getting better at what you've promised the marketplace. It means constantly improving the customer's experience. In the car business, improvement is most often viewed in terms of product. Product improvement generally falls into one of two categories. One is improving the general excellence of your products, how well they work, and their quality. The other is improving being the best at what you promise to be. Highest quality, Ultimate Driving Machine, a Different kind of Car Company, or whatever. Interestingly enough, the world will cut you some slack on overall excellence if you really excel at what you specifically promise. Some slack—time to improve your general excellence or quality—not a hall pass that says, "You don't need to worry about it."

Land Rover struggled with poor quality, yet sales still grew for a time even though quality problems seriously irritated its customers. Saturn coasted along with virtually no new products for a decade, getting by on humdrum products and the strength of the company's consumer-friendly retail approach.

For the best, the promise defines them while they evolve the experience. In 2005, BMW ran a commercial to introduce its new 3 Series sedan that said, "We invented the sports sedan in 1968, and have been re-inventing it ever since." While the commercial is far from breakthrough, it makes the salient point. We strive to be a better BMW with each new generation of car, and we have been doing this for almost forty years.

If you say it—promise it—you must mean it. BMW does. Each new generation of cars contains new technology and engineering with the sole goal of being the best. It is a self-acknowledged evolutionary approach. Each new BMW's steering, brakes, chassis, and engine improve upon the prior version's capabilities. This is no simple feat. BMW had the courage to invest in itself and to constantly raise the bar. The result is arguably the best automotive brand in the world. And guess what? It's also among the most profitable.

Competitors take aim at BMW all the time. Each year, car companies introduce an expressed or implied BMW fighter. For Lexus, it has been the IS300, now the IS350. Infiniti has enjoyed success with sporty offerings such as the G35 sedan and coupe and the M35 and M45. Yet, BMW continues to grow its business. The company refuses to rest on its laurels, impressive as they are. Do some of the competition's BMW fighters actually outperform real BMWs? From time to time they do—except in credibility, prestige, and trust.

What makes BMW such a wonderful example of patience and conviction is that the entire automotive industry knows exactly what BMW is doing. If, as we've said, it's a copycat world, why aren't more companies emulating BMW? Because it takes courage—courage to settle on a consistent, admirable vision, courage to say publicly that you will be best at something, and the patience to see it through.

Markets Change, Brands Evolve

At the end of 2004 and during the first half of 2005, we witnessed the market starting to move away from large SUVs. After Hurricane Katrina in 2005, when gas prices skyrocketed, interest in large SUVs declined dramatically. This was particularly tough on Ford and General Motors because their dominance of the truck segments generated the bulk of their profits.

After a brief respite, gasoline prices rose rapidly throughout the first quarter of 2006—smack in the middle of GM's launch of it new 900 series platform. The 900 series is a new architecture from which all of GM's big trucks and SUVs will be derived. While more fuel efficient than the vehicles it replaces, the 900 series may still be in trouble. The market appears to be losing interest in large SUVs and pickups as gas prices exceed $3 a gallon.

Markets can change slowly or overnight. A rapidly changing market can badly damage anybody's near-term plan.

A brand, on the other hand, should evolve. It can't change overnight to accommodate changes in the marketplace. Having virtually ignored cars for a decade—to concentrate on trucks and SUVs—the domestic automakers are now rushing to embrace them. Their car brands are not evolving, which should come as no surprise, because they didn't stand for much to begin with.

We can't always anticipate change, but we can interpret it within the framework of our brand promise. How will a change in market conditions require us to change—not our promise but rather the experience we deliver—so that we remain relevant to our customers?

An Enduring Conclusion

We've said that great brands start with a differentiating promise wrapped in an experience and that you need to build a culture that executes the vision. You need products or services that bring the promise alive, and you should build a conspiracy to get others to help you build critical mass. Consistency helps you cut through the clutter, and passion helps you become a winning team. All of which takes—requires—patience.

Your brand promise will take time to be understood and absorbed—and more time and experience to be believed. The majority of your competitors don't have the vision, courage or stomach to stand for something consistently over the years. Which means that your patience can create a major competitive advantage.

To set yourself apart, you must have the patience to prove over and over again, year after year, that you are who you say you are—building trust and letting the market come to you. Patience is the final test, and it's the one that most companies fail.

10

Brand Portfolios

"Here is what we will not stand for: Incremental change, avoiding risk, thinking short-term, blocking innovation, tying our people's hands, defending procedures that don't make sense, and selling what we have instead of what the consumer wants."

CEO Bill Ford, speaking of
Ford's "The Way Forward" Plan, January 23, 2006

A Test of Parenting

Few persons can build even one brand successfully. Many of those who can't, sad to say, are at the controls of important brand port-folios. You won't learn much from them, but this chapter offers our take on what you need to know in order to successfully juggle more than one brand at a time.

From the outset we have acknowledged the difficulty of building a world-class brand. Today, because of growth and ac-quisitions, more companies than ever find themselves faced with managing a portfolio of brands. In carrying out this task, most of them make Hogan's Goat look like a paragon of sensible organization and decision-making.

Successfully running a brand portfolio calls into play the best parenting skills. It requires seeing the brand children as individuals, knowing their strengths and weaknesses, giving them confidence, and encouraging them to have their own values and their own personality. It means sending them to play in an arena that capitalizes on their strengths. And the best parents accomplish all of this while remaining in the background.

Toyota, Honda, Nissan, BMW, and Hyundai—the fastest-growing automakers—have concentrated on building one, two, or at most, three brands. In our brand-saturated world, what does that say about the need to focus on what sets you apart? General Motors, on the other hand, currently markets eight brands in the US, and Ford is marketing seven, not including Mazda, which it controls. Given the level of competition and cost of supporting a brand in the marketplace, can anyone successfully manage this many brands?

Brand distinctiveness within most portfolios gets shredded daily through an overemphasis on efficiency. Bigness has led to a "supermarket brand" mindset—each brand must provide something for everyone. A supermarket brand that provides mass merchandise, a broad array of product, low prices, and thin margins may be just fine for one brand in your portfolio. Doing it with two is redundant and expensive.

And if you view your entire brand portfolio as your supermarket of brands, you're in more trouble than a man with a copperhead in his sleeping bag. If a portfolio is to add value and spread risk, each brand in it must focus on a specific and separate market. "Something for everyone," when everyone is seen as an individual, is the polar opposite of thinking "the same for everyone."

Pontiac's Sad Case History

Pontiac, GM's self-proclaimed "performance" or "excitement" brand, is an example of how confused one can get when running a portfolio of brands. GM Vice Chairman Bob Lutz admitted as much when he told analysts at the New York Auto Show in March 2005 that Pontiac was a "damaged brand." He later retracted his statement, but he was absolutely correct about the damage.

An *Automotive News* article in July 2005, said of Pontiac's lagging sales: " . . . disappointed dealers blame Pontiac's vague brand image, a car-heavy lineup, and Me-Too vehicles that resemble other GM products." Apparently Pontiac spells performance with a small "p." What has it gotten wrong? Just about everything. If you say you *are* something, wouldn't it be smart to deliver that something?

In 2004, Pontiac introduced its G6, an all-new car to replace the Grand Am, its most popular model. Well, all-new is not altogether accurate. The new car shares GM's Epsilon platform with the Chevrolet Malibu and the Saab 9-3. Forgetting the Saab for a moment, how do the Chevrolet Malibu and the new Pontiac G6 compare? After all, Chevrolet is GM's "supermarket" bread-and-butter family car brand, and Pontiac is a more expensive specialty brand, supposedly exuding excitement.

The G6 and Malibu look noticeably different, both outside and inside. The array of body styles is different as well. Chevrolet offers the Malibu as a four-door sedan or four-door hatchback, and Pontiac offers its G6 as a four-door sedan, two-door coupe, and two-door hardtop/convertible. And the Pontiac does *look* sportier. Yet mechanically they are twins. At the outset, in a bow towards its performance roots, Pontiac offered only a V-6 engine, while the base engine in the Malibu was a plain-vanilla four cylinder.

The Pontiac V-6 was an upgraded overhead valve engine that dates to 1980, when it was introduced on the GM X-body platform in the Chevrolet Citation and Pontiac Phoenix. The new generation variant produces 201 hp in 3.5 liter form. As introduced in the G6, it was mated to a four-speed automatic transmission. Pontiac's Japanese competitors all offer modern V-6 engines with dual overhead cams and variable valve timing that produce anywhere from 220 to 260 hp. They also offer five-speed automatic transmissions. And guess what? Not one of them claims to be a performance brand.

That same 3.5 liter engine is offered in the Chevy Malibu. So what happened to the performance superiority of the G6? Six months after introducing the G6, Pontiac added a 3.9-liter version of the V-6 and pumped its horsepower up to a claimed 240. Though still an old design, it at least has a competitive power output. And Pontiac even offered it with a six-speed manual transmission. But at the same time, GM introduced an SS performance version of the Malibu with guess which engine? Yup, the new 3.9.

In the summer of 2005, Pontiac brought out its halo car, the Solstice roadster. Patterned after the Mazda Miata, it is a smart looking two-seater. Score one for Pontiac, sort of. You see, GM's Saturn brand is also in trouble and needed a halo car, so Saturn will get its own version of the Solstice called the Sky. They share the new Kappa platform and will also share GM powertrains. Again, where is Pontiac's performance advantage?

But wait, there's more. At the 2006 Los Angeles Auto Show GM introduced a performance edition of the Solstice called the GXP. With a direct injection turbocharged high-tech four producing 260 horsepower, *this* Solstice will have real performance. The question is, can GM stop itself from giving the same powertrain to Saturn's Sky? Of course not. The new Sky will offer the same performance package later in 2006.

In fairness to GM, it has an undoubted hit on its hands with the Solstice. The issue again is one of discipline. Does GM want Pontiac to be its performance brand or not? And if so, what products will be unique to Pontiac that make it different from the other brands in the GM portfolio?

Can we possibly wander farther off the trail as to what products belong at an "excitement" Pontiac? Yes, Ollie, we actually can. In the spring of 2006, GM caved in to Pontiac dealer whines and gave them an entry-level car to join the sagging G6. The car? A rebadged Chevrolet Cobalt.

At this point you're saying, well, I'm sure Pontiac at least got its marketing right. Maybe the cars aren't everything they need to be, but never let the truth get in the way of a good story. In this case, however, the truth has pretty well bushwhacked a hard-hitting performance story. *Automotive News,* in April 2005, said: "General Motors doesn't like its own advertisements." It went on to say:

> In an evaluation, ad managers of GM's brands gave Pontiac and Buick ads a score of 3 on a 10-point scale, an executive close to GM says.
>
> Pontiac has started running a commercial for the G6 sedan that was produced by McCann-Erickson's Toronto office. That office created the G6 commercial for GM Canada.

It's an axiom in the ad business that good clients make good advertising. Or put another way, behind every bad ad lurks a bad client. How do you explain having to go to your Canadian ad agency to get a decent commercial for a product as important to Pontiac as the G6? Some would say this advertising unrest didn't happen for lack of trying. Since 2001, Pontiac has tried four tag lines on the public including: "We Build Excitement"; "Fuel for the Soul"; "Designed for Action."

And one more thing. Where did Pontiac introduce its new performance G6 sedan? Why, on that hotbed of automotive enthusiasm and excitement, Oprah Winfrey's television talk show. During Oprah's first show of the season, Pontiac gave away 276 new G6s to members of her audience. GM claimed it was a major marketing coup. Other observers said that it worked better for Oprah than Pontiac. We say, what in God's name is Pontiac's performance brand doing introducing a performance sedan on the Oprah show? How much of its target market watches the show? It is not quite the same as introducing the G6 on, say, the *Dale Earnhardt, Jr., Hour of Fender Banging,* if there was such a show.

Nine months later, Pontiac followed the Oprah breakthrough with a media buy on the Lifetime network, a cable channel that skews heavily female and saturates the air waves with stories of bad marriages and lurid extramarital affairs. No one confuses

Lifetime with the Speed channel. Listen to *Automotive News'* report on the deal:

> Pontiac teams with Lifetime on product vignettes . . . Shorts depict women's use of G6 in their everyday lives . . . .
>
> One vignette shows two women bringing suntan lotion and a beach ball to their G6, which has a large sunroof.

One can only image the sweat that broke out at BMW over in Munich when the marketing department heard news of this innovative selling of performance. Can it get much more confusing? Yes. Let's look at naming cars.

Car companies go one of two ways with names: word names (Ford Explorer) or alpha numeric names (BMW 330i). The Germans tend to like alpha numeric, and the Americans and Japanese lean toward words. Pontiac's decision is a split vote.

Pontiac owns some storied, performance-oriented, model names including Grand Am, Grand Prix, Bonneville, Trans Am, and GTO. Not a bad lineup. However, in the belief that its performance-inspired names are threadbare from long association with mediocre products, Pontiac decided to use an alpha numeric for the G6 and a word, Solstice, for the new sports car.

What has all this meant to G6 sales? Sales have picked up at the end of 2005, yet in historical terms they have been disappointing. Sales in 2005 of around 125,000 must be measured against 1999 Grand Am sales of 235,000.

How to spur sales? Simple, offer the G6 with the same lame four-cylinder engine found in the base Malibu. Now we're *really* talking performance. Don't laugh; Pontiac really did that.

Conventional Wisdom

"All we have to do is make the cars look different and then use branding to differentiate them. After all, most product differentiation is lost on the customer." It sounds backwards to us, yet this is how a lot of companies with brand portfolios think. Look at Ford and Mercury, Chevrolet and Pontiac, and at the deceased nameplates in Chapter 1 (Dead Brand Tales). This kind of thinking hastened the demise of Oldsmobile and Plymouth.

The industry is caught in a real bind trying to please multiple audiences. The stock analyst audience wants to hear about sharing—sharing of platforms, sharing of technology, and sharing of powertrains. Stockholders want to hear about growth and dividends. Consumers want to hear what makes a brand special—and sharing all of a product's mechanicals with one or two or three sibling brands doesn't sound special at all. It sounds like a shell game, which it is. Ford even calls it the top-hat strategy, the top hat being industry jargon for a car's outer skin.

The belief that customers won't know the difference is not currently supported by the plight of GM and Ford. The spectacle of continually escalating discounts while losing market share does not sound special at all. It does sound expensive.

Trends

The overall business environment impacts the way we might manage a portfolio of brands in ways both apparent and unseen. There are the obvious trends of consolidation, irrational belief in low risk/high reward, fierce competition, and cost reduction pressures. Customer expectations also affect our thinking in some surprising ways.

Consolidation

Beyond the obvious addition of more brands to manage, consolidation often reveals weaknesses in the acquiring organization. Few companies have the depth of talent required to focus effectively on additional brands. Furthermore, as discussed in Chapter 4 (Culture), the conquering company seems to eventually rape and pillage what it has acquired. As the takeover plays out, those within the acquired brand will spend more time worrying about the new parent than worrying about the customer.

When the inevitable downsizing begins, the new entity usually loses many associates who actually understand *their* brand. Hard-earned lessons and existing knowledge fall by the wayside, and corporate think starts to replace brand team think. Making things work for the corporation becomes paramount. For instance, Land Rover at the end of 2005 is not the same brand-focused team that it was before it suffered two iterations of being consumed and downsized by a new parent—once by BMW and once by Ford.

There are pluses and minuses to consolidation. Land Rover would have struggled to survive as a stand-alone brand. And based on some insightful product programs championed by Wolfgang Reitzle and which capitalized on Land Rover's image, Land Rover sales are setting records. Reitzle was the head of Ford's Premier Automotive Group (PAG) of which Land Rover became a part. Jaguar, Aston Martin and Volvo make up the rest of PAG's brand portfolio.

But questions remain about PAG's future. How does Jaguar's loss of nearly a billion dollars a year affect investment in the other brands? Jaguar enjoyed success during the early years of Ford ownership only to lose its way a few years later. Combining Land Rover and Jaguar sales and marketing into one operation in the US also raises issues of focus.

Loss of talent and focus seems to be an unintended yet inevitable fallout of consolidation.

Brutal Competition

Twenty-four million units of worldwide excess capacity can do weird things to a marketplace. Remember, a good year's worth of car and truck sales in the US is 17 million units. Collectively, the industry wants each year to sell far more cars than the market wants. Stimulating the market is the name of the game, and for many that means swinging the price machete instead of a lasso.

Over the past decade, overcapacity has taken its toll on a

number of companies and has led to numerous consolidations with more to come. Brutal competition continues to push companies into crisis mode.

Living 30 days at a time, fighting your way out of a crisis or crises, and managing a portfolio of brands ensure a tough environment. If any of the portfolio brands are performing poorly, brand building gives way to short-term sales programs that diminish brand equity. This leads to further sales declines, more short-term programs, and the cycle repeats itself. This is fatal.

Companies in crisis tend to move toward centralization of authority. In 2005 as GM went into crisis mode, GM Chairman Rick Wagoner declared that he would take over North American Operations because that was GM's biggest problem, and he should straighten it out. Brands need air to breathe, they need space, and they need to concentrate on being all they can be in the marketplace. Reporting to the chairman, which means even further centralized decision-making, works against creating brands with their own personality.

Cost Reduction Pressure

The ferocity of the competition has driven up marketing costs and has increased price discounting. This requires that companies examine their entire cost structure. Cost reduction becomes a tool for survival. One of the favorite methods to drive costs down is platform sharing. The concept itself is not daft; it cuts to the heart of efficiencies of scale, but the way it is applied determines whether it is good or bad.

Toyota uses the Camry platform to make both the Camry and the Lexus ES 330. These are reasonably well-differentiated cars, and both do a good job. Customers see them as different. Even so, this type of platform sharing is what makes Lexus a less authentic brand than BMW.

The industry is divided on this issue. One camp argues that it saves less money than people think. This is because it costs money to tool separate manufacturing locations and to add differentiation after the fact. The other camp says it costs a bloody fortune to build a platform these days, and one needs to milk it for all it's worth. What we know is that a per-car discount of $3,000 or more could easily cover the cost of desirable differentiation. Of course, discounting is faster.

Low Risk/High Reward

We have focused on the need for courage, yet many auto execs still believe that success lies at the end of a conservative, low-risk path. Let's agree on one thing: there is real risk in managing a brand portfolio. It takes resources, talent, time, and focus that might actually provide a better return if they were applied to a single brand.

This is what has happened to the Ford Division when the Ford Motor Company scattered its talent, resources, and focus across Jaguar, Aston Martin, Land Rover, Volvo and Mazda, not to mention Mercury and Lincoln. Toyota is beating the field, concentrating on one primary brand and two small brands initially restricted to the US market. In 2006, unless the earth opens up and swallows it, Toyota will overtake GM as the world's largest car maker.

It costs serious money to bring a brand to market. In the US, GM is marketing eight brands to Toyota's three. Could that be why Toyota is winning? Yet the evidence shows that persons within GM believe selling multiple brands with only slight differentiation is a low-risk strategy. Right. Yet GM's troubles persist.

Supermarket Brands

The vehicle market is mature and fragmented. New segments, new segments within segments, and the urge to compete in more and more segments have led to a supermarket approach to brand development. In our rush to grow, we examine every opportunity available—often without regard to our brand or to who we are and who we want to market to.

Porsche brings to market an SUV. Mercedes-Benz brings to market a small front-wheel-drive vehicle, its A-class, followed by the R-class minivan. Concerned that minivans are *declasse*, Mercedes obfuscated the intent of this addition by describing the R-class as " . . . combining the permanent four-wheel-drive capability of an SUV with the comfort and versatility of a luxury wagon . . . " In other words, a crossover. Or something.

Companies that have never built a single pickup truck are poised to bring them out in droves. Why? Because pickup trucks represent 19 percent of the market, and if we are going to grow, don't we need a pickup truck?

Thus the herd has decided that the supermarket approach to branding is the way to go. Let's offer something for everyone, and compete on price. Some, like GM, are finally learning that maybe they don't need more than one supermarket brand, Chevrolet.

Most brands have extended their product lineups. Brands such as Toyota, Chevrolet, and Ford are genuine supermarket brands and *should* offer a wide range of vehicles. The strategy is appropriate for them. For others, this movement stretches them too thin and reduces their brand's appeal.

The Smart "Smart" Customer

With each passing day, customers have more choice, more knowledge, and higher expectations—more choice as the result of proliferation and fragmentation, more choice as new manufacturers come to the US. At the 2006 Detroit Auto Show, the first Chinese exhibitor, Geely, revealed a car it plans to introduce in the fall of 2008. And as companies decide to expand their portfolios—as Toyota did recently with its Scion brand—there will be even more choice.

The Internet has opened up volumes of information that buyers can access as they shop for a new car. Information from manufacturers' sites, third-party sites, dealer sites, chat rooms, and the automotive press. You can learn the value of your trade-in and the invoice prices of vehicles that attract you. The typical new car shopper spends more than six hours doing homework, just on the Internet, before asking questions of John, the neighborhood car nut. ("Car nut" is our industry's sophisticated term for "expert" or "opinion leader.")

But here's the kicker: today's targeted consumers have higher expectations. Not only for the car industry but for every other industry they're exposed to. Some of those industries—consumer electronics comes to mind—make the car business look terminally dowdy. Customers expect more. And more. And more.

Not Enough Talent

Once, the car business seemed full of capable leaders. The domestic car industry's division—brand—structure was a marvelous teaching and testing ground. There always seemed to be a cadre of talented people running the car business.

Import companies siphoned off some of this talent even as the domestic car companies began increasingly centralizing their business. Today, fewer opportunities exist for middle managers to have real authority in reasonably autonomous profit centers working for strong leaders. Instead, the focus on short-term results, centralized authority, and lack of trust based on missed targets has increased pressure while reducing meaningful experience. We are burning out people we should be training for important work down the road.

A Brand Portfolio Primer

If we know how to make one brand a success, how do we apply those lessons to a brand portfolio? What are the key concepts and tenets that we must embrace?

The brands in a portfolio will compete with some brands that are stand-alone companies. Those companies live and die by what happens to their one and only brand. Bringing a single brand's level of focus and commitment to the portfolio is what it takes to successfully compete.

How can you optimize your brand portfolio? While we think of brand portfolios as spreading the opportunity, the financial community thinks of portfolios as spreading the risk. As fortunes rise and fall within consumer groups and segments, so will the fortunes of some of your brands. That is supposed to beat having all your eggs in one basket.

Brand Charter

Why do you want more than one brand? To appeal to buyers who are not interested in your first brand. In other words, to expand your reach. What brand promise and experience—fundamentally different from your current brand—would attract a new audience? Sounds obvious so far, yet all sorts of mischief can come into play.

Error one: can't I just expand my offerings to make myself more attractive to these different folks? Maybe yes, maybe no, but you run the risk of diluting your brand and alienating your core buyers. Volkswagen tried this with its $65,000 Phaeton and failed miserably, demonstrating that it was clueless about the image of its own brand. We call this brand extension.

Error two: can I create something from what I have and just *say* that I am different? You can, but you run the risk of diluting your focus and creating overlapping brands that add more incremental cost than incremental business. Ford and Mercury come to mind.

Welcome to the twin tests of market perspective and parenting. The test of perspective involves seeing the market as a battlefield filled with enemy forces. The goal is to array your forces (brands) in such a way that they are shooting at the enemy and not themselves.

Carlos Ghosn, CEO of both Renault and Nissan, told the *Wall Street Journal* in January 2006, that the Renault-Nissan alliance might someday add a third partner. "Why not?" he said, "we could use the same principles with more players." He went on to enumerate the principles—respect for each company's autonomy, cross-shareholdings to create common interests, and forbidding confusion among the brands.

Respect for autonomy and no confusion among brands. Effective thinking that is disarmingly clear but utterly absent at many large auto companies.

Which brings us to the test of parenting. What's critical to the development of a portfolio of desirable brands? Building strong separate brands takes tough love, and it takes discipline.

History shows what happens to weak brands that band together in an attempt to cost-cut their way out of trouble. The British car industry went through decades of consolidation, promising greater efficiency while losing market share with every merger. As one of our British colleagues loves to say, "We proved that one percent market share added to one percent market share equals one percent market share."

Charlie Hughes had the opportunity to lead a strategic think tank in the UK for Rover Group during BMW's ownership of the company. Ironically named Beyond BMW with Great British Brands, its charge was to select—from the long list of British brand names that BMW now owned—the brands Rover Group should develop. The team recommended consideration of four brands, selected because they were diverse and would appeal to separate audiences.

To codify the differences between the selected brands, the team created a charter for each brand. The charter defined where in the marketplace the brand would be positioned, what the essence of that brand would be, and to whom it would appeal. The goal was zero overlap.

A simple thought guided the team: the strength of a corporation lies in the power of its individual brands. And the team used the Brand Triangle^sm to aid it in conceptualizing a future brand portfolio strategy. The Brand Triangle^sm provides a good reality check in how different the brands truly are.

- Brand: Different audience? Different promise? Different experience? Any overlap?
- Culture: Nurtured by Brand? Brand centric or corporate centric?

- Product: Does each brand have its own strong technical point of view?
- Retail: Is each brand's audience seeking a different experience?

The Three Keys

If your goal is to have a portfolio of strong desirable brands, you must absolutely nail the first three of the seven components of great brands: differentiation, culture, and product. Demand that each brand be different and appeal to different customers; nurture separate cultures to support the desired differences in each brand; and invest in product that sets each brand apart from not only the other brands in the portfolio but, more important, from each brand's primary competition.

Doing this is no harder than riding an angry bull for ten minutes, but it must be done. Having a portfolio of brands is not an excuse to have a portfolio of second-place brands. To have multiple brands that are seen as best of their type takes courage, perspective, and an uncommon tolerance for decentralized leadership. Let's see how you can apply tough love to the seven key components of great brands.

Differentiation: Dare to Be Different, or Be Generic

On the surface it seems simple. To extend your reach into different markets with multiple brands, the brands should have different target markets, different competitors, different products, different marketing, different . . . you get the point. Too often they are the same brands in slightly altered clothing. Developing overlapping brands is the worst of all worlds, the proverbial triple threat. You double many of your costs, barely expand your appeal, and you create competition for yourself. You shoot yourself in the foot with a shotgun instead of a .22.

What are the hallmarks of an effective brand portfolio?

First, put the brands ahead of the corporation. Let the individual brands do the talking. Promote the brands, not the corporation. This will be news to many people in Detroit. Except for discussing corporate business results, the public relations, marketing, sales reporting, and other functions should be handled by the individual brands and should be specific to the brand.

Second, *clearly* define each brand. Each brand should make a promise important to its market and create an experience designed for its owners. In Chapter 3 (Differentiate), we emphasized the need for a brand's promise to be clear, compelling, and show real commitment. In the context of a brand portfolio, we add "distinct from its fellow brands."

Just as with one brand, each brand in a portfolio needs to strive to be the best in its category. Not the best we can afford, simply the best. Some of your competitors will surely bring their A game. You won't beat them with your B team. Ever.

Accept that selling basically the same car with different badges on it rarely saves money. Rather, it adds costs to vehicle design and duplicates your go-to-market expenses. That means before incurring the risk of bringing multiple brands to market, your brand portfolio strategy should include the specific technology game plan required to support each brand's market position and assure its competitiveness.

No company needs, nor can it afford, more than one supermarket brand. GM has Chevrolet, Ford has Ford, and Toyota has Toyota. Additional brands should pursue more targeted markets—accepting that their volume will be lower but that, done right, additional brands can mean additional profit.

To ensure the long-term differentiation of the brands in a portfolio, each brand needs a charter. That charter should include its target customers, its promise, its primary competitors, and its technological point of view. Each brand's strategy should be plotted using the Brand Triangle to design a specific experience for that brand's customers. Then the corporation must apply strict parenting to make sure that each brand develops along its intended path and is not encroached upon by sibling brands.

Culture: Who We Are and How We Do Things

Here's the dilemma: is "who we are" the brand we work on or the corporation we work for? Can it successfully be both? Where is the balance point? What values should we share as a corporation, and what aspects of culture need to be brand specific? These questions are not asked often enough, because most corporate heads obviously don't grasp the dilemma.

"We want to be one team with one culture." Is that so? Then what if, instead of a portfolio of automotive brands, you owned four sporting franchises—football, baseball, basketball, and hockey. Would you want one culture? One training camp? One group of talent scouts? Sounds ridiculous, doesn't it?

Some years back, GM decided that its field force would represent all its brands, not just one. This was a bad move. Customer expectations are different for each brand, just as they are for each sport. Fortunately it is moving away from this field force consolidation strategy.

If we want differentiated brands as well as customers who have different expectations, shouldn't "who we are and how we do things" drive those differences? Isn't it obvious that a single corporate culture acts as a homogenizer? Apparently not. If you treat having various brands as a shell game where brands are separated only by a thin marketing veneer, then rotating people from brand to brand and asking them to be one with their *current* brand makes perfect sense. Just don't expect them to have a clue as to what they need to do to make that brand a success. Passion for the corporation trumps passion for the brand. It wins the hand but loses the game.

What does it take to make each brand in the portfolio a success? A vision that sets the brand apart with the selected audience and a brand culture that makes it happen. Can you share some corporate values? Of course you can. But the prevailing attitude at the highest levels of the corporation should be brand centric not corporate centric. GM's slide in market share over the past 30 years can be traced to a company culture that went from being brand centric to corporate centric. Consolidating parts and manufacturing from division enterprises to large corporate groups started the shift away from brands. Soon, the drive for efficiencies began to hamper the individuality of the brands.

Roger Smith, the genius who choreographed much of GM's decline as its Chairman and CEO, rose through finance—a true born-again bean counter. He became chairman without ever having run a division. That gap in experience showed up every day of his reign. Unfortunately his legacy lives on. Believing that GM's existing revenue would go on forever, Smith's goal was to save as much money as possible as he pulled levers behind the wizard's curtain. He did not understand what was required to make a brand a success. He was wrong; a company's revenue base is never fixed, rather it has to earn its business everyday—even from a company's most devoted followers.

Under Smith's leadership, Pontiac and Oldsmobile at one point offered cars that had duplicate doors—exterior styling and all. How dumb did he think the public was? Twin brands is an oxymoron.

Smith's biggest crime by far, however, was creating a culture that thought in corporate terms. In GM's case, corporate is about as far removed from the marketplace—and frequently from reality— as you can get and still remain on this planet. GM started to defrock its divisions and castrate their division managers until divisions ceased being divisions and became "brands" with marketing managers in charge.

Under Ron Zarella, the madness went into high gear. Zarella brought in outside brand managers who couldn't tell a lug nut from a fortune cookie and told them to apply the cosmetics of difference. Parenthetically, Zarella was billed as a master portfolio manager but was the man who, among other missteps, vetoed the Cadillac Escalade. Zarella left, and the Escalade was not only approved but went on to become a best seller and help re-establish the Cadillac brand.

In a brutally competitive world you need people who see themselves as special, who want to belong to a team that loves its brand. A team that lives with its customers and knows what turns them on. Zealots who make their brand a must-have.

Does each brand need to be a stand-alone company? Of course not. But to be a brand-centric company, the principal operating committee needs to be populated by the brand heads. Corporate functions, all of them, should fall under a corporate services group. This group must be a service provider to the brands, and everyone should know its role is subordinate to the brand. It is the clearest way to say, "Our individual customers come first."

Each brand team needs to be responsible for all of the areas that contribute directly to its success. In the car business, that would include strategy that falls under the brand's charter, brand development, product development, retail, and culture. Functionally, that means marketing, sales, public relations, retail, and training, after sales (service), sales planning, product planning, finance (each brand should be a profit center), design, and vehicle development.

Areas that should fall under corporate services include legal, IT, human resources, corporate PR, treasury, insurance, purchasing, engineering, testing and certification, media buying (but not media planning), parts, physical distribution, and advanced technology and advanced manufacturing engineering.

The one wild card is manufacturing. BMW keeps manufacturing separate by brand, which appears to be an easy—and wise—decision because its cars (BMW, Rolls-Royce, and Mini) are so starkly different. Other companies have common manufacturing. There is a down side to this issue. When you centralize manufacturing, as GM did with the General Motors Assembly Division, the very next thought is how can we reduce costs by reducing complexity? Complexity often becomes code for those pesky product differences that set brands apart—the very things that make your brand desirable to *your* customers.

Each brand needs its own separate environment; grouping brands into a large corporate headquarters will only further homogenize them. You want each team to establish its own identity and spend its time looking at the competition—not waste effort looking over the shoulders of the other brands in the portfolio or worrying about who's pawing through its in-baskets. It is difficult to be different if you live in the same house with all your siblings and are constantly comparing yourself—and being compared—with them.

Understanding the nuts and bolts of how you do it is worthless if you fail to see the importance of culture to begin with. Unless you commit to the concept that great brands spring from driven cultures, your brand portfolio will wander in the wilderness like Moses. The good news is that it won't wander for 40 years but will die relatively soon.

Product: Choose between Distinct and Extinct

Within a brand portfolio, each brand's products must be distinct without obvious overlap. In the car business this means that each brand should have its own strong technology point of view—technology it uses to design and engineer cars that make its products arguably better than their primary competition.

Perhaps the car business is unique regarding the role of product in the marketing mix. A vehicle is, after all, a durable good—an *expensive* durable good that many buyers will spend more than five years paying for. For everyone, a vehicle represents independence; for many, it represents their very soul. American's love affair with the automobile is still in high gear.

For years, pundits have lamented the commoditization of cars and their conversion to passionless transportation devices. Toyota has been accused of leading this charge. That is unfair, because many Toyota buyers love their cars and trucks. But we are talking about a portfolio of brands. Even if you wanted one of your brands to appeal to the non-passionate, you wouldn't want *two* of them to do that. Would you?

Each brand in your portfolio needs products that suit its target market. The surest sign of overlapping brands is overlapping product lineups. We know all the arguments for reducing costs through platform and or component sharing. It can be effective when done intelligently and with a full understanding of what is important in a product to each brand's customer. But this discussion is secondary. To make each brand in your portfolio a winner, you must fulfill your promise with a product that is arguably better than that brand's primary competition. It is hard to do that by picking parts out of a corporate parts bin. Some will be okay, but others will be disappointing.

GM, in revitalizing Cadillac, has demonstrated that it knows how to build at least one competitive brand. Rebuilding Cadillac took vision, it took courage, and it took money. It took a new lineup of cars on their own platform using Cadillac powertrains. GM exercised its will to make Cadillac competitive with other world-class brands. Through 2005, GM has not demonstrated the courage to apply those lessons to its other brands. Perhaps the experience was more fatiguing than inspiring, for with the introduction of the new Buick Lucerne, GM is again offering the Cadillac Northstar V-8 in a non-Cadillac product—a shortcut to brand dilution.

We've said numerous times that the focus and investment required today to build a desirable and authentic brand may be so great that even the largest companies can effectively build no more than two or three brands. If so, could GM logically consider paring down to Chevrolet and Cadillac? We'll see.

Conspiracy: Who Wants to Be, Who Needs to Be, on the Inside

If you agree conceptually that each brand team needs to have its own mini-culture, encouraging that team to develop its own conspiracy should be simple. It's apparently not. Too often, the corporation's need for control and its drive for apparent—rather than real—cost reduction will smother the effort.

The need for creativity on the part of people who are attracted to your cause becomes even more important when you're part of a large corporation. The need for this creativity to reach critical mass is no less important. It is simply more difficult.

The degree of difficulty is obvious to all who have worked for

General Motors or Ford, or any number of large corporations. The "needs" of the corporation weigh on you like a wet overcoat. Doing business with or within these companies is challenging. Not because of the high standards being demanded, but because of a commodity mindset that demands virtually everything be bid, bought once, and then used across all divisions.

These constant beauty contests not only slow down the work flow, they dampen the enthusiasm of your potential suppliers. Much of the process is degrading, and little of it even begins to measure the true value and true cost of the work. Learning curves are steep, and the cost to both parties in terms of wasted time and missteps is enormous.

When you are buying aluminum ore or fertilizer, requiring bids makes sense. Advertising is not a commodity; PR is not a commodity; and neither are other creative contributions you need. Then there is the matter of chemistry. It is the brand team's task to find and develop suppliers, dealers—and also customers, of course—who are like-minded and who are just dying to be part of the team and its success story.

One final note: building a conspiracy requires inspired leadership. The successful talent search finds leaders mature enough to know their role in the corporation and perceptive enough to know that the success of the corporation is measured by the success or failure of each brand.

The people who head each brand in a company's portfolio need to be polished spokespersons for that brand. In their own way they need to be charismatic. They are the pied piper who brings everyone else along. They must be viewed as powerful people within the corporation. And, as they say in the hallways, positioned well above the corporate suits.

Consistency: Whoever You Are, Be That Everywhere

Consistency in a portfolio of brands follows the same tenets as for a single brand: each brand has its own distinct vision and promise, a well-designed and suitable owner experience, its own tone of voice, and most important, consistency of leadership.

Let's start with consistency of leadership. Large corporations can't seem to help themselves when it comes to rotating people in key jobs. Running a brand in a portfolio should be the most sought-after job in a company. The corporation must select its brand leaders with great care, knowing that only a handful of people have the experience and leadership skills to thrive in the job. And it must pay them world-class pay for world-class performance.

Guess what? Leaders are not interchangeable. Some people have a bent for bigness, which is perfect for running a supermarket brand. Some have a knack for specialty or niche brands. Some have a performance background, and some are truckers. Leaders have interests, histories, and personalities. They must be carefully matched to the brand they are to build. Once there, the tour of duty should be no less than five or six years with ten years the goal. What if we get it wrong, what if our new brand leader misses his sales targets? The corporation's primary job is to find and groom talent. Mistakes in this selection process are not acceptable. A company needs to invest in a reliable developmental selection process without churning people every 18 months in search of the perfect generalist.

Beware of the sanitizing process that trains people to be good corporate citizens. To successfully run a brand in today's punishing environment, you need leaders with character and who are characters. You want people who combine real expertise with personality. People with vision, people with entrepreneurial skills, and people who can fight for their brand within a large company. Independent-minded folks who love "their" brand and have the grit to grow it.

It is sad that many ambitious folks will read the above and say, "Why would I settle for being a brand manager when I want to run the corporation?" It's only a necessary whistle stop. Get my ticket punched and up, up we go. That attitude is sinking brands in portfolios every day. Is it any wonder that we don't have a clue as to what Buick or Mercury represent? More and more we have artificial brands led by corporate transients. Years ago in the packaged goods business this was called the P&G (for Procter & Gamble) Brand Management System. P&G abandoned it more than a generation ago. Why? Basically because it bred managers whose short-term thinking and tactics produced short-term gains at the expense of long-term brand goals. One of the key symptoms was—you guessed it—heavy, manic discounting.

As in most things, consistent, effective leadership makes things work. And part of being effective is sensitivity to the essence of the brand. Real brand leaders don't change the campaign, the tagline, and then the agency with the changing seasons. They clearly hear their brand's tone of voice and know that voice is working every day to advance the brand's fortunes. They know the power of consistency and believe that they will be in place long enough to see it work.

We have seen how difficult staying the course can be as the world changes in dramatic ways—as it so frequently does.

Two fuel crises in the 1970s and the spiking of gas prices in 2006 are examples. As the demand for better fuel economy grows, all brands in an automotive portfolio must respond. But their responses must be in character. In response to the second 1970s fuel crisis, GM allowed Cadillac to build the Cimarron off the Chevrolet Cavalier small-car platform. Wrong decision. This bit of badge engineering made Cadillac a laughing stock and badly wounded its image. What Cadillac did was akin to Burberry bringing out a line of cheap plastic raincoats—a move that, thankfully, Burberry has resisted.

The latest fad or trend is hybrids. Does GM need to get on the bandwagon? Yes. Does it need to offer them in every brand in the GM portfolio? No. GM should offer them where they support the brand promise and suit the brand's audience. Saturn is ideal, with Chevrolet right behind. Pontiac must take a pass, thereby avoiding the necessity of marketing a "performance hybrid." It is easy to see how, without discipline and over time, brands float out of character and become similar and less relevant.

Consistency at the brand level is dependent on a precise differentiation of the brand, reinforced by the parent's determination to keep it that way.

Passion: Energy, Enthusiasm, and Expertise

Passion is the fuel for building great brands. Passion for one brand among a portfolio of brands is no less important, just more difficult to generate. It requires corporate leadership that enjoys and encourages employees to demonstrate passion for their brand—in lieu of passion for the corporation. Being part of a corporation that you like should be rational. Being part of a brand team should be emotional. You compete in the market at the emotional level, and it is at that level that you win or lose.

Charlie Hughes worked at Cadillac in the early 1970s. When asked, he and his compatriots would say they worked at Cadillac. Not GM. The corporation was clearly in the background. GM was huge at the time, and most of its employees could not begin to get their heads around the corporation. But a single brand? That was something you could be proud of.

GM's brands were divisions back then, and they looked like stand-alone companies. No more. The continuous weakening of brands has led to ongoing downsizing. The steady move toward centralization and GM centric thinking has extinguished most of the passion that employees and customers alike once felt for the individual brands. If GM is to recover, this must change.

At the risk of repetitiveness, corporations must celebrate the distinctiveness and individuality of each brand in their portfolio, actively encourage each brand to live the brand in their culture, and demand products that live up to the brands promise—thereby laying the groundwork for passionate employees, suppliers, retailers, and customers. How in the world do you expect a customer to feel passion for a brand if the brand team doesn't?

To energy and enthusiasm, we need to add expertise—expertise in consumers, in products, in designs, and in technology. There must be widespread and effective expertise driving a brand to successfully be itself. The existence of passion for a brand that is part of a brand portfolio functions as a true test of differentiation.

Patience: Having the Courage of Your Convictions

Parenting is as much a test of tolerance as it is of patience. Do kids learn at the same rate? Do they mature at the same rate? Do they excel equally at school? Do they always stay out of trouble? Of course not, and it would be just as naïve to think that all brands will perform the same way as their portfolio siblings.

Portfolios are attractive because they extend your reach into different customer groups. Do these target markets grow at the same rate? Are they cyclically aligned? Do they all generate the same return on sales? Not likely, yet these are more examples of how unrealistic expectations can get in the way of success.

Patience is the final test, because unless and until you get the other components right you have little to be patient about. You can only be steadfast to a well-thought-out and properly executed strategy.

A portfolio strategy also spreads your risk. Having one of several brands encounter difficulty beats having your one and only brand struggle. At some time or other, they will each struggle. That's when the world will see whether you have the courage of your convictions.

We have defined patience as being steadfast to the vision and the plan for bringing that vision to reality. Focus and faith are required. Faith in the vision and in the plan. Focus on the individual brands, not the corporation.

Patience requires public commitment and large investments. Again picking on GM, if you say Pontiac is your performance brand, you cannot quit until you have reinvented the American muscle car and made BMWs seem like overpriced cars for poseurs and the recently divorced. Shout your intent and do not retreat. Being steadfast to the right idea can reward you beyond the dreams of avarice.

Putting It All Together

Managing a brand portfolio is Parenting 101. You must see each brand as an individual, with its own unique abilities and needs. Fairness and discipline are required. Each brand cannot have everything the other has, and it must be encouraged to develop along its own path. In this family we strive for individuality.

And, in the final analysis, isn't that what branding is all about? Do it well, and your portfolio can be greater than the sum of its parts. Do it poorly, and you'll just create a collection of products, not brands.

Remember Benjamin Franklin's line about the thirteen colonies need to hang together lest they hang separately. We'd reverse that in the case of brand portfolio management: "If we don't live—brand—separately, we will hang. Whether together or separately is of no consequence, but without separation, death is certain."

11

Fixing Ford and GM—
Some Modest Proposals

"Too many brands, too many dealers, too many plants, too many people."

Jerry Pyle, President of Friedkin Automotive, on the woes plaguing GM and Ford, Detroit Free Press, *May 14, 2006*

Is that the real problem? Too many brands, too many dealers, too many plants, too many people? No. The real problem is too few customers. A shortage of customers leads to all the other problems. Lest we forget, both Ford and GM at one time found ways to make themselves attractive enough to sell cars in sufficient quantity to support their brands, dealers, plants, and people.

The real question is: in an overbranded world, what does it take to attract more customers?

Conventional Wisdom

"All we need to do is work a little harder and execute a bit better." Too many companies that have utterly failed to differentiate themselves add this "wisdom" as another nail in the coffin.

A lot of companies are being outworked and outhustled in the marketplace. The Asian car companies have been tireless in outworking the competition. But the spectacle of a company spending 12 hours a day executing a poor strategy—and even Asian companies have done that—makes *Hamlet* look like a sidesplitting comedy.

Companies experiencing flat or declining sales for an extended time must make a clear-eyed assessment of what they're doing wrong—and they should begin by examining their basic branding strategy. A lack of differentiation, though not always the only reason, is frequently the cause. If you have been unable to get yourself noticed, ask yourself why? Timid strategy? Poor execution? Or some combination of both? Or you could simply admit that the competition is smarter and faster.

The Reality of the Situation

GM and Ford are in a struggle for their very survival. This pains us. Both authors grew up in the car business, and both worked many years in Detroit. We desperately want the domestic companies to succeed because we've worked for some of them.

Despite a lot of introspection and free advice, Ford and GM have yet to zero in on what is causing the erosion of their market share: they are not making themselves more desirable to customers than their key competitors. And their brand portfolios, instead of broadening their appeal, are draining the life out of them.

We're contrarians, so we see the domestic's brand portfolios as a potential competitive advantage. That said, does anyone outside of GM believe that GM can be successful in the US with eight brands and a market share of only 24 percent? Does Ford need, or can it afford, seven brands with an 18 percent market share? Toyota is moving past a 14 percent market share and has only three brands—and until two years ago it had only two.

GM and Ford have demonstrated their will to make tough decisions on the expense side of the profit ledger. Both companies, in the spring of 2006, were in the throes of reducing their employees by 25,000 to 30,000 each while shutting numerous plants. God knows, that is painful. But, as tough as this has been, they have steadfastly refused to make the tough calls on the revenue side by developing a brand portfolio strategy that culls out the losers. To say, "plants and workers are fair game, but brands are sacrosanct," only treats half of the patient.

Forbes Global 2000

Look at how GM and Ford are ranked on the Forbes Global 2000, compared with Toyota at one extreme and Porsche at the other. Toyota, with slightly lower sales then either GM or Ford, has four times the profit of Ford and a market value almost seven times greater than that of GM and Ford combined. Porsche's market value is almost equal to Ford's on one-twentieth of Ford's sales. The conclusion seems obvious. Those who focus their energy on a single or primary brand win. Doubt that? Little Porsche recently bought 20 percent of the Volkswagen group, a company that has dissipated its efforts through brand acquisitions.

	Toyota	Ford	General Motors	Porsche
Forbes 2000 Rank	12	133	526	526
Sales	$173.09	$178.1	$192.6	$7.97
Profits	$10.93	$2.25	–$10.6	$0.95
Assets	$227.05	$275.96	$475.28	$11.55
Market Value	$175.54	$15.21	$11.49	$14.74
Employees	265,753	324,864	324,000	11,878

*All dollar figures are in billions.

Drastic branding actions are a necessity, a matter of life and death. As farfetched as it would have sounded even five years ago, both are at risk of going out of business or being purchased. Both GM and Ford need to bang the kaleidoscope, create a new vision, and reinvent themselves. Their world has changed too drastically to accept thinking that says they can repair what they have. They don't have unlimited talent—or money—and time is against them. So far, we have heard lots of the same old rhetoric that boils down to "this time we will do it better." We feel they're missing the point: their revenue model is wrong, their brand strategy too complex, and they don't have the resources required to do it their way.

Reality-based thinking means seeing things—yourself and the market—as they are. No polite talk, no euphemisms. Just tough questions such as, what is the market telling you loud and clear? The marketplace will identify which brands are successes, which have potential, which are lost causes, and which don't fit in with your long-term goals. Some brands are walking cadavers that have been mismanaged for decades. Just shoot them and let them rest in peace. Reallocate those resources to conviction brands that are healthy and that can grow. Don't spread yourself so thin that you cannot win anywhere.

First, What about General Motors?

As we go to press, Kirk Kerkorian, who owns 9.9 percent of General Motors, has approached Carlos Ghosn, Chairman and CEO of Renault and Nissan, to buy an interest in GM. Fresh eyes might well help General Motors, but whoever is in charge will have to address GM's surplus of brands. And it won't be easy.

General Motors is one hard nut to crack. Historically the world's largest automaker, the General has struggled with the global brand concept. It's difficult to believe, but GM does not have a world-dominant brand. Until recently, it essentially sold its biggest volume brand, Chevrolet, only in the Americas.

When you look at the brands GM sells worldwide, you could argue that the company has clung to a regional instead of global brand strategy. With the distraction of selling eight brands in the US, it took Chevrolet 19 years to outsell Ford in 2005 and become the number-one selling brand in the country. Is Chevrolet a global brand like Ford? No, not really, and it will be tough to make Chevrolet a global brand because GM has a big mass merchandise brand in Europe called Opel. In 2005, Opel was the third-largest seller behind Volkswagen and Renault and ahead of Ford and Peugeot.

Well, that is not entirely accurate. To become number three, GM must combine Vauxhall with Opel. Vauxhall is GM's British subsidiary, which makes tiny changes and applies the Vauxhall badge to Opel models.

GM's brand mess is not relegated to the US. Now, to make life even more interesting, GM has decided to make Chevrolet a global brand. A first step was to badge Daewoo models built in Korea as Chevrolets and import them to Europe. They now have three brand names to market in Europe. And who does Chevrolet compete with among others? Well, there's Opel and Vauxhall, of course.

Thinking just about the United States, can GM make sense of this mess? GM should start by concentrating on its two lead brands, Chevrolet and Cadillac, not with words but with tough pruning actions that cut off the saplings preventing Chevrolet and Cadillac from growing. It's time to get rid of internal competition, be it competition for product development resources, marketing budgets, dealer attention, or competing for the same customers. Maintaining that level of internal rivalry is nuts.

Growing Chevrolet means getting rid of the second entry-level brand, Saturn. Turning Saturn into Opel West, as Bob Lutz has suggested, benefits only Saturn. It drains resources and would create a product lineup that had to be imported or adapted for the US market. Sell Saturn lock stock and barrel to one of GM's Chinese partners. That would give some Chinese manufacturer a strong brand name, a great dealer body, and a competitive plant in Spring Hill, Tennessee. A tightly focused and well-funded Chevrolet can more than offset the loss of 200,000 Saturn sales.

At the same time, GM should sell Hummer and sell or close Saab. This pair's combined sales in 2005 were less than 100,000 units. Hummer is GM's fourth truck brand behind Chevrolet,

GMC, and Cadillac. Is fragmenting one's effort to market four truck brands an impediment to growing market share? Yes it is.

GM has made noises about combining Cadillac, Hummer, and Saab at the retail level. This is insane. Cadillac is competing with BMW, Mercedes-Benz, and Lexus, all of which depend on the tight customer focus applied by their exclusive dealers. Luxury car buyers want the attention exclusive dealers provide. In 2005, Cadillac had 1,482 dealers to BMW's 339, Mercedes-Benz's 407, and Lexus's 215. Cadillac has far too many stores already—the average Cadillac dealer sold only 108 cars in 2005 compared to 712 at Lexus dealers. GM cannot afford to dilute its resources this way.

Hummer is one of GM's most successfully differentiated brands, but its potential is small, and it's a distraction. However, Hummer is an intriguing brand and could likely be sold for a profit. A major issue, of course, is that Hummer products are based on GM truck platforms, so unbundling Hummer may be challenging.

Saab is a sad case and a lost cause. From the beginning, GM has made a complete hash out of Saab, and it is time to let Saab go. There may be a group of Swedish investors, much like the British group that bought and lost on Rover, who want to give Saab one last try. If not, GM should just shut it down. They already plan to shut down the last Saab plant in Sweden.

These moves would free GM to focus the necessary energy to make Chevrolet and Cadillac winning brands.

In the middle, GM is moving to combine Pontiac, GMC truck, and Buick at the dealer level. That way each brand can be who GM has claimed they could be. Pontiac and Buick could stop building overlapping, badge-engineered products to feed two dealer bodies. Resurrecting Pontiac and Buick is a world-class challenge; Bob Lutz was right when he said they were damaged brands.

Is it possible? The issue is this: can GM effectively develop even five brands? Does it have the leadership and financial resources? Is GM serious about making Pontiac and Buick conviction brands that make a market for themselves? If so, GM must deliver authentic genuine products for each brand—products that are like nothing else GM sells and are highly desirable in the marketplace. What we are talking about here is nothing less than a near-total attitudinal shift within the GM culture.

And what effect does pouring resources into Pontiac, GMC, and Buick have on the two primary brands, Chevrolet and Cadillac? We'd hope that the money generated by selling Saab, Hummer, and Saturn would offset that in the short term. But, as we said at the beginning, GM is a tough nut to crack.

Multiple brands, overlapping brands, and no real global brands portend a dark future for GM. The existing GM brand strategy lacks focus, clarity, and energy. Which of GM's brands makes a clear promise? How many of its brands have thought through the entire ownership experience and made it memorable? To make a strong comeback, GM must grapple with these issues. Quickly. The company is squandering a fortune marketing undifferentiated brands that have no global scope.

Ford: Is There a Solution for ANYONE?

Using the tenets set forth in *Branding Iron*, we will lay out a possible brand portfolio strategy for Ford Motor Company. Our strategies are radical, controversial and, to borrow a Ford phrase, "Bold Moves," far bolder than Ford's "The Way Forward" initiative. We recognize the practical difficulties that argue against some of our solutions. However, we also recognize the pain and suffering that accompany bankruptcy and failure. If anyone reading this feels that radical problems can be solved by halfway—or half-baked—strategies, you've wasted your money on this book.

Our proposed strategy for Ford results in a more manageable number of brands and puts the spotlight on their volume brand. The attraction of the Ford proposals is that each remaining brand could be a force in the global market. The recommendations focus on revenue generation through clear differentiation of each brand in the portfolio and in the market.

Our goal is to concentrate on fewer and stronger brands that have no overlap. The personality and strength of each brand would grow rapidly with fewer sibling distractions. Balancing global circumstances with US market needs makes our plan a natural. But we would say that, wouldn't we? We call this the Dearborn Plan:

> Ford Motor company should move to three worldwide brands: Ford, Volvo, and Jaguar. Sell Land Rover, Aston Martin, and Mazda. Shut down Mercury and Lincoln altogether.

Brands to Build

We would like to think the reasons why Ford should choose these brands is obvious, but let's leave nothing to chance. With the exception of Land Rover, these are Ford's three strongest brand names, and they nicely fit a strategy that says the Ford brand comes first as a dominant world player—as a supermarket brand. Ford is solid and basic. Volvo will be a clear step up that has no conflict or overlap with Ford and appeals to an entirely different audience. Jaguar will become a true luxury offering that is genuinely attractive to affluent people throughout the world.

Despite its corporate problems, Ford remains one of the world's strongest auto brands. Eleven automotive brands appeared on the 2006 list of the top 100 brands as judged by Millward Brown's Optimor, a brand consulting service. Of Ford's seven brands, only the Ford brand made the list, finishing just ahead of Chevrolet but trailing Toyota (at number 10, the highest-ranking automaker), BMW, Mercedes-Benz, and Honda. If the Ford Motor Company placed the lion's share of its focus, energy, creativity, and funding into the Ford brand, how far could it go?

Above Ford but below Jaguar, we'd put Volvo, a clearly differentiated cut above Ford. Volvo's family appeal and reputation for safety have made it a world brand that can be grown in all major markets.

At the top of Ford's three brands, Jaguar can again be a standout luxury brand with worldwide credentials. It has suffered through "expansion" efforts by Ford that have diluted its luxury stance, but its core attributes for success remain. It has also been artificially limited by having Aston Martin and Land Rover as stable mates. By selling Aston Martin and Land Rover, Ford would be able to pursue making Jaguar a true rival to BMW and Mercedes-Benz—a no-excuses rival that could push the Germans to the limit.

All three brands, based on heritage alone, have the seeds of a genuine brand promise, and each can develop relevant and differentiated experiences for their owners.

What makes this strategy so compelling is that all three brands appeal to entirely different audiences. They are successful world brands that can be even more successful. There is no overlap between the brands, and each can conquest sales from the competition, growing and prospering in separate sectors of the market.

Brands to Discard

Given its drive and talent, we believe that Ford could challenge for worldwide supremacy if the company put its heart and all its ammunition into the effort. That would require far more discipline than its leadership has demonstrated for more than two decades. It would also require euthanizing two confection brands, Lincoln and Mercury, which have been badge-engineering exercises at best and don't have the brand image of a sack of potatoes.

In the first four months of 2006, the nation's 1,968 Mercury dealers sold 68,000 units, down five percent from last year. That's less than a dozen cars per month per dealership. Dealers had six models to sell: Milan, Montego, Grand Marquis, Mariner, Monterey, and Mountainer. The parent company had to not only design, engineer, and tool for those models, it also had to advertise and market them. Each of the models is a triumph, if that's an appropriate word, of badge engineering.

Meanwhile, in the same period, it required 1,361 Lincoln dealers to sell 44,000 units, up six percent from last year. As with Mercury, Lincoln needed to engineer, tool, build, and market six models: Zephyr (now the MKZ), LS, Town Car, Mark LT, Aviator, and Navigator. In 2005, Ford spent $299.3 million to advertise Lincoln and Mercury, or $935 per unit (319,000 total sales).

Is this crazy or what? To sell 319,000 Toyotas would have required only 197 dealers. Could the message be any clearer?

We know Ford would correctly say that Lincoln and Mercury vehicles are sold at dualed dealerships within Ford, achieving at least some efficiency, and it would also say that those brands contribute to its bottom line. In a funny accounting way, perhaps, but at what price? The costs in lost opportunity and duplicated efforts are astronomical. Imagine a Ford driven to be the biggest brand in the industry on the offensive. No more road maps to recovery, no more wasted energy trying to make sense of Mercury and Lincoln. Just pure Ford throughout the world.

As we mentioned earlier, we're hardly unaware of the problems inherent in executing this strategy, not the least of which is what to do with all those Lincoln-Mercury dealers. The question remains, however: can Ford afford *not* to do something about a division that drains resources of all kinds? If Ford doesn't take action on Lincoln and Mercury, the marketplace surely will.

Disposing of Winning Brands

It is emotionally difficult to sell a brand that is a winner, and Mazda, Aston Martin, and Land Rover, each in its own way, are winning brands. But even winners require energy and financial resources to maintain, and they can conflict with other parts of a company's brand portfolio.

It hurts to suggest that Ford sell one of our all-time favorite brands, Land Rover. Our sadness is somewhat mitigated by Land Rover's having just finished dead last in the J.D. Power 2006 Initial Quality Survey. Emotion aside, Ford should stick to three brands, and those three should be the strongest brands in its portfolio. Land Rover has the most limited potential. Furthermore, its presence has prevented Jaguar from becoming a full-line luxury brand. Sell it.

Aston Martin is Ford being a dilettante, dabbling at being a specialty manufacturer. Owning it is pretentious and sends the signal that mass merchandise vehicles are somehow beneath you. The head of Aston Martin, Ulrich Bez, is an extremely talented man. Although he is not British, he would be a sane choice to lead Jaguar in the early years of its reformation. Soon, Jaguar coupes wouldn't have to look likes sub-par Aston Martins. Meanwhile, sell Aston Martin to some sheik.

The final part of the strategy requires that Ford sell its interest in Mazda. Mazda is an entry-level brand, and Ford does not need two of them; it needs to concentrate on the big one. Ford management has helped turn Mazda around, and there's no doubt that Ford has effectively mined the relationship. Still and all, Mazda gets in the way of making the Ford brand world dominant. And it would relieve Ford of having to balance the interests of the Ford and Mazda brands in major growth markets such as China.

Because Mazda, Land Rover, and Aston Martin are successful and profitable, selling them would generate cash that could be invested in developing a more resolute and successful company.

The New Brand Portfolio

With those dispositions made, the Ford brand would become top gun within the Ford stable, and it could become that in the world market. Ford needs to reinvent itself as an aggressive "we build the best cars for the money in any segment you might want" company. It should set its sights on beating Toyota—a noble mission worthy of its finest efforts. Clearly this would take a seismic change in thinking at Ford, but Ford took on Toyota with the first Taurus, and it whipped them.

Volvo, positioned as near-luxury, European, family, and the safest vehicles on earth, should aim for worldwide volumes approaching a million units a year within the coming decade.

In a 2006 interview with *Fortune's* Alex Taylor III, Volvo CEO Fredrik Arp said: "Volvo can be as big as Mercedes or BMW, but we have to be committed over time, consistent, and decisive." He's right. And where have we heard that before?

"We aren't as individualistic as BMW or Mercedes," Arp continued. "We lean more toward the family, but we're still a prestigious brand of car. If we can grow in a good way, then why not? We have some good opportunities." Right again.

In the new Ford Motor Company, Jaguar can become a highly desirable and authentic alternative to Mercedes and BMW. The goal should be a Bentley level of luxury and prestige at a BMW price—a pure conviction brand that believes it knows more about style, luxury, and living well than the Germans or Japanese—as well it should. Jaguar should not be in the small car business, so its growth goals of necessity would be more modest—in the 300,000 range globally.

The war Jaguar wants to win is prestige that can't be found on every street corner. We're sorry, but a Jaguar should not be "accessible." Achieve a high standing in the prestige market, and high profits will follow.

To make this strategy work requires concentrating talent at each brand and making substantial investments in product and marketing. But most of all, it demands that Ford clear the deck of superfluous brands and get down to the business of making these three brands the best in the world. The seeds of greatness are there. It is easy to see a clear compelling brand promise and a differentiated ownership experience for each of the three. Only commitment is missing.

Culture

For Dearborn Reborn to work, radical changes in culture that go beyond believing beyond that "culture eats strategy for breakfast" must be made at Ford. The company must overcome its embedded preference for centralized management, its frequently observed climate of fear, and its decades-old penchant for treating its suppliers as outsiders and second-class citizens. Or, more succinctly, like garbage.

Ford Motor Company would have to recast its own view of itself. The new Ford would see a global corporation with each of its three strong brands having its own structure and leadership. Each brand's leadership would sit on Ford's board of directors. That alone would make a powerful statement.

Synergies would come from a federal structure in which Ford Corporate would provide shared services that add efficiency without impinging upon a brand's ability to differentiate itself in the marketplace. We've discussed the potential split of responsibilities in Chapter 10, and there is no rulebook on how to make it work. But the default position should be desirability before efficiency—a complete reversal from how Ford has historically worked. The brands simply need to be responsible for their own differentiation and efficiency—and their own success.

The above philosophy sets the stage for encouraging each brand to design and nurture its own brand culture—the "who we are and how we do things" part of the equation that so profoundly affects the ownership experience.

Embracing decentralized management is critical to success. That will not happen with all three brands "working together" in Detroit. That's another reason why these three brands are a naturally strong lineup, for the three don't sit comfortably in one location, and if they did, the location surely wouldn't be Detroit, Michigan.

It is tempting to suggest moving Ford Corporate Headquarters away from Detroit. When corporate staffs and line staffs work in proximity, corporate control always seems to win out. GM's former chairman, Jack Smith, when he headed GM Europe, limited its staff to 300 and moved them to Zurich, away from the temptation to meddle with Opel. He understood the issue. Can a Ford Corporate Headquarters and a reborn Ford brand prosper together in Dearborn? And what effect would that have on Volvo and Jaguar? We say move the corporate headquarters to Chicago, which would give the new strategy a chance to take root and signal to one and all that Ford is serious about its new strategy.

On the other hand, Ford Group Services—which could include such functions as engineering services, corporate power train, advanced engineering, purchasing, manufacturing process design, parts supply chain management, and the like—should be located in Dearborn with operations in Cologne and China for Ford and in Sweden and the UK for Volvo and Jaguar. Although a support group, it needs to be fully committed and involved with each brand team.

The Ford brand must be led by a single strong management team responsible for the brand's performance worldwide. They should be located in Dearborn with regional headquarters in Dearborn, Cologne, and China. The Ford brand would become a single group as is the case with its major Japanese competitors. Ford's culture would be a natural extension of the giant it has always been— once it's purged of fear and careerism. People would move freely within the Ford brand, but they would not take ticket-punching excursions to Volvo or Jaguar "to broaden their experience."

Volvo would headquarter in Sweden. However, to become more aggressive in North America it would need an expanded presence here. The North America headquarters would be in the New York area, affording easy access to Sweden. Ideally, a Swede would lead Volvo, and its culture should be Swedish with a small "s."

Jaguar would be located in the UK, in Coventry. Ideally, a talented Briton would lead it and would lure the best British designers back to the motherland. Style has been and should always be a Jaguar hallmark. The Jaguar culture should be stylish, educated, refined, and tasteful. Jaguar must cultivate a profile of being the top luxury brand in the world, and that must be lived inside the company. Casual Friday would not include jeans or khakis with T-shirts. Not even if they came from the Ozwald Boateng shop in Mayfair. Jaguar would be proud of its British heritage, but again writ with a small "b."

As with Volvo, Jaguar would have a strong design and engineering presence in the US, and its North American headquarters should remain in New Jersey.

Product

To elevate all three brands to world-class standards will require that each brand's product programs be largely bespoke. We know, we know, where are the synergies? Learning from Ford's own sad history with Mercury and Lincoln, the corporation's philosophy should be to concentrate on shared processes and allow more autonomy of design based on each brand's DNA. The synergies that occur within a single brand can be more important than synergies within a corporation.

Let's use BMW as an example. Its planners drive cost reduction by designing a basic platform such as the 3 series and then spinning as many variants off that investment as possible: four-door sedans, coupes, convertibles, wagons, and crossover SUVs. Powertrains are shared throughout the range, and even when BMW designs a sports car, major components such as suspensions, brakes, and powertrains are common with other BMWs. That is vertical sharing—sharing *within* a brand—at its best.

But BMW is much larger than either Volvo or Jaguar, so each would have to share more, right? No. Not if you want to be competitive with BMW and grow both brands. Volvo and Jaguar already have unique architecture. The goal would be to apply that architecture to more variations, thereby spreading the cost of basic design work and broadening their appeal in the market.

Jaguar has world-class architecture in its aluminum XJ platform used in the 2007 XK. It needs to be further applied to all Jaguars, meaning ways must be found to drive down the cost through ongoing engineering and economies of scale. Without this kind of strong technical differentiation, Jaguar will never escape Ford's shadow and compete with the world's best.

So each brand would continue to perfect its unique architecture in two sizes that would be used throughout their product range.

"You're dreaming," people within the industry will say to us. Yes, we are. Our dream is of three highly desirable brands that do not cannibalize each other, that don't require 7,000 dealers to lose money in North America, and which are free to grow as fast as they can by aggressively making a promise and delivering on it. There are material benefits from being members of the same family, and a staggering amount of effort can be shared—but without cannibalizing sales or sinking to badge engineering. Some examples follow.

Gasoline powertrains should be brand specific. Diesel power trains can be corporately sourced, but their applications should be brand specific. Hybrids and new technology power trains should also be corporate creations, but their application should be adapted to a brand's position in the market.

Product synergies would come from sharing the processes for designing vehicles, the design and simulation software, testing standards and methods, manufacturing processes, non-brand specific components, collection and interpretation of government standards, and purchasing.

In moving to three brands, we make the assumption that the Ford brand is, in 2006, being held back from building the world's most desirable mainstream vehicles by the distractions it faces. But there is a big caveat. Ford must drop its habit of believing good enough is good enough, an attitude stemming from a decades-long history of daft badge engineering. Ford designers and engineers could now pour their talent and energies into making superior products. Nothing less than superior is going to win.

Ford must have a "we build the best" attitude in every segment it enters. Not a midsize car based on a Mazda platform and a full-size car based on a Volvo platform. A Ford should be built on a Ford platform, the way Toyota does it. Like Volvo and Jaguar, the Ford brand needs to cultivate its own point of view on technology. Ford needs to redeploy its "cleverness" in sharing platforms across a brand portfolio to sharing basic—and superior—architecture within the Ford brand.

And Ford needs to enter—aggressively—all of the mass-market segments. No more half-hearted efforts on minivans or eternal life spans on small cars. Ford must drive the market in all the segments it competes in.

We will know that Ford has turned the corner when, at some future time, the press hails its new-generation Camry fighter, built on a new Ford platform, as the best and most beautiful car in the segment. No ifs, ands, or buts. Pouring into the single Ford brand the energy, funds, and creativity Ford now puts into three versions for the Larry, Curly, and Moe brands of Ford, Mercury, and Lincoln will put Ford on the road to becoming the number-one car brand on the globe.

Volvo needs to continue on its stylish, family, safety path with a wider array of offerings. It must fight to be viewed always as the builder of the world's safest cars. Safer even than Fords and Jaguars. Volvo should invest in upgraded powertrains, more crossovers, more wagons, more convertibles, more cars that are Volvos. It should also enter the minivan market and use a Volvo platform.

Jaguar needs to perfect its aluminum platform and build cars that compete with BMW's 5 and 7 series. They need two sizes of sports car, two shooting brake wagons, and two sizes of crossovers. These vehicles must be sumptuous, fun to drive, and quiet as the proverbial Rolls-Royce. And they must be gorgeous— as viewed by the public, not howled about in Jaguar advertising. Above all, they must be Jaguars.

Retail

The Ford brand retail structure in the US is the messy part. Ford has too many dealers, and Lincoln and Mercury have *far* too many dealers. Lincoln dealers sold an average of 90 cars in 2005 while Mercury dealers averaged 99. Does Ford really believe it needs 1,361 Lincoln dealers and 1,968 Mercury dealers? If there is any good news, many of these dealers are dualed with Ford. Draining this quagmire will be difficult, but it must be done.

To put the issue in perspective: In 2005, Toyota sold 1,800,916 vehicles through 1,215 dealerships, each of which averaged 1,613 units. Ford sold 2,634,061 vehicles through 3,777 dealerships, an average of 696 units. Which group do you think was more excited, more driven? Can having more dealers than Toyota be an advantage? Yes, if you have maybe 400 more, but not 2,500. Hell's bells, there are only 27,000 *post offices* in this country. Reducing the dealer count is a major issue for Ford, even before contemplating the issue of dropping Lincoln and Mercury.

Ford stores need to follow the big box concept. Given the array of models they need to sell, large inventories are the key to selling vehicles in large volumes. The stores need to emphasize convenience and speed of service. On a given Saturday they must be able to handle hundreds of customers, not dozens. The dealerships must also have the service capacity to take care of their many customers without long waits for an appointment.

Want proof this is possible? Visit Longo Toyota in El Monte, California. The store's sales goal for the month we finished editing this book was 2,400. Based on current sales, that equals the number of units sold by 24 Mercury dealers in a year.

Volvo needed 348 dealers to sell 124,000 vehicles in 2005, while Lexus sold 303,000 units with only 215 dealers. Too many dealers make it difficult for any one dealer to make the kind of profit that attracts dealers willing to invest in premium facilities and top-rank people. For instance, the best luxury car facilities in places like Orange County, California, can cost more than $20 million. Volvo does not need to be in that league, but it needs dealers who are in good, well-located facilities.

Volvo should incorporate the essence of the Volvo brand into the retail experience. A good place to start is establishing an environment that is family and kid friendly and which offers a living demonstration of safety and the automobile.

Jaguar has 177 dealers and needs more to do a greater volume of business. Unfortunately, Ford has been pushing Jaguar and Land Rover dealers to dual, and this is another mess that will take time, money, and most of the lawyers in North America to straighten out. But to compete with BMW, Mercedes, and Lexus, Jaguar needs a dealer body with the dedication that those brands display and with the facilities to match.

The obvious Jaguar retail theme is understated British luxury and style. These stores would be fun to design and even more fun to visit.

What's Stopping Ford?

A lot of things. Its history, being a family-controlled business, lack of vision, centralized management, ego, a hostile financial community, a culture of fear and careerism, a bloated dealer body, no ingrained drive for excellence, and insufficient courage to make a dramatic change from the past. Very little on that list separates Ford from a host of other large companies struggling with their brand portfolios. The difference is that we believe Ford could fix it.

We have used Ford as an example of how a dysfunctional brand portfolio could be improved. There are a number of alternative solutions that might work as well or even better, but they would all take vision, courage, patience, and incur sizable risk and expense. We would argue, however, that the risk is less than that inherent in the present course and in Ford's insistence that it can make its current kennel of brands work.

The Ford brand has a brilliant legacy, and many good and talented people work there. They need to be turned loose and told to bring to life a brand strategy they can win with . . . to reignite their energy and enthusiasm by making bold moves that show a determination to leave Ford's mark on the auto business . . . to prove once and for all that Ford can compete with and beat the best the world has to offer.

Ford could have a future in its future.

12

Steel in Your Britches

"Don't let it end like this. Tell them I said something."

Last words of Pancho Villa

By now you know that we love the Old West, and we've alluded to it as often as we felt you'd tolerate. That freewheeling period captures the essence of what we feel it takes to build a world-class brand. It was a time full of vivid imagery, and the stories resonate with us today. People had grit, called a spade a spade, and made maverick a household word.

In *Branding Iron* we have tried to be equally candid, starting with a simple premise: most executives don't have what it takes to build a world-class brand. What's more, they can't handle the truth about what it does take. Most of us know this and in our hearts strive to do much better. We don't want to end up like Pancho Villa—saying "Tell them I said something."

We believe passionately in the power of branding. We have built strong brands and labored over weak ones. Throughout

Branding Iron we have shared with you what we have experienced and learned about building world-class brands. The challenge is to do it in an overbranded world.

We hasten to add that building a world-class brand is anything but a sterile academic exercise. There's plenty of bloodshed involved. Yours, in many cases.

Great brands are a promise wrapped in an experience. An experience those managing the brand try to improve every day. And those managers who do it right bask in the sunlight created from their public commitment to be who they are.

You are now thoroughly versed in the seven key elements that go into great brands. Successful brand leaders know the importance of differentiation, culture, product, conspiracy, consistency, passion, and patience. You also know how to use the Brand Triangle to evaluate your brand and to design what your brand can become.

If you have assimilated the collective wisdom in this book, application becomes the issue. It is worth revisiting one last time the issues of perspective, leadership, culture, and courage using some of our favorite Old West quotes.

Perspective

> "When you discover that you are riding a
> dead horse, the best strategy is to dismount."
>
> *Dakota tribal saying*

Successful branding takes uncommon perspective and an accurate market focus. Many folks in the car business are riding horses deader than the founding fathers of Tombstone, and they steadfastly refuse to dismount. The dead horses include failed strategies and mortally wounded brands.

Charlie Hughes once had a boss, Jim Fuller—a victim of the Pan Am 101 tragedy—who loved to say that every golf course has its own club rules. Fuller was particularly fond of a rule in force at the Rangoon (Myanmar) Golf Club: "Play the ball where the monkey drops it." Truly a perspective for life.

As we wrote *Branding Iron*, we, of course, could not possibly know the personal set of circumstances confounding you who read it. Are you trying to set a school apart, a bank apart, or just your career apart? Whatever your task, play the ball where the monkey dropped it.

Start with a brutally frank assessment of your brand and what is holding it back. Concentrate on understanding the people part. Pogo was right when he said, "We have seen the enemy, and he is us." Not a bad assessment for a possum.

One of Dr. Edward Deming's fourteen points demands that you "drive out fear in the organization." This is tough to do. If people are afraid to tell the truth, how do you get an honest assessment of your situation? The necessary candor must start at the top, both in terms of speaking the truth and listening to it.

Move on to the brand's closely held beliefs. Throughout the book we have had fun with conventional wisdom:

- *Customers are smart*—some are, many aren't.
- *Product is King*—a simplistic answer to a complex question that most executives don't act on anyway. And finally,
- *More brands create more synergies*—no, just more complexity and less focus.

Then there are the trends that affect you. Perhaps the most vexing and greatest area for potential exploitation is *More Choice/Less Choice*. And as sure as spurs hurt, the trends you face today will be replaced with newer and perhaps more daunting trends tomorrow.

It is easy for us to suggest that you see the world clearly and seek opportunity in a crowded marketplace. But it's damned difficult to do. If we knew an easy way, we'd tell you. We don't think there is. And by now we hope you don't think so either. Focusing on this reality is a fine place to begin the next day of your career.

With this fresh perspective comes the most critical question: "What are you going to do about it?"

Leadership

> "You can choose to run with the herd or you can set out to run the herd. One makes your mamma proud; the other don't."
>
> *Marvin "Sidewinder" Abernethy*

Yes, you can choose to run with the herd, which is certainly the path of least resistance. Throughout most of our careers we have witnessed the sad truth that it is inevitably easier to do the wrong thing, a temptation you and all your fellow travelers must resist if you're not going to end up wandering in a metaphorical desert moaning, "Where is everybody?"

We were once in a meeting where a top executive, widely respected in his industry, said; "If I say what we all know to be self-evident to the president without an iron-clad set of facts, I will be fired." When dealing with the future, facts are rarely clad in iron. Only a good historian can be a worthwhile forecaster, and after 30 years of outstanding service with a company, you would expect that such a person's opinion would carry some weight. Sadly, at most companies, you would be wrong.

Business is tough, business is bruising, and not everybody is in it for the good of the brand. Yet business responds to aggressive leadership, strong vision, and undaunted courage. You must navigate through conventional wisdom, identify harmful trends and capitalize on good ones, and insofar as possible relentlessly steer human nature in a positive direction.

You must be a leader, and you must declare and role-model your leadership every day. You must do so with intelligence, humor, insight, and steel in your britches.

Culture

> "Nobody never run no cattle drive by his
> own self."
>
> Ned "Schoolhouse" Tubbs

Successful leaders know that the key, the secret weapon, is culture. Vision, of course, is the prerequisite for differentiation—the art of being special in a world of the commonplace. A half-second behind vision comes culture, from which everything else proceeds.

Both leaders and half-bright subordinates have the sense to know that all too often the "who we are and how we do things" is the roadblock. Ego, hubris, tyranny, self-interest, instant gratification, ignorance, fatigue, and resistance are common and overlapping themes in business today. Not one is easy to deal with. All, with the possible exception of ego, are harmful.

We urge change management. You must change a culture if it is not engaged and is not working for the good of the brand. Such cultures can be characterized by a resistance to change fierce enough to make Charles Darwin rethink his theories.

Winners work everyday to cultivate brand-centric cultures, and that is especially true of winning brand portfolios. Winners are unafraid to move to a decentralized organization. "Who we are and how we do things" must reflect in every way what our customers expect from us.

The car business is big, the car business is mature, and the car business is tired. The trends of High Growth/Low Reality, Low Risk/High Reward, Consolidations and Downsizing have taken their toll. You must build your culture with full appreciation of these issues.

Informal dress, cell phones, laptops, email, pagers, PDAs, and a 24/7 mentality have blurred any distinction between work hours and private hours. Many people would gladly sign up for a 60-hour week if the hours were capped at that. Most people we have worked with are not afraid of hard work or long hours, but they do fear unending work and unending crises. They're willing to remember the Alamo and to step across a line in the sand, but make them fight Santa Ana day in and day out, and you'll lose the battle.

The wheels are about to come off an entire generation of management: the Baby Boomers. The best brands live life as a marathon finding ways to keep life fresh. The losers are in a constant sprint. Culture needs to be ethical, engaging, and nurturing. Companies, whose callousness lays waste to an entire generation of management, are being seriously mismanaged.

If yours is a legacy culture, plan on serious work. Every floundering brand has a passive-resistant group, nests of drones who need to find a new home to destroy. You must weed them out. On the positive side, concentrate on the work environment. Find ways to make it feel like the brand. Make sure that persons rising through the organization stay in key jobs long enough to know what they are doing.

And remember, culture is the most difficult thing to change. You will need raw courage, and plenty of it.

Courage

> "You can't lead a cavalry charge if you think
> you look funny on a horse."
>
> *Unknown*

Courage is a personal issue, a look-in-the-mirror issue.

We know a number of folks who could build a world-class brand, but like the Lion in the Wizard of Oz, they lack courage. Courage to go against the norm, to fight conventional wisdom, to laugh at some of the appalling mistakes they have been supporting, and the courage to speak up when they know that what they're hearing is nonsensical or destructive.

We know the level of tension involved, just visualize the movie *High Noon* on replay. Each day full of showdowns that can make or break a company. Showdowns inside the company and showdowns in the marketplace. These confrontations can be bloodier than a switchblade fight.

When the trail dust settles, when the team is aligned, the never-ending external showdowns will seem less threatening and more challenging—in a healthy way. But there's a lot to be faced down before you achieve getting all your enemies outside corporate headquarters and off company property.

Branding has been diluted, but not because the concept has lost its way. The concept behind a standout brand is as strong as it ever was. It's the practitioners who are groping their way on the dark side of the moon. Every day, we witness the contrast between those who understand and those who don't. The gap is as big as the difference in desirability between BMW and Buick.

Closing that gap takes bravery. It means doing the unexpected and avoiding what's safe. *You* must risk everything, stick your neck out, and stand for something. You cannot be hesitant, let alone spineless.

Branding Iron has guided you on a quest to build a brand that leaves a real mark, one made the old-fashioned way—burned in with a red hot iron. We have identified the acceptance of mediocrity for what it is, an act of cowardice. We have railed at conventional wisdom, candidly assessed the trends that impact brand development, and declared a saturated market to be the perfect place for smart, stout-hearted executives to build a five-star brand.

It has been our goal throughout to stimulate your imagination and inspire your dreams. And in the process, to pointedly ask you: Do you have the courage to leave a real mark on this world?

INDEX